Poverty in Haiti

Also by Mats Lundahl

THE DISTORTED ECONOMY (*with Hans C. Blomqvist, 2002*)

Poverty in Haiti

Essays on Underdevelopment and Post Disaster Prospects

Mats Lundahl

palgrave
macmillan

First published 2011 by
PALGRAVE MACMILLAN

Palgrave Macmillan in the UK is an imprint of Macmillan Publishers Limited, registered in England, company number 785998, of Houndmills, Basingstoke, Hampshire RG21 6XS.

Palgrave Macmillan in the US is a division of St Martin's Press LLC,
175 Fifth Avenue, New York, NY 10010.

Palgrave Macmillan is the global academic imprint of the above companies and has companies and representatives throughout the world.

Palgrave® and Macmillan® are registered trademarks in the United States, the United Kingdom, Europe and other countries.

ISBN 978–0–230–28941–3 hardback

This book is printed on paper suitable for recycling and made from fully managed and sustained forest sources. Logging, pulping and manufacturing processes are expected to conform to the environmental regulations of the country of origin.

A catalogue record for this book is available from the British Library.

Library of Congress Cataloging-in-Publication Data
Lundahl, Mats, 1946–
Poverty in Haiti : essays on underdevelopment and post
disaster prospects / Mats Lundahl.
p. cm.
Includes bibliographical references.
ISBN 978–0–230–28941–3
1. Haiti—Economic policy. 2. Haiti—Economic conditions—
1971– I. Title.
HC153.L85 2011
338.97294—dc22 2010042401

10 9 8 7 6 5 4 3 2 1
20 19 18 17 16 15 14 13 12 11

Printed and bound in Great Britain by
CPI Antony Rowe, Chippenham and Eastbourne

For Bo, who put me on the track

Contents

Part IV A Future for Haiti?

List of Tables and Figure

Tables

Chapter 6

Chapter 13

Figure

Chapter 10

Preface

This book collects a number of articles that I have written on Haiti since 1992. They deal in different ways with the question of why Haiti has failed so badly in terms of economic and social development during its entire existence as a sovereign nation. Basically, the reason is twofold. Even with the best government in the world, the country has an extremely severe erosion problem – the worst in the Western Hemisphere – caused by the growth of the population. The second reason is that Haiti never had the best government in the world. Ever since independence, it has been plagued by a series of rulers that have paid little attention to the vast majority of the people. These two themes form the backbone of the book.

The different chapters range from an analysis of the economic history of Haiti to a number of current problems. The failure of policy reform is brought out, and an effort is made to identify possible ways out of the stagnation and retrogression that has characterized the country during the recent decades. Finding bright spots has always been difficult, and after January 12, 2010 the task is more daunting than ever. The final chapter brings the analysis of Haiti's plight up to date (mid-2010) and attempts to identify the main challenges and priorities that Haiti must deal with during the next couple of decades.

I came to Haiti for the first time in August 1969. At that time, I was a 23-year-old university student of business and economics at Lund University. One of my economics teachers was Associate Professor Bo Södersten, later Professor of International Economics at Lund. He had been to Haiti for a week in September 1968, and it was he who urged me to go there. His urge was the beginning of a more than 40-year affair with the country. In spite of all the dark aspects of Haitian life I have never regretted it. This book is dedicated to Bo.

Virtually all the chapters in the book have been published in different contexts, given at the end of each chapter. They are reprinted by permission of the various publishers. My secretary Lilian Öberg, as always, has had to shoulder a heavy load in the preparation of the manuscript. Needless to say, I am very grateful to her.

Stockholm, June 5, 2010
Mats Lundahl

Prologue: Will Haiti Rise From the Ashes?

Haiti is one of the least enviable countries in the world. Two-thirds of its people are peasants who have to eke out a living on less than 1 hectare of land. Over three-fourths of the population have to make do on less than two US dollars a day, around fifty percent on less than one. Haiti never had a decent government. The country has always been governed by kleptocrats. It is no coincidence that two military interventions by the United States took place during the twentieth century.

The country is regularly hit by hurricanes, no less than 4 in less than 3 weeks in 2008. On January 12, 2010, Haiti suffered its worst catastrophe yet. The capital, Port-au-Prince, with a population of more than 2 million, was devastated by the strongest earthquake ever registered in the country. The world reacted immediately. Money poured in to mitigate the effects of the catastrophe. Suddenly, Haiti became everybody's concern. But for how long? Internationally, Haiti has always been a pariah, a country where nothing works and that no one wants to get engaged in. The interest flares up in connection with elections or natural disasters, but thereafter it quickly fades again, and Haiti falls back into lethargy and mismanagement.

Between 1957 and 1986, Haiti was ruled by François 'Papa Doc' Duvalier and his son Jean-Claude, 'Baby Doc', two of worst Latin American dictators ever. After a chaotic 4-year period with military rule, Jean-Bertrand Aristide was elected president in 1990, with an absolute majority of the people behind him. Aristide had been a priest in a poor parish, and he lit the hope of democracy and a better future. Unfortunately, the hope never came true. The military threw him out the following year and when he returned in 1994 it was as one more link in the chain of predatory presidents. In 2004 he had to leave the country once more. Aristide had chosen to forfeit the opportunity to change the history of the country.

It is difficult to qualify Haiti as anything but a failed state. Aristide's successor René Préval did not do much to change this fact. Without the presence of UN military and police Haiti in all probability would have sunk into total chaos. In 2009, a poverty reduction strategy for the country was finally presented. It never left the office desk. The earthquake cleared the agendas of the international organizations completely.

Haiti's fundamental problem is the fragile ecology of the country. It has the most severe erosion problem in the Western Hemisphere. Nine million people on a surface as large as that of Belgium or Maryland have slowly but steadily pressed food crop cultivation up the mountainsides and seen to it that the country is almost devoid of forest. When the tropical downpours arrive, exactly when it is time to sow and plant, the soil is washed down into the valleys. New land must be used for food cultivation, and so on, in a cumulative process which has depressed rural incomes for an entire century.

As a consequence, Haiti has almost ceased to be an agricultural exporter. Today, four-fifths of its exports derive from the textile industry, the only organized production sector in the cities. The export industry broke down during the military rule 1991–94 but recovered gradually thereafter. Unfortunately, with a single significant exception, all the factories were located in the capital. Hence, after the earthquake, the Haitian industry ground to a halt. The visit by Bill Clinton and the American businessmen in 2009 therefore failed to produce any results.

The government and the administration have been eliminated. The ministries do not exist anymore, nor does the parliament or the communication network. Maybe it does not matter. Politics in Haiti has always been characterized by fights between small cliques who think that the people exist for the benefit of the government and not vice versa. The easiest way to define a political party is as a leader and his followers. Politics has nothing to do with ideas. It is based only on vested interests. In this, there has never been any room for dialogue and opposition. To win an election is not just a question of getting the majority of the votes. It's about crushing the adversaries completely.

I have followed events in Haiti since 1969, and I have never been optimistic with respect to the future of the country. In order to break the political trend, the leading actors must break completely with the entire political history of Haiti. *Kole zèpòl ak zèpòl* – to work shoulder to shoulder – is necessary. Unfortunately, the prospects are not good. At the end of February 2010, parliamentary elections were to be held, elections that had to be postponed. Fifty-two (!) parties had registered. Préval has already been president twice and cannot be re-elected. Someone must succeed him, but where are the new leaders? In the best case, they may emerge from the crisis, but I am not so sure.

The Haitian dream is to emigrate to the United States. The number of boat people will probably increase in the near future – a development not desired by anyone – but with an economy in shambles there are few alternatives for common people. The international community must therefore step in. Catastrophe assistance during 2010 is not enough, but the economy must be rebuilt, a giant task in a country which now lacks virtually all infrastructure, where the damage done to the capital stock is so significant that much of it probably is more or less worthless. The only abundant factor is labor – the survivors – but they must be employed.

Unfortunately, the foreign assistance to Haiti never worked well. When the World Bank closed its Port-au-Prince office temporarily at the beginning of the new millennium, it concluded that it was impossible to contend that the loans that had been given to Haiti had improved the situation in the country. Will the Haitian politicians manage to cooperate and will the international donor community and the international investors get long-run, self-sustained growth going? Will Haiti ever rise from its ashes?

Voltaire saw the 1755 Lisbon earthquake as an indication that God was not good. Which conclusions may we draw from the 2010 Port-au-Prince earthquake?

* * *

Human and socioeconomic consequences of the disaster

The immediate toll of the earthquake amounted to between 250,000 and 300,000 dead,[1] 300,000 injured, 1.3 million in temporary shelters in the capital, and over 600,000 who left the affected areas for the countryside.[2] Of the latter, most (162,500) went to the Artibonite valley. Large currents also left for the Grande Anse and Sud departments (the southwestern tip of the country) and the Centre.[3] Some 105,000 homes were completely destroyed, over 208,000 were damaged, more than 1300 schools were destroyed, more than 50 hospitals, and other health centers were wiped out, the Port-au-Prince harbor was rendered inoperative, the presidential palace, the parliament building and the majority of the public administration buildings lay in shambles. Eighty percent of the city of Léogâne was destroyed.[4]

The first, preliminary, assessment by the Haitian government indicates that the growth impact of the earthquake is a decline by 8.5 percent in GDP.[5] With a population between 9 and 10 million, a natural population growth of around 2 percent and a death toll of 300,000, this is tantamount to a per capita decline of about 7.5 percent. These figures are of course nothing but crude estimates and have to be read as such. Still, they provide a clear indication of the severity of the situation.

The assessment makes a distinction between damages, losses, and needs.[6] The damages are defined as the replacement value of the destroyed assets, losses as the reduction of 'the economic flow' that results from the temporary absence of the damaged assets, and the needs 'include the recovery, reconstruction and rebuilding of Haiti'.[7] Given these definitions, the total damages and losses have been estimated to US$7.9 billion (70 percent in the private sector) or 120 percent of the Haitian GDP in 2009, 4.3 in damages, and 3.6 in losses. Around 40 percent of the damages and losses are due to the destruction of houses, 8 percent derive from the trade sector, and 6 percent each from transportation and public administration on the one hand and education and health on the other. The needs, in turn, were estimated to US$11.5 billion: 50 percent for the social sectors, 17 percent for infrastructure, including housing, and 15 percent for environment and risk and disaster management.

The Inter-American Development Bank has also published an estimate of the economic damage to Haiti from the earthquake.[8] This estimate is based on regressions using data for 2000 natural catastrophes between 1970 and 2008, fetched from the Emergency Events Data Base (EM-DAT) of the Center for Research on the Epidemiology of Disasters at the Catholic University of Louvain in Belgium.[9] These catastrophes include earthquakes (also tsunamis), floods, and windstorms. Regressions were run both for the data set as a whole and just for the earthquake category, with and without inclusion of industrialized countries, and thereafter a calculation was made of the likely damage in a country with Haiti's characteristics.

These results as well need to be interpreted with caution, since, as the authors of the report underline, the earthquake in Haiti was 'the most destructive event a country... [had] ever experienced when measured in terms of the number of people killed as a share of the country's population' (since 1970), 'and it has affected the capital city of the country: the center of commerce, government and communication', and it was not possible to control for the destruction of 'many priceless buildings'.[10] The Haitian catastrophe involved as many as 20,000–25,000 people killed per million inhabitants (actually more), to be compared with some 4000 during the 1972 earthquake in Nicaragua and 3700 in the one in Guatemala in 1976 (number 2 and 3 on the list in terms of severity) or 1800 in Sri Lanka and 772 in Indonesia as a result of the 2004 tsunami (number 6 and 10, respectively).[11]

The dependent variable in the (OLS logarithmic) regressions was the direct damage in (2009) US dollars and the independent variables were a measure of the intensity of the events (the number of people killed or missing), the level of economic development as measured by lagged real GDP per capita and country size, in terms of population, land area, or lagged real GDP. To this was added a linear trend to control for improved reporting of events, regional dummies, and dummies for each of the three types of catastrophes. The results obtained were robust to the exclusion of industrialized countries. When regressions were run just for earthquakes, it was also possible to control for the strength of the latter, using the Richter scale. These regressions turned out to be consistent with the baseline results.

When the regression results were used to predict what would happen in a country with Haiti's characteristics, the basic prediction was that an earthquake causing 250,000 dead would yield an estimated damage of US$8.1 billion, with an upper limit of 13.9 billion, using a 90 percent confidence interval.[12]

A disproportionally vulnerable society

Haiti was not the only Latin American country to be hit by an earthquake in 2010. A mere month and a half later, on February 27, disaster struck in Chile as well, a much stronger earthquake, but with consequences that do not in any way compare to those in Haiti. That Haiti was hit so severely hardly comes as a surprise. In the first place, in Haiti the quake struck at the worst possible place. Its epicenter was located a mere 25 kilometers from the capital, the largest concentration of population and buildings in the country, and at a depth of a mere 13 kilometers, to be compared with the much stronger (8.8 on the Richter scale) quake in Chile, 35 kilometers deep, offshore Maule, but 335 kilometers from Santiago and 60 and 65 kilometers, respectively, from the nearest major cities: Chillán and Concepción. The Chilean disaster took place near a relatively sparsely populated area. In spite of the fact that the energy released at the epicenter was 501 times as strong in Chile as in Haiti, the death toll the former case hence is counted in the hundreds, whereas in Haiti hundreds of thousands of people were killed.[13]

The above are the most important factors behind the magnitude of the catastrophe in Haiti, but they are not the only ones. Even in *ceteris paribus* terms, Haiti was likely to take a much more severe beating than Chile. The earthquake in Haiti struck in the poorest and most underdeveloped country in the Western Hemisphere. This explains why the consequences were as grim as they turned out to be. Haiti was much more prone to disaster than Chile, for a number of reasons. As pointed out in a recent publication, 'Haiti is a prime example of a Caribbean country that is vulnerable to hazards. Without an adequate national response system or governmental agencies to prepare for and manage environmental disasters, the country is unable to protect its citizens from the impacts of natural hazards.'[14] Also, 'One cannot overlook the various social, economic, and political factors that play a part in Haiti's vulnerable conditions.'[15]

Rosenfeld et al.[16] have identified seven such factors, which have been applied to the Haitian situation by Crystal Andrea Felima:[17]

1. Poor health and nutritional status made individuals more vulnerable.
2. Governmental irresponsibility and lack of state financial support had created a situation where the Ministry of the Environment, with a mere 2 percent of the total government budget[18] had next to nothing to invest in assessments of environmental degradation and measures to prevent this. The result of this was nothing short of alarming:

   > Haiti's national development framework is extremely weak. While national disaster plans exist on paper, national disaster management capacity is inexistent. Currently, the government's role is limited to declaring a state of emergency once a disaster occurs and to soliciting international relief and reconstruction assistance. This may not solely be due to a lack of political will to invest in risk reduction, but also [to] the mere fact that Haiti is faced with tackling so many fundamental issues of daily survival that disaster mitigation simply remains a luxury the country cannot afford.
   >
   > Extremely weak institutions for governance result in inefficient public policies. The many changes in government led to a high turnover that in turn led to loss of institutional memory and capacity. The country has not been able to 'learn from experience' due to a lack of resources to do so. As a result the same disaster losses happen over and over again when some could easily be prevented.
   >
   > Haiti's national disaster plan is non-functional. Due to a variety of problems the government has to address, disaster management remains severely under-funded. No early warning systems exist, no evacuation plans have been implemented on the municipal level.[19]

3. The polarization between rich and poor in Haiti had created a situation where the urban poor, and especially those in the capital, were

living in overcrowded areas with next to no infrastructural amenities, like safe drinking water and adequate sanitation.
4. The size and growth of the Haitian population had had a serious environmental impact.[20]
5. The growth of the population had led to unplanned urbanization with buildings on unsafe land.
6. The social service delivery – sewage, water, electricity, health care, and education – was completely inadequate.
7. The deforestation caused by the population pressure made for landslides and washing down of soil and dirt into the cities.

On closer inspection, these factors can be reduced to two: population growth and political irresponsibility. Income and wealth *differences* as such played no role. What mattered was rather the *absolute level* of poverty among the Haitian population, caused mainly by the combination of population growth and government inertia (and outright plunder).[21]

The chapters of this book provide an analysis of the factors that rendered the situation after the earthquake so difficult. The earthquake itself and the future of Haiti will be dealt with in the last section of the book. In order to arrive at a proper understanding of the consequences of the quake and the formidable challenge that lies ahead of both the Haitians and the international community, however, a number of basic analytical points must be made. Part I of the book, 'History', deals with the historical factors that made Haiti an underdeveloped country. Part II, 'Contemporary Problems', analyzes the main contemporary causes. Part III, 'The Failed Transition', analyzes the failure of the Haitian governments to make the transition from a kleptocratic to a modern, democratic state after 1986. Part IV, 'A Future for Haiti?', discusses what will happen in Haiti after the devastating earthquake.

Notes

The first part published in *Svenska Dagbladet* (Swedish version), January 16, 2010.

1. *Telegraph* (2010).
2. Government (2010), p. 7.
3. République d'Haïti (2010).
4. Government (2010), pp. 6 7.
5. Ibid., p. 46.
6. Ibid., p. 7.
7. Ibid.
8. Cavallo et al. (2010).
9. http://www.emdat.be/.

10. Cavallo et al. (2010), p. 3.
11. Ibid., p. 4.
12. Ibid., p. 11.
13. Bajak (2010); USGS (2010a), (2010b).
14. Felima (2009), p. 11.
15. Ibid., p. 17.
16. Rosenfeld et al. (2005).
17. Felima (2009).
18. Ibid., p. 18.
19. Eichler (2006), p. 7.
20. cf. Lundahl (1979), Chapter 5.
21. Lundahl (1979), (1983), and (1992).

References

Bajak, Frank (2010), 'Chile Earthquake 2010: Why the Haiti Earthquake Wasn't as Strong, but Far More Devastating', *Huffington Post,* February 27, http: www.huffingtonpost.com/huff-wires/20100227/cb-tale-of-two-quakes/. Downloaded March 27, 2010.

Cavallo, Eduardo A., Powell, Andrew and Becerra, Oscar (2010), *Estimating the Direct Economic damage of the Earthquake in Haiti.* February. IDB Working Paper Series # IDB-WP-163. Washington, DC: Inter-American Development Bank, Department of Research and Chief Economist.

Eichler, Lisa (2006), *Community-Based Environmental Management: A Tool for Natural Disaster Risk Reduction in Haiti?* Master Thesis, Nicholas School of the Environment and Earth Sciences, Duke University, Durham, NC.

Felima, Crystal Andrea (2009), 'Haiti's Disproportionate Casualties After Environmental Disasters: Analyzing Human Vulnerabilities and the Impact of Natural Disasters', *Journal of Haitian Studies,* Vol. 15, 6–28.

Government of the Republic of Haiti (2010), *Action Plan for National Recovery and Development of Haiti: Immediate Key Initiatives for the Future.* March. N.p.

Lundahl, Mats (1979), *Peasants and Poverty: A Study of Haiti.* London: Croom Helm.

Lundahl, Mats (1983), *The Haitian Economy: Man, Land and Markets.* London and Canberra: Croom Helm.

Lundahl, Mats (1992), *Politics or Markets? Essays on Haitian Underdevelopment.* London and New York: Routledge.

République d'Haïti (2010), Haïti: Summary of the PDNA after the Earthquake. Damage, Losses and General and Sector Evaluation. Prepared by the Government of the Republic of Haiti, with the Support of the Inter American Development Bank, the United Nations System and the World Bank. March 12. Power point presentation at the Technical Preparatory Conference for Haiti, Hotel Santo Domingo, Santo Domingo March 15–17.

Rosenfeld, Lawrence B., Caye, Joanne S., Ayalon, Ofra and Lahad, Mooli (2005), *When Their World Falls Apart: Helping Families and Children Manage the Effects of Disasters.* Washington, DC: NASW Press.

Telegraph (2010), 'Haiti's Earthquake Death Toll Revised to at Least 250,000', April 22. http://www.telegraph.co.uk/news/worldnews/centralamericaand

thecaribbean/haiti/7621756/Haitis-earthquake-death-toll-revised-to-at-least-250000.html. Downloaded May 18, 2010.

USGS (United States Geological Survey) (2010a), 'Magnitude 8.8 – Offshore Maule, Chile', http://earthquake.usgs.gov/earthquakes/eqinthenews/2010/us2010rja6/. Downloaded March 27, 2010.

USGS (United States Geological Survey) (2010b), 'Magnitude 7.0 – Haiti Region', http://earthquake.usgs.gov/earthquakes/eqinthenews/2010/us2010tfan/. Downloaded March 27, 2010.

Part I
History

Chapter 1, 'Five Decisive Events in the Economic History of Haiti', was published in 1995. The chapter analyzes five important historical events and their consequences. The first is the European discovery of Haiti in 1492 which resulted in the extinction of the indigenous population and the exhaustion of the alluvial gold of the island. The second is the destruction of the French plantation society during the wars of liberation 1791–1803 which prepared the ground for a smallholder society. The third is the redistribution of land from 1809 which completed this society and initiated the degeneration of politics. The fourth is the American occupation 1915–34 which created an army that was to have a strong voice in politics. The fifth is the dictatorships of the two Duvaliers, Papa Doc and Baby Doc, 1957–86, which resulted in the worst plunder in the history of Haiti. The final section offers some speculations with respect to the possibility of a post-predatory society in Haiti.

Chapter 2, 'Economic Interests Are Color-Blind: On Class Divisions in Haitian History', was published in 2007. It discusses the thesis advanced by David Nicholls: that skin color was a divisive and decisive factor when it came to shaping Haitian politics during the nineteenth century. It advances the alternative thesis that economic interests were as decisive and that these interests were largely color-blind. The creation of the social classes in Haiti cannot be seen simply as a result of differences in skin color.

Chapter 3, 'Poorest in the Caribbean: Haiti in the Twentieth Century', was published in 2001. The chapter explains why Haiti was the poorest Caribbean nation during the twentieth century. At the most fundamental level, we find the tendency for per capita income to decline secularly, caused by the growth of the population, operating during the entire period. This also operated to create an anti-export bias in the agricultural sector, a bias that was also reinforced by dubious government interventions. Over time, as a result of population growth and soil destruction, Haiti lost whatever comparative advantage the country possessed in agriculture. Instead, the labor-intensive assembly industries emerged as the main export sector. Economic policy, as pursued in Haiti, was concentrated on plunder of the citizens by the government, and latter-day reform efforts failed for political reasons. The degeneration of the state also led to a failure to accumulate social capital, a failure to work for common purposes, and a failure to develop education. This degeneration has made it difficult to develop the most efficient sector, industry, beyond the low-skill, low-wage segment.

1
Five Decisive Events in the Economic History of Haiti

The present chapter deals with the historical reasons why Haiti is caught in what appears to be a secular economic decline, which in all probability has been going on for at least a century.[1] There is a strong case for approaching Haiti's economic plight from a historical standpoint. The chapter singles out what I believe to be the five most decisive events in Haiti's economic history so as to reconstruct an interrelated series of historical phenomena which explain the country's current economic disaster.

The European discovery

The first event, of course, is the discovery of Hispaniola by Columbus in 1492, during his first voyage. We are all familiar with the story of how *El Almirante*, on his way from Cuba, arrived on 5 December, at the northwestern tip, at present-day Môle St. Nicolas, how he continued from there along the north coast, until the Santa María was shipwrecked on Christmas morning east of present-day Cap-Haïtien, and how, using the planks of the wreck, the crew constructed the Navidad fort. What started out as an enterprise of discovery was rapidly transformed into one of conquest and subjugation. Some 40 men were left behind when the two remaining caravels left for Spain. They clashed immediately with the Taino Indians, and when Columbus returned to Hispaniola in November 1494, he found that all of them had been killed.

From then on, however, the odds turned steadily against the Indians, and the discovery of gold in Hispaniola sealed their fate. 'Spain's major gift to the New World was the destruction of its people', writes Ralph Davis.[2] The impact of the discovery could hardly have been more drastic. The exact number of inhabitants in Hispaniola in 1492 is not known with any precision. Estimates range between some 100,000 and

8 million.[3] The exact number matters little, however. The importance of the discovery lay in the fact that it created a population vacuum. In 1508, no more than 60,000 Tainos remained, and 40 years later less than 500 were left.[4] During the course of a single generation, the native population of Hispaniola, for all practical purposes, had become extinct, as a result of European diseases and forced labor.

The Spaniards combed the neighboring islands for people to replace the Tainos as a source of labor, completely depopulating the Bahamas in the process.[5] This was of little avail, however. Labor continued to be a scarce factor of production, and as early as the beginning of the sixteenth century, the first African slaves were imported to Hispaniola. This would pave the way for the first component of today's economic problems: the creation of a group that would become the future Haitian peasantry.

The gold that was discovered in Hispaniola would soon be exhausted. This left few incentives for European immigration, and when rumors of the fabulous riches of Mexico and Peru reached the island, an exodus of whites began. The remaining population was concentrated on the eastern side, especially in Santo Domingo, while the western side (present-day Haiti) remained more or less unpopulated for almost a century.[6] The European population vacuum was gradually filled by the French, who, with the island of Tortuga as their base from 1630, began to penetrate the Hispaniola mainland as well.[7]

After the Treaty of Ryswyck in 1697, the French were in complete control of the western third of Hispaniola. During the course of the next century, the French colony of Saint-Domingue developed into the most profitable colony not only of France, but worldwide. The basis of this wealth was the plantation economy created by the French, with sugar, coffee, cotton, and indigo as the main crops. This economy rested on the backs of African slaves. The French followed the labor pattern established by the Spaniards. Slaves from almost 40 different African regions were imported,[8] at an increasing rate: 4000 per annum in the 1720s, 5000 in 1753, 10,000 in 1771, 27,000 in 1786, and 40,000 every year from 1787 to 1789.[9] On the eve of the French Revolution, Saint-Domingue had around 450,000 African slaves.[10] The future peasants were in place.

The destruction of the plantation society

On the night of August 14, 1791, a voodoo ceremony was held at Bois Caïman, in northern Haiti.[11] This ceremony would prefigure the events that would put an end to the French colony. A week later, the slaves rose up against their masters, and a war, or rather a series of complicated wars of liberation began that would last for more than 12 years.[12] When these wars came to an end, following the defeat of the French invasion army under the command of Napoleon's brother-in-law, General Leclerc, by Haitian forces and the ravages of yellow fever, the once-prosperous plantation society was in shambles.

The plantation economy had built on intensive use of two production factors: labor and capital. The most important plantation crop was sugar (although on the eve of the French Revolution Saint-Domingue was supplying some 60 percent of the world's coffee), and with the sugar technology prevailing in the eighteenth century, the critical moment in sugar production, the harvest, revolved around the crushing mill.[13] The sugar cane had to be cut when it was ripe. If not, the sugar content would decrease. The harvested cane had to be brought to the mill within a few hours, for the same reason. The mill, in turn, had an optimum size which was determined by certain economies of scale. This made for a certain necessary concentration of capital, and it also determined the optimum size of the plantation, somewhere in the 150–300 hectare range,[14] and the, consequently large, size of the labor force which was necessary to keep the mill going virtually round the clock during the harvest.

The wars of liberation completely undermined the viability of the plantation system completely, although the death blow, as we will see below, did not come until later. They did so by dramatically reducing the available stocks of both capital and labor. Between 1790 and 1805, the size of the population fell from 520,000 to 380,000 as a result of the expulsion of the French and the losses due to the war.[15] If we discount the European casualties altogether, the available labor force was reduced by more than 20 percent. In practice, the figure was far higher, since many ex-slaves also chose to hide in the mountains where they were beyond the reach of the *autorités*.

The capital stock was also extensively destroyed by war. Reports from 1803 paint a clear-cut picture of wholesale destruction and burning of both plantations and sugar mills. Tadeusz Lepkowski summarizes the situation which prevailed at the end of the wars of liberation:

> In November 1803, almost the entire colony, formerly flourishing, was a big cemetery of ashes and debris. Tens of thousands of cultivators and soldiers-cultivators had died. The huts, if they were still standing, were deserted. The cities were burned out, the sugar mills

> had been demolished or showed the stumps of the carbonized beams, the majority of the plantations had been reduced to ashes. Only the small plots planted with coffee and food crops spoke of life in the country.[16]

Export statistics from the period reflect the impact of destruction. In 1795, sugar exports were down to 1.2 percent of their 1789 level, coffee exports to 2.8 percent, and exports of cotton and indigo had all but been wiped out at 0.7 and 0.5 percent, respectively, of their previous levels.[17] After a strong recovery for all four crops except indigo up to 1802, the French invasion that year brought a new downturn, with sugar at 34, coffee at 40, cotton at 43, and indigo at 4 percent of their pre-revolutionary levels in 1804.[18]

Despite the recovery from the all-time lows of 1795, it was fairly clear that the plantation system had been severely undermined. In fact, what was left of it had only survived thanks to extraordinarily drastic measures. In order to understand these measures, we need to recognize the second component of what would become Haiti's political problem. Part of this component had been created during the colonial period: the mulatto *affranchis*, that is, the manumitted offspring of the French colonists with their slave mistresses. This group, many of whom had become the owners of slaves and other property already before the 1791 revolution, clearly aspired to elite and ruler status. The second component was a direct product of the wars: the upper ranks of the new Haitian military, whether black or mulatto.[19] Together, these two groups were to constitute the new Haitian upper class, and from this group, the first Haitian rulers were recruited.

These rulers faced a twofold problem which made it necessary to attempt to conserve the plantation system. On the one hand, they needed weapons and ammunition in the event of a French return to reconquer the lost colony. These had to be purchased from outside, which in turn made exports necessary. On the other hand, the upper class wanted an income without having to work on the land themselves. Land was plentiful in Haiti, and after the 1791 uprising, the slaves were free. Free peasants and freely available land, however, cannot be reconciled with a non-working upper class extracting a surplus from the peasants.[20] The peasants could always escape unless they could be controlled. Accordingly, the new rulers chose to bring them back to the plantations where they had to work under military control. Thus, from the very first moments of freedom from the French – already during the wars of liberation – the ruling clique preyed on the masses. With the crystallization of the new elite, the precedent was set for the future predatory state. It would, however, take yet another event for the typical pattern of predatory activity in Haiti to emerge.

The 1809 land reform

The Haitian land reform of 1809 was the first of its kind in the history of Latin America.[21] The return to the plantation system had been initiated by Toussaint Louverture in the middle of the wars of liberation.[22] The system had been further developed by the first ruler of the new nation of Haiti, Jean-Jacques Dessalines, who turned all the land owned by whites and a lot of the land owned by mulatto *affranchis* into state land which was thereafter leased to the new elite.[23] The population was divided into two classes: soldiers and workers, and anyone who was not a soldier was put to work under military supervision on a plantation which he or she could not leave without permission. Once again, Haiti found itself in a situation where the many toiled for the benefit of the few.

The forced labor system survived Dessalines, who was murdered in 1806, by a mere 3 years in the south, and another decade in the north. (In 1807, Haiti had been divided into two rival states: a northern kingdom under Henry Christophe and a southern republic under Alexandre Pétion.) In 1809, Pétion made one of the most crucial decisions in the history of Haiti: that of dividing the large estates. He could hardly have done otherwise. We have already pointed out that the plantation system was under tremendous pressure from the supply (factor) side. There was pressure from the demand side as well. The traditional French market had been cut off by the wars of liberation, and the Napoleonic wars made trade with Great Britain and the United States equally difficult. The system buckled under its own weight. It simply became too costly to maintain export production with the aid of troops.

Finally, the slaves were free to shape their own destiny. Gradually, over the course of the nineteenth century, Haiti was transformed into a peasant nation. Subsequent efforts to revert to the large estates failed completely, and with inheritance laws building on the *Code Napoléon*, which conferred equal rights on all children, it was inevitable that a process of subdivision would be set in motion, with farm size growing smaller and smaller for each generation until reaching today's exceedingly tiny 0.75 hectares or less.[24] Thus, the land reform gave Haiti an agrarian structure which differs substantially from the majority of Latin American countries, where it is common to find very large holdings alongside very small ones. In doing so, and in creating the peasantry, it set the stage for the current erosion drama, where an increasing population is literally mining the soil, with fatal consequences for future generations.

The land reform also had a second – completely unexpected and completely negative – consequence. It made politics degenerate into a fight over the spoils of the presidential office.[25] In other words, it created a full-fledged predatory state. This may sound far-fetched, but we only have to go back to the dilemma facing the new-born elite once the French had been driven out to see why. With military supervision being a thing of the past, the peasants free and plenty of land for them cultivate, there was no longer any room for a non-working upper class living off the fat of the land. Thus, the upper class had to devise new ways to avoid working while maintaining a substantial income, and if the peasants could not be exploited directly, they could always be taxed – not very systematically, given the weakness of the administration – and the taxes could go into the pockets of the ruling party.

Accordingly, politics in Haiti took a sharp downhill turn during the nineteenth century. Small cliques – distributional coalitions in the sense of Mancur Olson[26] – fought each other in order to gain control over the government treasury. As a rule, these cliques paid more attention to rapid gains than to remaining in office for long periods. Most of the time, they were too small to be safe from outside contenders for power.[27] Hence, they were quickly overturned by the next clique, for exactly the same purpose: making a quick profit from the perquisites of presidential office. This, in turn, explains why Haiti had so many presidents and coups during the nineteenth century. From 1843 to 1915, the country was ruled by 22 presidents, 11 of whom stayed in office for less than a year. Only one managed to retire peacefully. Four died of 'natural' causes while in office. The remainder were deposed more or less violently.[28] The same period saw more than a hundred coups and attempted coups, uprisings, and so on.[29] Those rulers who managed to stay in office for longer periods[30] succeeded in doing so only because they chose to deliberately invest in extraordinary security measures: police, spy networks, and so on.

Thus, already toward the end of the nineteenth century, the most important mechanisms of underdevelopment were in place in Haiti: the interplay between population growth and soil erosion on the one hand and the kleptocracy which exploited the masses on the other. This is why it is fitting to call the nineteenth century 'crucial'.[31] What followed was more a case of 'fine tuning', to borrow an expression from the jargon of economic policy.[32]

The American occupation

In 1915, the US Marine Corps moved into Haiti and occupied the country for the next 19 years. The reasons for the occupation are disputed, but it appears clear that President Wilson feared increased German influence in Haiti, not least given the strategically location of Môle St. Nicolas, opposite Guantánamo in Cuba. Economic factors presumably played a minor role. At the time, American investment in the country was relatively limited. The same was true of American commercial interests.[33]

The American occupation, above all else, represents a hiatus in the history of Haiti. The first few years were spent securing internal peace and order, and only in 1921 did the occupation enter into what may be labeled 'a constructive phase'. As could be expected, the occupation forces met with resistance. Just before the landing of the Marine Corps, President Vilbrun Guillaume Sam was killed by a mob, and his torn limbs were paraded through the streets of the capital. This was further proof of the fact that Haiti continued to be torn by inner dissension and domestic strife, and that the country had, in fact, been in a more or less continuous state of civil war for 70 years, where loyalties were the only variable.

The occupation put an end to all that. Prior to the occupation, Haiti had not one but many armies whose only purpose was to fight each other. The pattern which had developed since the removal from office in 1843 of Jean Pierre Boyer (the last president to rule firmly for a long period – since 1818) was a predictable and repetitive one: with a would-be president hiring a mercenary army to march on the capital, failing or succeeding to topple the sitting government, and in the event of success going straight for the contents (if any) of the treasury.[34] Should the vaults happen to be empty, there was a remedy for that as well – that of floating a loan in the international or domestic market, more often than not at a tremendous discount, with repayment being passed on to future governments and generations. Foreign loans were taken in 1874, 1875, 1896, and 1910. Thereafter, Haiti's creditworthiness abroad was exhausted, and the last governments before 1915 had to make do with what they could squeeze out of the domestic capital market: in 1912, 1913, and 1914 – the latter year, four loans.[35]

The Americans put a stop to the political and financial merry-go-round, but this was not to be a lasting achievement. As soon as the occupation came to an end, the old tendencies raised their ugly heads again. Other constructive efforts of the occupation were also short-lived. The Americans concentrated on forcing the Haitians to repay the foreign debt which their rulers had contracted for them, on constructing physical infrastructure and on providing education, along American lines.

They were infinitely more successful in the first area than in the second, and much more successful in the second than in the third. Debt repayment was given absolute priority, since Haiti's entire foreign debt had been concentrated in American hands, beginning in 1922. Between 1924 and 1930, the external debt was effectively halved, and in 1947 it was completely paid off. (The United States continued to exercise financial control after the end of the occupation as well.) The legacy of the second effort was above all an improved transport network, which was left to slowly deteriorate once the Americans pulled out of Haiti. Finally, vocational education, not least agricultural, modeled on black schools in the United States, was superimposed on the Haitian, French-inspired system, which favored *belles-letters* and classical studies, with few, if any, lasting results.[36]

What *would* last was something of an entirely different nature. It took the Americans 4 years to pacify Haiti, and pacification could not be achieved without first putting down, with considerable effort, a major uprising, led by Charlemagne Péralte.[37] Once the armed resistance had been silenced, the Americans set out to do what they had done in all the other countries in the region where they had an immediate influence on domestic affairs (Cuba, Nicaragua, and the Dominican Republic). They created a modern constabulary – which consisted of both an army and a police corps – under Marine supervision. This constabulary, the *Gendarmerie d'Haïti*, would in time develop into the regular Haitian army of the late 1930s, the 1940s, and the 1950s, the *Forces Armées d'Haïti*, monopolizing police duties and calling the political shots all the way up to the 1957 elections.

With the creation of the modern army, Haiti turned into a praetorian state where the effective power was being exercised by the military in the sense that it was the armed forces who, from the late 1930s onward, decided how long a sitting president would remain in office.[38] The particular significance of the new army was that regional forces, such as those which had been fighting each other during the nineteenth century, no longer had any say. The political system was centralized in the capital and in the hands of whoever controlled the army. During the nineteenth century, no one group had been strong enough to control the others. Power had shifted from one group to another in a stochastic fashion.

With a strong army in place, this was less and less the case. The post-occupation presidents shared the same predatory characteristics as their pre-occupation colleagues, the only difference being that the probability of their remaining in office was now determined by a group which was in principle exogenous to them and which insisted on a substantial share of the political spoils. This feature brought a certain measure of stability to Haitian politics. Presidents were deposed, but in a completely bloodless way, when the army felt that it had had enough and another candidate who had the tacit approval of the armed forces was brought into the presidential saddle. Another group of actors who continued to have a strong imprint on Haitian political life until very recently had entered the drama of Haitian underdevelopment.

The predatory climax: The two Duvaliers

From the early 1940s until 1957, the army played a decisive role in Haitian politics. Presidents Lescot (1941–46), Estimé (1946–50), and Magloire (1950–56), the latter a military man himself, all attempted to stay on in office after the end of their constitutional presidential terms. They were all removed by the army. All of them were solid kleptocrats who did not hesitate to use the power of office to fill their own pockets. By the time Magloire was forced to leave, he had supposedly amassed $12–28 million.[39] Haiti was right back in the nineteenth-century tradition. The American occupation had been a hiatus in this respect as well.

The crowning act in the predatory drama was yet to unfold, however. It would come with the creation, in 1957, of what would prove to be the longest rule in Haiti's history since Boyer: the Duvalier dynasty. When the turbulent election campaign of 1956–57 came to an end, François Duvalier (Papa Doc) had been elected president, with the support of, among others, the Haitian army. His record when he came into office was a comparatively clean one, as far as could be judged at that time. He had campaigned on a social program and on promises to put the financial house in order and wipe out the corruption in the state apparatus.[40] This was a promising beginning.

However, it would not take Papa Doc very long to prove that he had been a very perceptive student of Haitian society – as an independent intellectual in the 1930s, as Minister of Public Health and Labor under Estimé and when he had gone into hiding during the Magloire years. Duvalier probably understood the predatory state and its logic better than any other ruler in Haiti's history. During the nineteenth century, the presidents had faced a trade-off between quick profits and a possibly longer stay in office. When Papa Doc came to power, he immediately set out to shift that trade-off to higher levels of both income and security, ruthlessly persecuting all forms of opposition – imagined as well as real.

His most brilliant insight was that the central role in the Haitian drama had been conferred on the army. Accordingly, he began to change this. The leading officer, General Antoine Kébreau, who had been instrumental in obtaining the necessary support for Duvalier during the election campaign, was retired the following year. Thereafter, the army was in for a major overhaul. Every top-brass officer who was in any way perceived as a personal threat to the president was retired, sent abroad or to some godforsaken place inside the country, or simply liquidated. A completely new chain of command was created, with officers who all had one thing in common: they owed their promotion, and hence their absolute allegiance, solely to Duvalier.

The army had been nothing but the first step. Subsequently, Duvalier brought all the principal domestic bodies and organizations under complete control: the Church, the business community, the judiciary, the parliament, the media, and the administration. None of these entities, with the partial exception of the Catholic Church, with its foreign backing, would pose any threat in the future, all of them being solidly packed with ardent *Duvaliéristes*.

Simultaneously, Duvalier worked on the construction of a new support structure. This structure rested on three pillars: the dreaded *tonton macoutes*, the voodoo clergy and the administration at the most local level – the *chefs de section*. The *tonton macoutes* not only served to intimidate and liquidate people. They also infiltrated all the national institutions – not least the administration – and vice versa: to prove their loyalty to the regime, government officials had to join the *macoutes*. The *houngans* and *mambos* (priests and priestesses) and the *chefs de section* (the local 'sheriffs'), in turn, acted as the arm of the government in the local community. The voodoo clergy had traditionally wielded a strong influence over the rural population, and Duvalier, who was an ardent student of voodoo, used this to his advantage, by placing himself at its head, insinuating that he had divine powers. Finally, the *chefs de section* were already more or less synonymous with the state on the local level. Often, the same persons played all three roles: a tremendous concentration of power, accountable only to Duvalier.

When Papa Doc died, in 1971, he stood out as a tremendously successful ruler – on terms that he himself had defined, and which, in the economic arena, corresponded very closely to the tradition established during the nineteenth century, pocketing altogether some $150 million through an unbelievably varied repertoire of tricks, all of which served to tax the population.[41] He had managed to build a new and efficient power structure which was completely concentrated in his own hands.

This concentration of power was to create problems for his son, Jean-Claude (Baby Doc), who succeeded him in 1971 and who, of course, could not count on the same personal allegiance as his father, never having made any effort to gradually assume responsibility. Papa Doc's system had not been built in such a way as to ensure a smooth transfer on this count. Baby Doc realized this and hence chose to opt for his own strategy: what very much amounted to reverting to the situation which prevailed before his father's time. Duvalier *père* had crushed all the traditional power structures, but Jean-Claude could not do without them. His rule became more technocratically oriented than that of his father, and the old *Duvaliéristes* were gradually pushed aside. The technocrats came from the traditional elite groups with whom Jean-Claude had been to school and he married the daughter of an *arriviste* businessman, who helped to organize his rackets. In particular, he made extensive use of government monopolies of various kinds, both in public services and in direct production and sales.[42] When Jean-Claude Duvalier was finally ousted in 1986, his family was suspected of having pocketed no less than $1.6 billion.[43] The predatory state had reached an all-time high in Haiti. Jean-Claude, in a perverse sense, stood on the shoulders of previous giants in the exploitation business in a game where he and his father had 28 years to bleed the nation dry.

Towards the post-predatory state?

What would have been reasonable to expect after the fall of Baby Doc? It should be absolutely clear from the foregoing that the two Duvaliers did not constitute any exception to the Haitian tradition. They were the logical culmination of one-and-a-half centuries of kleptocracy, simply better organized (Papa Doc) and more finely tuned to predation (Baby Doc) than their predecessors. Only therein lay their historical importance. It goes virtually without saying that whoever would follow would also be likely to aim for nothing but plunder.[44]

This is exactly what occurred. The road from Baby Doc to Aristide was not a smooth one, but one which attested to the negative selection of politicians that had been going on in Haiti for 182 years. When Magloire fell in December 1956, political chaos ensued. This lasted until Duvalier was sworn in, in September the following year. In the interim, Haiti had three provisional presidents. When Baby Doc fell, some 30 years later, the country was once more thrown into turmoil: one provisional government council, one provisional president, one dupe head of state, and two generals, until finally Jean-Bertrand Aristide was elected president with a solid two-thirds majority in December 1990. In September, 1991, Aristide was ousted by the military. Once again, the nineteenth century had made a come-back. Aristide remained in exile until he was reinstated by the Americans in September 1994. The obvious question is: 'What will happen next?' Will democracy finally take root in Haiti, or will the tragically shortened Aristide presidency represent yet another hiatus in the troubled political history of the country? Predatory states seldom turn developmental unless outside pressure compels them to do so.[45] This pressure is clearly present in contemporary Haiti. The United States has moved in and occupied the country for the second time, with the support of the United Nations and the international community in general. The army which the Americans created during the first occupation, 1915–34, is being reorganized. Most important, a police corps under civilian control, independent of the army, is in the process of being recruited and trained.

Still, the process may not work unless it is given time. Whatever one might feel about the presence of foreign troops inside a sovereign country, it would be a serious mistake to withdraw prematurely. Haiti in 1995 is in an inherently unstable situation. The supporters of the 'old' regime have either gone into hiding or are keeping a very low profile. There is very little else they can do. Nevertheless, they could easily reappear. In 1996, the bell will toll for Aristide, who according to the constitution cannot be re-elected immediately, and presidential elections will then have taken place.

Haiti's future rests on the outcome of these elections. Unfortunately, however, the electoral process will involve more than just the ardent defenders of democracy and development. The 'old guard' will also attempt to make it back in the saddle, on whatever pretext – but essentially for the exactly same reasons as their predecessors, ever since 1804. As I have tried to illustrate, political evolution in Haiti has always been a process of negative selection, and it will take considerable time to get rid of the corrupt 'old guard' and breed new generations of politicians who are firmly anchored in the great democratic tradition. This process cannot be left to itself. The present equilibrium is far too unstable for that. The eventual displacement could be in any direction. Hence, foreign supervision will have to continue for quite some time until it is certain that peace, democracy, and honesty have the upper hand over violence, dictatorship, and plunder. The entire history of Haiti is crystal clear on this point.

Notes

Published in *Historia y Sociedad*, Vol. 8, 1995–96, by Departamento de Historia, Facultad de Humanidades, Universidad de Puerto Rico, Recinto de Río Piedras. Reprinted by permission.

1. See in particular Lundahl (1979), (1983), and (1992).
2. Davis (1973), p. 55.
3. Lundahl (1980), p. 276; Cook and Borah (1971), Chapter 6; Bethell (1984).
4. Logan (1968), pp. 10–11.
5. Sauer (1966), pp. 159–60.
6. Peña Pérez (1980), (n.d.).
7. See e.g., Crouse (1940), Chapter 5; Crouse (1943), Chapter 5; Peña Batlle (1951); and Funck-Brentano (1979), for details.
8. Leyburn (1937).
9. Rotberg and Clague (1971), p. 34.
10. Leyburn (1966), p. 18.
11. Whether the ceremony actually took place, and if so, when, is in dispute. See Thylefors (2009).
12. See e.g., James (1963); Ott (1973); Heinl and Heinl (1978), Chapters 2–5; and Brutus (1969), for details.
13. Davis (1973), pp. 257–58.
14. Lundahl (1979), p. 258.
15. Moreau de Saint-Méry (1958), p. 28; Leyburn (1966), p. 33.
16. Lepkowski (1968), p. 91.
17. Ibid., p. 75.
18. Leyburn (1966), p. 35.
19. For a discussion of race and color in the history of Haiti, see Nicholls (1979).
20. Domar (1970).
21. Lundahl (1979), Chapter 6.
22. Lundahl (1985a).
23. Lundahl (1984a).
24. PNUD, Unité de Coordination et de Suivi de l'Environnement (ECMU) (1994), p. 10.
25. Lundahl (1979), Chapter 6; Lundahl (1985b).
26. Olson (1965), (1982).
27. Lundahl (1985b).
28. Ibid.
29. Heinl and Heinl (1978), p. 404.
30. Faustin Soulouque (1847–59), Fabre Geffrard (1859–67), Lysius Salomon (1879–88), Florvil Hyppolite (1889–96), Tirésias Simon Sam (1896–1902), Pierre Nord Alexis (1902–08).
31. Mintz (1966), p. v.
32. Danielson and Lundahl (1994). Cf. Maingot (1986–87), p. 83.
33. For the occupation, see above all Schmidt (1971) and Castor (1971).

34. Lundahl (1985b).
35. For details, see Lundahl (1979), pp. 366–70.
36. Ibid., pp. 463–67.
37. For details, see Gaillard (1984), (1987), (1981a), (1981b), (1982a), and (1982b).
38. Lundahl (1985b).
39. Rotberg and Clague (1971), p. 186.
40. Lundahl (1984b).
41. Ibid. The tricks included taxation of agricultural produce, 'voluntary donations' from the citizens, kickbacks from foreign investors and from the provision of Haitian workers to the Dominican Republic, the use of unbudgeted accounts as well as blackmail and intimidation.
42. Danielson and Lundahl (1994).
43. Lundahl (1989), pp. 2–3.
44. Cf. Lundahl (1995).
45. Gunnarsson (1993), Gunnarsson and Lundahl (1996).

References

Bethell, Leslie (1984), 'A Note on the American Population on the Eve of the European Invasions', in: Leslie Bethell (ed.), *Cambridge History of Latin America, Volume 1, Colonial Latin America*. Cambridge: Cambridge University Press.

Brutus, Edner (1969), *Révolution dans Saint-Domingue*. Two volumes. Bruxelles: Éditions du Panthéon.

Castor, Suzy (1971), *La ocupación norteamericana de Haití sus consecuencias (1915–1934)*. México: Siglo Veintiuno.

Cook, Sherburne F. and Borah, Woodrow (1971), *Essays in Population History: Mexico and the Caribbean, Volume One*. Berkeley, CA: University of California Press.

Crouse, Nellis M. (1940), *French Pioneers in the West Indies, 1624–1664*. New York: Columbia University Press.

Crouse, Nellis M. (1943), *The French Struggle for the West Indies, 1665–1713*. New York: Columbia University Press.

Danielson, Anders and Lundahl, Mats (1994), 'Endogenous Policy Formation and the Principle of Optimal Obfuscation: Theory and Some Evidence from Haiti and Jamaica', *Comparative Economic Studies*, Vol. 36, 51–78.

Davis, Ralph (1973), *The Rise of the Atlantic Economies*. Ithaca, NY: Cornell University Press.

Domar, Evsey D. (1970), 'The Causes of Slavery or Serfdom: A Hypothesis', *Journal of Economic History*, Vol. 30, 18–32.

Funck-Brentano, Frantz (1979), *L'Île de la Tortue*. Paris: Librairie Jules Tallandier.

Gaillard, Roger (1981a), *Les blancs débarquent. Vol. 3, 1915, Premier écrasement du cacoïsme*. Second edition. Port-au-Prince: L'Imprimerie Le Natal.

Gaillard, Roger (1981b), *Les blancs débarquent. Vol. 4, 1916–1917, La république autoritaire*. Port-au-Prince: L'Imprimerie Le Natal.

Gaillard, Roger (1982a), *Les blancs débarquent. Vol. 5, 1917–1918, Hinche mise en croix*. Port-au-Prince: L'Imprimerie Le Natal.

Gaillard, Roger (1982b), *Les blancs débarquent. Vol. 6, 1918–1919, Charlemagne Péralte le caco*. Port-au-Prince: L'Imprimerie Le Natal.

Gaillard, Roger (1984), *Les blancs débarquent. Vol. 1, La république exterminatrice, première partie: une modernisation manqué (1880–1896)*. Port-au-Prince: L'Imprimerie Le Natal.

Gaillard, Roger (1987), *Les blancs débarquent. Vol. 2, 1914–1915, Les cent-jours de Rosalvo Bobo ou une mise à mort politique*. Second edition. Port-au-Prince: L'Imprimerie Le Natal.

Gunnarsson, Christer (1993), 'Mercantilism Old and New: A Transaction Cost Theory and Developmental States in Europe and East Asia', Paper presented at the Conference 'Public Choice Theories and Third World Experiences', London 17–19 September.

Gunnarsson, Christer and Lundahl, Mats (1996), 'The Good, the Bad and the Wobbly: State Forms and Third World Economic Performance', in: Mats Lundahl and Benno J. Ndulu (eds), *New Directions in Development Economics: Growth Environmental Concerns and Government in the 1990s*. London and New York: Routledge.

Heinl, Robert Debs, Jr. and Heinl, Nancy Gordon (1978), *Written in Blood: The Story of the Haitian People, 1492–1971*. Boston, MA: Houghton Mifflin Company.

James, C.L.R. (1963), *The Black Jacobins. Toussaint L'Ouverture and the San Domingo Revolution*. Second edition, revised. New York: Vintage Books.

Lepkowski, Tadeusz (1968), *Haiti. Tomo I*. La Habana: Casa de las Américas.

Leyburn, James G. (1937), 'The Making of a Black Nation', in: George Peter Murdock (ed.), *Studies in the Science of Society*. New Haven, CT: Yale University Press.

Leyburn, James G. (1966), *The Haitian People*. New Haven, CT and London: Yale University Press.

Logan, Rayford W. (1968), *Haiti and the Dominican Republic*. London: Oxford University Press.

Lundahl, Mats (1979), *Peasants and Poverty: A Study of Haiti*. London: Croom Helm.

Lundahl, Mats (1980), 'Population Pressure and Agrarian Property Rights in Haiti', *Statsvetenskaplig Tidskrift*, Vol. 83, 275–83.

Lundahl, Mats (1983), *The Haitian Economy: Man, Land and Markets*. London and Canberra: Croom Helm.

Lundahl, Mats (1984a), 'Defence and Distribution: Agricultural Policy in Haiti during the Reign of Jean-Jacques Dessalines, 1804–1806', *Scandinavian Economic History Review*, Vol. 32, 77–103.

Lundahl, Mats (1984b), 'Papa Doc: Innovator in the Predatory State', *Scandia*, Vol. 50, 39–78.

Lundahl, Mats (1985a), 'Toussaint L'Ouverture and the War Economy of Saint-Domingue, 1796–1802', *Slavery and Abolition*, Vol. 6, 122–38.

Lundahl, Mats (1985b), 'Government and Inefficiency in the Haitian Economy: The Nineteenth Century Legacy', in: Michael B. Connolly and John McDermott (eds), *The Economics of the Caribbean Basin*. New York: Praeger.

Lundahl, Mats (1989), 'History as an Obstacle to Change: The Case of Haiti', *Journal of Interamerican Studies and World Affairs*, Vol. 31, 1–21.

Lundahl, Mats (1992), *Politics or Markets? Essays on Haitian Underdevelopment*. London and New York: Routledge.

Lundahl, Mats (1995), 'Economic Underdevelopment in Haiti: Some Fundamental Causes', in: *Themes in Development Economics: Essays on Method, Peasants and Government*. Aldershot: Avebury.

Maingot, Anthony P. (1986–87), 'Haiti: Problems of Transition to Democracy in an Authoritarian Soft State', *Journal of Interamerican Studies and World Affairs*, Vol. 28, 75–102.

Mintz, Sidney W. (1966), 'Introduction', to James G. Leyburn, *The Haitian People*. New Haven, CT and London: Yale University Press.

Moreau de Saint-Méry, Médéric-Louis-Elie (1958), *Description topographique, physique, civile, politique et historique de la Partie Française de L'Isle Saint-Domingue*. Three volumes, Paris: Société Française d'Histoire d'Outre-Mer.

Nicholls, David (1979), *From Dessalines to Duvalier: Race, Colour and National Independence in Haiti*. Cambridge: Cambridge University Press.

Olson, Mancur (1965), *The Logic of Collective Action: Public Goods and the Theory of Groups*. Cambridge, MA and London: Harvard University Press.

Olson, Mancur (1982), *The Rise and Decline of Nations: Economic Growth, Stagflation, and Social Rigidities*. New Haven, CT and London: Yale University Press.

Ott, Thomas O. (1973), *The Haitian Revolution, 1789–1804*. Knoxville, TN: University of Tennessee Press.

Peña Batlle, Manuel Arturo (1951), *La Isla de la Tortuga*. Madrid: Ediciones Cultura Hispánica.

Peña Pérez, Frank (1980), *Antonio Osorio: monopolio, contrabando y despoblación*. Santiago de los Caballeros: Universidad Católica Madre y Maestra.

Peña Pérez, Frank (n.d.), *Cien años de miseria en Santo Domingo, 1600–1700*. Santo Domingo: Editorial CENAPEC.

PNUD, Unité de Coordination et de Suivi de l'Environnement (ECMU) (1994), *Haiti 1994. Indicateurs environnementaux de base. Étude préliminaire*. Mimeo. Projet HAI/92/001. Port-au-Prince: PNUD.

Rotberg, Robert I. and Clague, Christopher K. (1971), *Haiti: The Politics of Squalor*. Boston, MA: Houghton Mifflin Company.

Sauer, Carl Ortwin (1966), *The Early Spanish Main*. Berkeley, CA and Los Angeles, CA: University of California Press.

Schmidt, Hans (1971), *The United States Occupation of Haiti, 1915–1934*. New Brunswick, NJ: Rutgers University Press.

Thylefors, Markel (2009), ' "Our Government is in Bwa Kayiman:" A Vodou Ceremony in 1791 and Its Contemporary Significations', *Stockholm Review of Latin American Studies*, No. 4, 73–84.

2
Economic Interests Are Color-Blind: On Class Divisions in Haitian History

In Haiti, foreigners are often called *'blan!'*. The unknown person is identified in the simplest possible way. He does not even have to be white. Haitians often refer to each other as *nèg*. This sounds strange for those not used to it. In the worst case, they interpret it, wrongly, as derogatory. But *nèg* simply means 'man' or 'hey, you!' *Nèg*, however, also means black, as opposed to *blan* or *milat*. Skin color has never been registered in Haitian censuses, but the overwhelming majority of all Haitians are black. Less than 10 percent are mulattoes, and then there are less than a thousand Levantines – Palestinians, Lebanese, and Syrians – who arrived in Haiti toward the end of the nineteenth century and at the beginning of the twentieth, and who have mainly married within their own group.

Among the first things that strike the foreigner in Haiti are the enormous social gaps. The members of the upper class are people who are as educated and cultivated as ever the Europeans, frequently even more. As everywhere else, the Haitian elite are sophisticated and amiable. Most of the time, they are relatively light-skinned, and rich. Frequently, they are also incredibly difficult. This is the case not least when it comes to their association with the population at large. Most Haitians are peasants. Haiti is a 'classic' peasant nation, and anthropologists, sociologists, and economists frequently write about peasant society. The peasants have nothing to do with the elite. They belong to what the French economist Gérard Barthélemy calls *'Le pays en dehors'* – the outside society.[1] The Haitian elite often pretend that the peasants do not exist. They do not identify with poor black devils who attempt to make a living for themselves and their families on infinitely small land plots. The gap between the upper and the lower classes often appears to be insurmountable, but why does it exist? Does skin color have anything to do with it, as in so many other parts of the world?

In 1979, the English priest and political scientist David Nicholls published a book which attracted a great deal of attention, *From Dessalines to Duvalier: Race, Colour and National Independence in Haiti*,[2] where he made a sharp distinction between race and skin color. According to Nicholls, race was always a unifying factor among the Haitians. All of them view themselves as linked by the African biological heritage, and the racial factor was an important component of the wars of liberation against the whites. Skin color, on the other hand – black or mulatto – has served to split the nation. Nicholls saw the social class divisions and the fight for power that characterized the entire nineteenth-century history of Haiti as a struggle between blacks and mulattoes. '...politics in Haiti from 1804 to 1915 was largely concerned with a struggle for power between two elite groups, designated principally by colour', he writes.[3]

Unfortunately, Nicholls' thesis does not work. Not even in the case of the colonial society so impregnated by racism that existed until the slave uprising in 1791 is it possible to explain the social divisions only in terms of skin color. They were also economic. The whites, of course, were found at the top of the colonial hierarchy. Below them were the manumitted slaves – the *affranchis* (mainly mulattoes, the offspring of the French) – but their status was based not only on skin color. It was also economic. They were often both land and slave owners. (Altogether, they owned up to one-third of all land and one-fourth of all slaves.) At the bottom of the pyramid were the 450,000 slaves. When the independent nation of Haiti was proclaimed in 1804, after the French had been killed or driven out, the *affranchis* saw themselves as their natural successors. They were economically important, and they liked to identify themselves with European culture. This view was, however, not shared by everybody. The revolutionary leaders had mainly been black slaves, and they of course also aspired to elite status.

In addition, there was a difference between northern and southern Haiti. It was in the northern parts, on the plains around Cap Français (present-day Cap-Haïtien) that the colonial sugar economy developed. That was where the greatest number of slaves were found and where the position of the whites had been strongest. It was also in the northern part of the country that the uprising against the French had begun. The southern part was more mountainous, which made sugar cultivation difficult, and the number of slaves was lower, comparatively speaking. The *affranchis* were strong there. The geographic differences between northern and southern Haiti were mirrored in the differences between the military and the economic elites.

In his book, Nicholls provides an account of the rise of two different historiographic traditions in nineteenth-century Haiti. The mulatto writing of history to a large extent was concerned with justifying the dominant position of the very mulatto elite in Haitian society. It depicted the black Haitian rulers as despots who did their best to suppress the mulattoes, and it opposed military intervention in politics because this intervention simply led to (black) autocracy. Divergences of interests between different groups in society were downplayed. The ideal would be if the nation could be united under enlightened and civilized (mulatto) leadership, the leadership of the fittest. The most able, those characterized by intelligence, courage, and integrity, should lead the nation.

The black history tradition was perhaps not always as explicit or unequivocal, but to the extent that it existed, it put the blame of all evil on the mulattoes and explained the shortcomings of the black heads of state on the fact that they were secretly governed by the mulattoes, what in Haiti is known as *politique de doublure*. This view preferred paternalistic (black) rule to elite rule, and in this, the army had a given role to play.

Not too many people were, however, influenced by more or less ideological writings. On the practical level, the writing of history was carried out by people who were not too bothered by book-learning. Often they were illiterate – and they had other interests. The problem with Nicholls is that he does not have any consistent thread in his skin color reasoning. Time after time, the analysis comes to a halt. The skin color question is reduced to something which is secondary in the given historical situation, and he is forced to resort to *ad hoc* explanations all the time. Skin color is always present in Haitian politics, but often it is an excuse, one of many factors – and moreover a subordinate one.

The history of nineteenth-century Haiti is complex, but above all, it is a story of power struggles. In 1843, Jean-Pierre Boyer, who had been president since 1818, was toppled. Thereafter a period of prolonged unrest began, with 22 presidents up to 1915. Only one of them finished his period. Four died during their presidencies, for more or less natural reasons. The rest were toppled: 11 held office for less than a year. Altogether, the country experienced more than a hundred more or less successful revolutions, coups or attempts during this period. This fact cannot be explained in terms of skin color. The political parties were not based on ideologies but they stood and fell with their leaders. It is difficult to find any systematic color patterns in the political constellations. Even Nicholls himself is forced to admit that this was the case at the beginning of the twentieth century.

If you want to explain the power struggle in nineteenth-century Haiti, it is a great deal more meaningful to view it as a struggle between different economic interests. In 1807, Haiti was divided into a northern kingdom under the black autocrat Henry Christophe and a southern republic under Alexandre Pétion, and until the death of Pétion in 1818, the relation between the two was in principle one of war. Paradoxically, it was Pétion, the elite mulatto, who in 1809, through his decision to dissolve the plantation system and redistribute the land, would do more than any other Haitian ruler to increase the economic and social equality – although probably without realizing the consequences that his decision would have. This led to the creation of a nation of smallholders, a nation that differed radically from the rest of Latin America with its polarization between immense latifundios and ridiculously small minifundios.

Pétion's decision, however, also had an undesirable political consequence. The new elite were not interested in eating their bread in the sweat of their brows. Now, however, the slaves were free peasants, and land was plentiful so they could not be converted into tenant farmers or agricultural workers. On the other hand, they could be taxed, but this required control of the political power. The struggle for the presidency was converted into a fight over government revenue, for the sake of private gains. Haiti was governed by a never-ending chain of kleptocrats, all the way up to the present time. Some of these predators were more light-skinned than others, and, as shown by Nicholls, skin color made regular appearances in politics, but it was never a fundamental force in the political game. Economic self-interest ruled, and that was color-blind.

What makes the analysis difficult for Nicholls is that it is not possible to meaningfully separate skin color from the other criteria that constitute social groups in Haiti. Almost 40 years before his book came out, Yale sociologist James Leyburn had published his classic *The Haitian People*.[4] He also had a thesis: Haiti was no class society. Reality was far worse. It was a caste society, with two groups which differed radically in virtually all respects. According to Leyburn, the elite did not amount to more than 2–3 percent of the population at the beginning of the 1940s, and over 90 percent of all Haitians were peasants. 'They are as different as day from night, as nobleman from peasant; and they are as separate as oil and water', he wrote.[5]

Leyburn identified a number of characteristics that distinguished the two groups. The elite did not work with their hands, but were mainly engaged in politics, since the road to riches went mainly through the latter. The masses were peasants. These peasants spoke nothing but *kreyòl*, the popular language which had emerged when slaves from more than 30 African nations had been forced to live together under French supremacy. The elite of course also spoke *kreyòl* but in addition, and by predilection, they spoke French. The third line of division was economic: the elite were rich, the masses were poor. 'The elite wear shoes', answered the American Marine Corps general Smedley Butler laconically, when during the American occupation of Haiti (1915–34), he was asked by a US Senate committee what the main difference was between the social classes in the country. It was only a slight overstatement. The peasants furthermore lived in the countryside whereas the elite were urban. The latter married formally, in church, while the masses lived in *plasaj ònèt*, a common-law marriage without sanction by the Catholic Church. The religion of the elite was Catholicism. The masses stuck to voodoo. Finally, 'the . . . most complicated distinction',[6] the skin color of the two groups differed, but Leyburn cautioned of false generalizations. There were black elite members and light-skinned peasants, although both were exceptions, not the rule.

Leyburn labeled the Haitian society a caste society. It was not based on skin color, because it was the totality, not each one of the criteria, in isolation, that determined status in society, but the characteristics tended to go hand in hand. In principle, the elite were endogamous. They would never marry anyone with a mass background, possibly white foreigners. According to Leyburn, Haiti came dangerously close to India's classic caste society, characterized by both social and economic immobility.

Leyburn's caste society thesis was challenged by Jean Price-Mars, Haiti's leading intellectual, in a review which occupied an entire issue of the *Revue de la Société d'Histoire et de Géographie d'Haïti*.[7] It made as much sense to contend that the United States, where the legislation was partly racist, was a caste society. In Haiti, after independence, no legislation had ever discriminated against either blacks or mulattoes (only whites). Price-Mars questioned the three fundamental elements of the caste system: its rigidity, its permanence, and its heredity, as well as their inevitable sequel: endogamy. There was no question about the fact that Haitian society was split, along the division lines indicated by Leyburn, but these lines could be redrawn, with some effort. Haiti was a class society, not a caste society.

Leyburn exaggerated the extent of rigidity in Haitian society. One of the things he overlooked, and which Nicholls stresses, is the emergence of a black middle class and new ideas – *négritude* – about Haiti's African heritage precisely during the period when he was working on his book. Nothing of the kind would have been possible in a caste society. This middle class was to become one of the most important actors when Dumarsais Estimé became president in 1946, the first black president in 30 years, and when François Duvalier, 'Papa Doc', who nurtured a number of 'ethnologic' ideas with respect to skin color, was elected in 1957.

Leyburn's analysis of what determines the social gap, on the other hand, is correct. It is only on a superficial level that the social lines of division coincide with differences in skin color. *'Nèg rich, se milat. Milat pòv, se nèg'* – 'A rich black is a mulatto. A poor mulatto is black' – summarized Jean-Jacques Acaau, legendary insurrection leader in the 1840s. It is still like that. The social gap is deep, and above all, it is economic. The upper class is rich, often fabulously rich, and the masses are poor. Today, three-fourths of all Haitians live on less than two dollars per day, one-half on less than one, and the distribution of income is as skewed as the one in South Africa or Brazil.

Does skin color not play any role at all, then? It certainly does, it always did, and it continues to do so today, but it is impossible to reduce the structure of Haitian society or history only to a problem of the relationship between blacks and mulattoes. All Leyburn's categories must be brought into the picture, and even David Nicholls had to admit that after the death of Papa Doc in 1971, skin color played a far less important political role than it had done during the preceding 25 years. In his final chapter, he writes that not enough effort had been put into 'studying the concrete social, economic and political structure of the country'.[8] This is exactly what he should have done himself instead of insisting on watching the Haitian society through his pre-adjusted *'lunettes bicouleures'*.

Notes

Published in *Axess* (Swedish version), No. 9, 2007.

1. Barthélemy (1989).
2. Nicholls (1979).
3. Ibid., p. 8.
4. Leyburn (1941).
5. Ibid., p. 4.

6. Ibid., p. 7.
7. Price-Mars (1942).
8. Nicholls (1979), p. 243.

References

Barthélemy, Gérard (1989), *Le pays en dehors: Essai sur l'univers rural haïtien*. Second edition. Port-au-Prince: Éditions Henri Deschamps.

Leyburn, James G. (1941), *The Haitian People*. New Haven, CT and London: Yale University Press.

Nicholls, David (1979), *From Dessalines to Duvalier: Race, Colour and National Independence in Haiti*. Cambridge: Cambridge University Press.

Price-Mars, Jean (1942), 'Classe ou caste? Étude sur "The Haitian People" (Le peuple haïtien) de James G. Leyburn', *Revue de la Société d'Histoire et de Géographie d'Haïti*, Vol. 13, No. 46, 1–50.

3
Poorest in the Caribbean: Haiti in the Twentieth Century

To the memory of David Nicholls – my sternest critic

Some statistical facts

Let it be said at once: Haitian statistics have never been good. Given the large probable margin of error,[1] they tell us little about Haiti's plight. The most recent data derive from the IMF.[2] According to these, GDP per capita amounted to US$524 in 1998, which, if true, represents an improvement of no less than 13 percent over 1996–97[3] and of more than 100 percent over the fatal year 1994,[4] when in the wake of the international sanctions following the military coup against President Jean-Bertrand Aristide in 1991, the figure had dropped by an estimated 30 percent.[5]

It is quite obvious that these figures make no sense. The changes are far too large for that. Still, there should be no question about the fact that Haiti is the poorest country in the entire Western Hemisphere and hence also the poorest in the Caribbean.[6] The available estimates of the long-run trend also tend to point to stagnation in the best case and decline more generally, ever since the 1920s.[7] As we will find below, there are good economic reasons for this to be true.

Even assuming that the IMF estimate of GDP per capita is correct, the figure is a mere average, and it hides the fact that some 80 percent of the rural population (which accounts for about two-thirds of the total) live below the poverty line (1995).[8] The human development index for Haiti in turn, which takes into account not only income but also longevity and education[9] has improved slightly, from 0.3 in 1990 to 0.4 in 1998, but Haiti has been relegated from the 137th position among those countries for which data are available to the 150th, which places Haiti on a level comparable to the poorest nations in Sub-Saharan Africa – an alarming finding.

Looking at the individual components of the human development index, we find that the life expectancy at birth was somewhat less than 54 years in 1998, an improvement over 1970 (below 48 years). The improvement is due to drastic reductions of the infant (under 1 year) and under 5 mortality rates, whereas the percentage of 15-year old who will die before they reach the age of 60 (the adult mortality rate) increased for both men and women in the late 1990s. The latter figures are the highest in the Western Hemisphere: 340 per 1000 for females and 432 for men. They are related not least to the nutritional situation, with an average daily calorie intake of 1869 in 1997 (80 percent of the standard recommended by the FAO) – a figure that is lower than the estimated intake in the 1960s: 2140 in 1962 and 2000 in 1966.[10]

The absence of adequate health facilities is another factor responsible for the high mortality rate. The number of physicians per 1000 people was no more than 0.2 in 1995, an improvement over the 0.1 in 1990 – a figure that had been stagnant since the beginning of the 1970s and which was not much higher than the 1952 figure.[11] Likewise, the availability of hospital beds per 1000 people in 1995 (0.7) was approximately the same as that reported in 1952 and lower than the corresponding figure for the early 1970s.[12] Again, Haiti ends up at a level comparable to that of the poorest African countries.

As far as the third component of the human development index, education, is concerned, the combined primary, secondary, and tertiary enrollment ratio gives a low total and a drastic decline from level to level. In 1998, 64 percent of the relevant age group was enrolled at the primary level, 15 percent at the secondary level, and a mere 1.3 percent at the tertiary level (1995 figure). In spite of this, it is reported that the adult (15 years and above) illiteracy rate has been reduced from 78 to 80 percent in the early 1970s to 52 percent in 1998[13] – a development hard to believe when it is taken into consideration that primary enrollment rates in 1985, 1990, and 1995 were between 12 and 20 percent lower than in 1960, and the percentage of repeaters was higher in 1995 than in 1980. At the primary level, 80 percent of the pupils go to private schools where they are taught in a resource-poor environment by teachers only 1 percent of whom are formally qualified and 67 percent of whom have not themselves finished their primary education.

Why does Haiti present such a dismal picture at the turn of the millennium? The rest of the chapter will attempt to provide an explanation of this, covering as much of the twentieth century as possible, but before embarking on that venture a suitable starting point for the analysis must be found – and that brings us to the nineteenth century.

Creating the setting: The nineteenth century

It is impossible to understand modern Haiti without going back to the nineteenth century – for two reasons. The first is that during the nineteenth century, the system of property rights that still prevails was created, and this in turn shaped the export pattern for a long time to come. The second is that during the nineteenth century, the Haitian political tradition was shaped. Both these events date from the crucial year 1809 – the year of the first 'land reform' of Latin America – and cannot be separated from one another. The same forces that put Haiti on the road to a peasant society created a predatory state. These two interacting and opposing forces are, in the main, those responsible for the state of utter underdevelopment that characterizes Haiti almost two centuries later.

Independent Haiti emerged out of an almost completely hierarchical society based on large properties and slave labor.[14] In the French colony of Saint-Domingue, there was a clear pecking order running from the *grands blancs* (large plantation owners, high government officers, wealthy merchants, etc.) to *petits blancs* (shopkeepers, small planters, artisans, etc.) to *affranchis* or *anciens libres* (manumitted ex-slaves, mainly mulattoes) to unfree *gens de couleur* to black slaves, and among the black slaves from *nègres créoles* born in the colony to *nègres bossales* imported from Africa.[15] The wealth of Saint-Domingue, the richest of all the French colonies, was generated mainly by the large sugar plantations, but to an increasing extent, also by the cultivation of coffee on, relatively speaking, smaller estates. By the time of the French Revolution, coffee had almost caught up with sugar in terms of export value.[16]

The protracted wars of liberation between 1791 and 1803[17] broke up the plantation society, but once the French yoke had been thrown off, the new Haitian rulers chose to go back to *la grande culture*.[18] This, however, lasted only until the decisive year in Haiti's history – 1809 – the year when the course of the next two centuries was decided, politically as well as economically. At that point, the plantation economy crumbled under its own weight.[19] The demand for Haitian export products had been reduced by the loss of the main market – France – and the Napoleonic Wars. The labor force had been reduced with around 140,000 people. The managerial and administrative competence had been lost with the expulsion of the French. The capital equipment which had been one of the most crucial components of the sophisticated economy of Saint-Domingue had to a large extent been destroyed. The remaining workers – the ex-slaves – had settled for subsistence food cultivation whenever the opportunity presented itself.

In this situation, Alexandre Pétion, president of the southern part of the country, decided that the time had come to begin a redistribution of the land (which after independence in 1804 had been state property), in favor of his officers and soldiers. In 1819, the ruler of northern Haiti, King Henry Christophe, followed suit – also under the pressure of both demand and supply forces.[20] The rest of the nineteenth century was to witness a rapid lapse of agriculture into peasant farming. The agricultural 'frontier' that was created by the sudden loss of population during the wars of liberation was closed at some point during the last quarter of the nineteenth century, and from then on, Haiti's agricultural history was reduced to a Malthusian race between population and food production, with disastrous long-run consequences for environment and living standards.

The events that began in 1809 saved Haiti from sharing the fate of most Latin American nations: that of a polarization between large and small properties, with the later strongly dependent on the former. However, it had another, unfortunate, consequence in the political sphere. The fact that an agricultural frontier existed where land was available at virtually zero cost for whoever chose to occupy it made it impossible for the new rulers and their polity to extract any surplus above the implicit wage accruing to those who worked the land.[21] In other words, the existence of a free peasantry with free land at its disposal precluded the creation of a work-free income for the power holders.[22]

The solution to this dilemma was taxation.[23] While the new elite had no business in their capacity of landowners unless they cared to soil their hands themselves, they could squeeze a surplus out of the peasants in the form of more or less randomly imposed taxes *provided that they possessed the political power*. This, the elite clearly understood, and they were to demonstrate it time after time, *ad nauseam*, all the way until the beginning of the American occupation of Haiti, in 1915. Politics in nineteenth-century Haiti turned into a negative-sum game using up resources in the fight over the spoils of the presidential office – a game where the winner took everything and did his best to humiliate and crush those he defeated. A predatory state was created which became the private property of those who ran it. The only purpose of politics was to grind out private incomes for the clique that happened to be in the saddle at whatever particular moment in time, at the risk of suddenly being overthrown by the next, even greedier faction. Between 1843 and 1915, the Haitians had to witness more than a hundred coups, revolutions and uprisings, with highly variable results.[24]

To sum up, at the end of the nineteenth century Haiti's economic fate was in a sense already sealed. Two powerful mechanisms were at work that would inexorably depress the living standard of the average Haitian and turn what had once been the jewel in the French crown into the poorest nation of the Western Hemisphere. The events of the twentieth century may rightfully be regarded as logical consequences of the structures that were built up between independence and the American occupation. In this chapter, we will look into seven different aspects of Haitian political economy, namely, the Malthusian erosion process, the continued degeneration of politics, notably the gap that has opened between the state and the nation, the failure to develop a growth-generating export basis, both in agriculture and in manufacturing, the consequences of politics and population growth for education, the absence of social capital, and, finally, the subservience of economic policy to selfish political goals. Altogether, these mechanisms have contributed to locking Haiti into a downward cumulative process of economic deterioration and political deadlock that has created incomes for the few at the expense of the many that constitute the Haitian nation and without whom the existence of the few would not have been possible.

Man versus nature: The process of soil destruction

The most fundamental of the mechanisms that have contributed to making Haiti the poorest country in the Western Hemisphere is the interplay between the growth of the population and the destruction of the arable soil.[25] Since the land is much more evenly distributed in Haiti than in other Latin American countries, it means that this process hits the agricultural sector more or less 'across the board' – with few exceptions. The overall rate of population growth is not exceedingly high in Haiti, but given the rugged topography of the terrain, the figure is high enough to have disastrous consequences in terms of loss of soil fertility.

The process works via the composition of agricultural production. In Haiti, a distinction may be made between export crops and food crops. Among the former, traditionally, we find coffee, sugar, cocoa, sisal, and so on.[26] Among the latter, we find beans, peas, rice, and corn. Both these categories of crops are in Haiti produced mainly with the aid of land and labor only while the input of capital tends to be negligible. The rural sector therefore very much resembles the two-by-two textbook economy producing two commodities using two factors of production. The main distinction between the two groups is that export crops tend to be land-intensive while food crops are labor-intensive.

This description of the rural economy in turn opens for the application of one of the standard theorems of international trade: the Rybczynski[27] theorem. This theorem, which is one of the most useful in economics, states that if the two production functions are linearly homogeneous (no economies of scale exist) and the endowment of one of the two factors increases, at constant relative commodity prices, the output of the commodity using the growing factor intensively will increase in absolute terms while the output of the other commodity will fall, relatively and absolutely. This has to do with the fact that if relative commodity prices are to remain constant so must relative factor prices and the factor intensities employed in each sector. Thus, when the labor force increases in rural Haiti, this increase must be absorbed by food cultivation, but if the land–labor ratio is not to be altered there, enough land must be taken out of export production together with some labor, so as to ensure that techniques remain the same in both lines of production. The theorem thus predicts that food crops will be substituted for export crops over time.

This is precisely what took place in Haiti at least during the second half of the twentieth century, and presumably the same tendency was at work during the first 50 years as well. It should be noted that a rise in the relative price of export products should theoretically be capable of reversing the sequence, but at least from around 1950 this was hardly the case. On the contrary, adverse trends in the world market prices of export goods combined with increased demand for food to give a further impetus to food production at the expense of export crops.

This sequence is not an innocent one in the Haitian context. The problem is that of the topography. The most important substitution is the one of food crops for coffee. This takes place on hill and mountain sides which are often very steep. The coffee plant is a tree with roots and a canopy which contributes to binding the soil and protecting it from the direct impact of rain and wind. It is furthermore perennial. Food crops do not share these characteristics. They either tend to be annual or they are harvested more than once during the year. As a rule, a given plot carries a number of food crops at the same time, which contributes to the rapid loss of nutrients, and in general, the ground is cleared during the harvest and when the time comes to plant or sow.

Unfortunately, the latter time happens to coincide with the rainy seasons, which is when the ground is soft enough for putting in the plants or the seeds.

The result is that when the tropical downpours set in the soil is easily washed off the steep mountain sides and into valleys and streams, that is, the substitution of food crops for export crops increases the likelihood of soil erosion. What is more, once this process has been set in motion, it feeds itself without any further need for population growth to stimulate it. The destruction of the soil simply amounts to running the Rybczynski theorem in reverse. The land shrinks and the output of the good using land intensively, that is export crops, must then contract while that of food crops increases, since food production has to absorb the labor that is taken out of export production, together with some land. For each round in the process more land is destroyed, the rural economy moves further and further into food production, and per capita income falls in the countryside. At the same time, the population continues to grow which means that the Rybczynski process receives further stimulus from this side as well. The process thus tends to accelerate and become cumulative.

The process of soil erosion receives a stimulus also from tree-felling for the purpose of getting firewood or making charcoal (the most commonly used fuel in Haiti, for which there is no economical substitute) and for the construction of houses. Together, the two mechanisms have contributed to the gradual destruction of the forest cover of the country, to the conversion of soils clad with perennial vegetation into barren land which cannot be used for anything. Little by little, Haiti is being turned into a naked rock with no capacity to nourish the population and give it an income.

Shaky as they may be, the statistics are revealing. In 1938, there was an estimated 540,000 hectares of 'good arable soil' in Haiti. In 1954, this figure had shrunk to 370,000, and in 1970, it was down to 225,750 hectares.[28] The figure reported for 1985 was 205,000 hectares,[29] and there are no indications that the trend should have been reversed thereafter. On the contrary. In the mid-1980s as much as 6000–10,000 hectares of arable land were lost each year,[30] and in the early 1990s, the figure was 6000–15,000 hectares.[31] Haitian agriculture continues to be what Sébastien Hilaire has called a mining agriculture.[32]

Why is nothing done to stop soil erosion? Is the Haitian peasant so myopic that he does not understand what is going on with his lands? Of course not. The peasant is no fool, but the incentives that he is facing are such as to force him literally to saw off the branch on which he is sitting. The core problem when it comes to erosion control is that the erosion process contains strong negative externalities.[33] Haiti is an extremely mountainous country, even more so than, for example, Switzerland. The population long ago grew to the point where the cultivated fields extended from the plains into the mountains. As a result, it does not pay a peasant to undertake erosion control, for example, in the form of terracing, unless his neighbors – notably those above him – do the same. If not, he simply incurs costs without ever seeing any benefits. The terraces will be washed away. The Haitian peasants are in the classic Prisoners' Dilemma situation, where they could be better off if they cooperated but where there are no incentives to do so.

To this must be added that the peasant tends to discount the future very heavily. Average income is low in the countryside, and the erosion process lowers the level over time. Thus one should perhaps expect the peasants to value additions to future incomes more than addition to present incomes, but that is hardly the case, since the Haitian peasant is so desperately poor that he has enough to do with trying to stay alive today. Increasing your incomes 10 years down the road does not sound like an interesting proposition unless you can feed your family today. The long and the short run collide with each other, and in this clash, the short run always pulls the longer straw. Tree planting and conservation of standing trees is not interesting as long as you need the wood here and now.

Food versus export crops: The failure to develop exports

One of our main findings so far is that there is competition between food and export crops in Haiti. The peasant export crop – the cash crop *par excellence* – is coffee. The production of this crop was well developed already toward the end of the colonial period, when coffee accounted for almost as much as sugar in value terms.[34] However, as we have seen in the foregoing, over time coffee has been fighting a losing battle against population growth and food crop production.

Coffee has, however, not been the only export product in Haiti.[35] During the course of the twentieth century efforts were made to push a number of other crops as well. Toward the end of the nineteenth century, Haiti exported coffee, cotton, cocoa, and logwood. Cotton prices had increased drastically during the American Civil War and stimulated production in Haiti, and from the late 1880s to the beginning of the 1920s, Haiti experienced a logwood boom. Cocoa had been cultivated already during the colonial period but had not received any real stimulus until world market prices went up in the mid-nineteenth century. From the 1890s to World War I, it was one of Haiti's most important export crops, due not least to the high quality of the output. In addition to this, coffee prices had been high in the 1890s, but fell toward the end of the decade, to remain low up to World War I.[36]

The export base was not overly strong at the beginning of the American occupation in 1915. Coffee dominated the picture, but prices were down, the logwood reserves were being depleted, and the increases in cotton and cocoa exports could not compensate for this.[37] The Americans made an effort to stimulate exports, not least because during the nineteenth century Haiti has accumulated a large foreign debt which had been consolidated into American hands. The repayment of the debt constituted the first priority of the occupation and for this export incomes were needed. The occupation administration attempted to stimulate American investment in large-scale farms in Haiti and to this end in 1918 changed the Haitian constitution which forbade foreign ownership of land.[38]

The effort failed, however. Few American companies could be made to enter Haiti, and when the occupation came to an end in 1934 only a large-scale sugar plantation venture, the Haitian American Sugar Corporation (HASCO), and the sisal producing Plantation Dauphin, later the world's largest sisal producer, stayed in Haiti. Coffee remained the most important export product, and the peasant economy continued to display the same features as it had during the nineteenth century: essentially a combination of food crops and coffee. During years with good coffee prices, like 1924–28, the country's import capacity increased, but once the depression hit and prices fell, export incomes were drastically reduced. The decision by Brazil to refrain from keeping the coffee price up during the 1930s dealt a further blow to Haitian exports.[39]

The 1930s also saw the introduction of a new export crop: bananas. In 1935, the Standard Fruit and Steamship Company from New Orleans was given exclusive rights to purchase and export bananas in all of Haiti, with the result that banana exports increased substantially during the rest of the 1930s. The momentum lasted until 1947 and conferred a certain prosperity on the Haitian countryside. However, in the mid-1940s, the company and the Haitian government got into a dispute, in 1946 President Estimé put an end to the monopoly concession and Standard Fruit decided to leave Haiti. Banana concessions were distributed right and left, to a number of small, not too serious companies, who in just a couple of years managed to ruin the reputation of Haitian bananas in the world market. In 1948, banana exports had been cut in half, and this was followed by a steady downward trend until bananas disappeared from the countryside as an export product.[40]

The latter half of the 1940s was a good period for exports with increasing coffee and sisal prices. The Korea boom in 1950 and 1951 also meant high coffee prices and an increased demand for sisal, but from late 1951 to the summer of 1952, sisal prices were halved. The year 1953 saw a very small coffee harvest, and the following year coffee prices fell drastically. The same year Haiti was hit by hurricane Hazel which destroyed 40 percent of the coffee harvest and 50 percent of the harvest of another export product: cocoa.[41]

In 1955, coffee was Haiti's dominant export product, accounting for over 65 percent of the total export value, followed by sisal with almost 16 percent, sugar with more than 3.5 percent, cocoa with almost the same share, and essential oils with 3.0 percent.[42] In 1971, Plantation Dauphin gave up sisal production, after a persistent fall in export prices since the early 1960s. Sisal had simply been out-competed by synthetic fibers. A brief revival until the mid-1970s proved unsustainable when prices fell again. A decade later, sugar had disappeared from the export list, also to make a brief, but futile, comeback to the mid-1980s. The sugar content of the cane had declined steadily since the 1940s, prices had been stagnant between 1948 and 1973, and at the beginning of the 1980s, it was clearly more profitable to grow food crops than sugar. The marginal tax rate on exports by the main private sugar company, HASCO, was increased drastically at the end of the 1960s and the early 1970s, while two competing, mismanaged and corrupt, government competitors benefited from substantial tax incentives. In the mid-1980s, Haiti had turned into a net importer of sugar, under the impact, among other things, of smuggling from the Dominican Republic. Cocoa, in turn, threatened to be out-competed by food crops from the mid-1950s to the mid-1970s, because of the operation of the Rybczynski effect, but an improvement of the relative price of cocoa made export increase again during the next decade.

Essential oils (vetiver, lime, and amyris) began to be produced in Haiti around 1940, and exports displayed an upward trend from the late 1950s to 1974, when they accounted for 9 percent of the total export value, and then declined again during the next 15-year period. The reason for this appears to have been the creation in 1975 of a government export monopoly which managed to price Haitian products out of the market, especially in the United States.

In the late 1950s, the American Reynolds company began to export bauxite from Haiti, and bauxite exports rose steadily until the early 1980s. In 1962, bauxite was already the second most important export item, after coffee, and 17 years later it almost accounted for 18 percent of the total. In 1983, however, bauxite production came to a total stop. The reasons were, on the one hand, the decision by a number of Caribbean bauxite producers to increase taxes and royalties on bauxite production by 700 percent in 1974 and 1975, and on the other hand, the reduction of the size of the bauxite reserves in Haiti.

Coffee, finally, displayed a decreasing export trend during the 1950s and 1960s, as a result of the Rybczynski effect in combination with a falling price of coffee in relation to food crops. Improved coffee prices and reduced taxes in the early 1970s combined to increase exports, and during the first half of the 1980s exports fell again, for reasons that are not completely clear, but which definitely include the interplay between population and soil erosion. The further decline of coffee exports, up to 1994, was a result of unfavorable prices and profitability in relation to food crops,[43] soil erosion, and the international sanctions imposed between 1991 and 1994.

The only alternative to primary or primary-based exports in Haiti has been the products of the light small-scale assembly industry.[44] This industry experienced rapid growth from the mid-1960s to the beginning of the 1990s. It is no exaggeration to say that it constituted the only bright spot in the Haitian economy during this entire period. The labor force, which consisted mainly of women, amounted to 46,000 in 1990, distributed across some 250 firms. Each one of these employees supported about three or four other people, mainly in the capital.

The assembly industry, which has been concentrated on the American market, and which to a large extent was American-owned, has rested on imported raw materials, and has been concentrated to such branches as toys, electronics and textiles, is based on Haiti's main comparative advantage: low wages. Its share of the total export value grew from less than 5 percent in the mid-1960s to more than two-thirds in the mid-1980s. Thereafter, however, the assembly sector suffered a hard blow. When President Jean-Bertrand Aristide was ousted after the military coup against him in 1991, international sanctions were imposed on Haiti. The sanctions wreaked severe havoc on the small-scale industry. The unavailability of oil made energy costs soar. Spare parts and inputs disappeared from the market and the customers were suddenly gone. At the beginning of 1995, after the return of Aristide a few months earlier, no more than 5000 workers were left in the sector.

Thereafter a long march back has begun, but markets have been lost, and many of the former companies have either fallen by the roadside or left the country. The international competition is hard, and from the competition point of view the 1990s by and large were a decade lost for the assembly industry. When in 1995 a study was made that compared the competitive position of Haiti with that of other countries in the Caribbean, Central America, and China, the outcome was not good.[45] Basically, Haiti had a competitive edge only with respect to Cuba, and in some respects, it was at par with the Dominican Republic. Possibly, this situation can be improved, but then Haitian politics, which has been irrational and chaotic for a long time, must take a turn for better. As long as physical safety cannot be guaranteed and the political process is developed mainly in the streets, expansion will prove difficult. We will come back to the political problem below.

As the twentieth century ended, in 1999, the share of agricultural products in total exports had fallen to 11.4 percent.[46] The main contributor here is coffee, with about 6 percent, followed by essential oils with around 2 percent.[47] In terms of volume, the 1999 coffee exports represent around two-thirds of the average for 1981–86 and less than half the average figure for 1950–55.[48] The light manufacturing industry, in turn, accounted for 84.2 percent of total exports, which represented a more than threefold increase in value terms since 1995.[49]

In other words, Haiti had become a pronounced industrial exporter. The comparative advantage of the country had changed from agriculture to manufacturing during the course of the twentieth century. This is far from as paradoxical as one may believe. In fact, it is precisely what one should expect to happen sooner or later, given the long-run population growth interacting with soil erosion. Haiti's agricultural exports have been relatively land-intensive. It is even possible that the country to an increasing extent has been exporting commodities in whose production it has had a comparative disadvantage, once the costs for society as a whole are taken into account. Export producers have not taken the cost of environmental degradation into account, and as is well known from the theory of distortions, this may result in exports of the 'wrong' product.[50] However, with the passage of time, production possibilities in agriculture have deteriorated, to the point where the labor-intensive products of the light assembly industry have become the main export item and agricultural products are being increasingly marginalized. This, of course, has implications for the choice of development strategy. We will come back to these below, but before we do so, we must take a look at some issues of economic policy and politics.

Politics versus economics: Economic policy problems

Long-run economic development generally presupposes an economic policy which on the one hand provides suitable incentives for growth and on the other hand provides a stable macroeconomic policy environment that does not create uncertainties and obstacles in the short run. In this respect, the twentieth century did not begin well for Haiti.[51] During the course of the nineteenth century, a number of governments had taken up loans abroad: in 1825, 1874, 1875, and 1896. With the exception of the first one, which was the result of an indemnity forced upon Haiti by France, these were floated for a variety of shady purposes which all had in common that they provided the cliques that governed Haiti with private incomes at a high cost for the state, since none of them could be floated except at a high discount. They were complemented by a variety of domestic loans on similar conditions. The disastrous loan policy continued during the pre-occupation years of the twentieth century. In 1910, a further foreign loan – the last one before the occupation – was floated at a 38 percent discount, and between 1912 and 1914, this was complemented with six domestic loans that killed whatever was left of Haiti's creditworthiness.

The disastrous loan policy was directly responsible for the economic policy of the American occupation administration: a policy that first and foremost saw to the interests of the American bondholders into whose hands the debt had been consolidated between 1922 and 1925. The external debt was paid off at an extremely rapid pace which continued also after the end of the occupation, since the United States continued to exercise supervision of Haitian finances until the last amortization had been made in 1947. The scrupulous record of debt repayment, paying off the debt ahead of time, in addition building up cash reserves for future payments, however, did Haiti no good when it came to obtaining new funds. The only instance was a loan from the Export-Import Bank in 1938, for public works by an American company, which as it seems squandered the money.

The American-directed repayment policy made it extremely difficult to free money for development purposes. The only project that was launched before the end of World War II ended with a fiasco. The project was a direct outcome of the war: an effort to grow cryptostegia – a domestic vine rubber – by an American company, Société Haïtiano-Américaine de Développement Agricole (SHADA), when the rubber plantations of Southeast Asia had been lost to the Japanese. An American loan of $5 million was obtained and 150,000 hectares were put at the disposal of the company, at the expense of local peasants. However, no rubber was ever exported, since growing conditions turned out to be unfavorable, and the project ended up as a major loss maker.[52]

The first postwar years saw a return to more or less complete passivity, with a UNESCO project in the Marbial Valley near Jacmel as the major exception. The project aimed at basic education, including literacy, which would facilitate an improvement of living standards in an isolated community. This project failed as well. Corruption, incompetence, and lack of funds combined with the unfortunate selection of an isolated area to make progress impossible.[53]

During the first half of the 1950s, a weak effort toward planned economic development was made, but the plan for 1951–56 was a mere want list which besides did not contain the most important ventures, notably the Artibonite Valley project. The latter aimed at damming the Artibonite River for irrigation purposes and for electricity generation. The end result was that $29 million (as compared to the planned 21 million) were spent before the project was interrupted in 1958. At that point three-fourths of the targeted area was irrigated but the projected hydroelectric power station had not yet been begun. Rampant corruption had squandered the money.[54]

In the meantime, François Duvalier (Papa Doc) had become president, in 1957. During the coming 30 years, the Haitian economy would be completely mismanaged. The public purse would be made completely subservient to the interests of the presidential family, with disastrous results for the economy. As was made clear in the introductory section of this chapter, plunder was nothing new to Haiti. On the contrary, the predatory aspects always dominated Haitian political life. However, there are degrees also in Hell, and in the Haitian case, plunder and corruption reached unprecedented heights during the rule of Papa Doc (1957–71)[55] and Baby Doc (Jean-Claude Duvalier, 1971–86).[56] Papa Doc was an innovator in the field of predation, using all conceivable means, notably the unbudgeted accounts of the Régie du Tabac et des Allumettes, the tobacco monopoly, which collected taxes on a number of goods other than tobacco and matches, and whose funds were channeled into the pockets of the president and into the paramilitary thug organization known as the *tonton macoutes*. His son, in turn, relied more on the various notorious loss-making public enterprises that had been set up as further conduits of money.

During the chaotic years that followed the fall of the Duvalier dynasty, things did not improve very noticeably.[57] For one thing, the macroeconomic situation had deteriorated sharply. The budget deficit amounted to 7 percent of GDP in 1984–85, inflation was rampant, the state-run enterprises made huge losses, inefficient import-substituting industries produced behind tariff walls or protected by quantitative import restrictions, coffee exports were struggling against high taxes, other taxes were generally evaded, and what tax revenue there was could be collected only at high cost.

This situation called for drastic reforms, and reforms there were.[58] The budget deficit was reduced and inflation brought down. The coffee export tax was abolished, and so were the quantitative import restrictions. The latter were replaced with tariffs and tariff levels were brought down. A reform of the tax system was initiated. For a short while, it looked as if the situation would improve, but when the presidential elections that had been scheduled for late 1987 were violently interrupted by ex-*Duvaliéristes* the situation again got out of hand. The international donor community withdrew its support, and the reform effort foundered. The country was back to where it had been when Baby Doc fell.

Since then, economic policy making in Haiti has been dominated by the twofold problem of how to achieve stabilization and growth at the same time. Another attempt was made in 1991, after the inauguration of Jean-Bertrand Aristide as the new president of Haiti. The second reform package included balancing the budget, controlling domestic credit, increasing the efficiency of tax collection, reducing smuggling, trimming the corrupt pubic administration and maintaining a strict monetary policy. Again, macroeconomic indicators began to look more favorable, but the effort lasted a mere 8 months – until Aristide was ousted by the military.

Once again the clock had been turned back, and it was not until after the invasion in September 1994 that brought Aristide back that a third reform effort could be launched, only that at that point real per capita income had fallen with an estimated 30 percent as compared to before the coup. At the same time the major macroeconomic imbalances had come back: an increased budget deficit, negative public saving, declining tax revenue due to a breakdown of the tax collection system, declining public investment, non-payment of the public debt, a balance of payments deficit instead of a surplus, a currency which had depreciated with two-thirds vis-à-vis the dollar and an inflation rate of over 50 percent on the eve of the invasion.

The new Aristide government launched a new stabilization effort, beginning with an emergency recovery program and continuing with a medium-term economic strategy which emphasized trade and capital movement liberalization, fiscal reform, government expenditure reduction, restrictive monetary policy and privatization of the mismanaged public enterprises. This program was inherited by the government of René Préval who took over as president in 1996. For the third time, the cycle repeated itself. The macroeconomic indicators began to look favorable exactly as during the first two programs. However, for the third time the process was wrecked by political factors. A fight ensued over the privatization program, with Aristide suddenly declaring that he was against it, but this was only the nominal issue. The real issue was that the ex-president had begun to stage his come-back in the 2000 elections and to that end wanted to appear as a savior of Haiti as the country emerged out of chaos – a chaos that the ex-president himself had been instrumental in creating. In the end, the political process broke down. The opposition claimed that the 1997 parliamentary elections were marked by fraud. In the aftermath, Haiti was without a prime minister for one-and-a-half years, until December 1998, and in January the following year, the parliament was closed by presidential decree. Lacking a political base that was independent of Aristide, Préval could not produce an efficient government. In December 2000, Aristide was elected as president for the second time, in elections where the opposition refused to take part. The country continues to be politically paralyzed.

Government versus citizens: The continued degeneration of politics

One of the main conclusions to be drawn from our survey of economic policy in Haiti is that the advent of the twentieth century did not put any end to kleptocratic rule. Quite on the contrary. The first 15 years were nothing but the accelerated continuation of the pattern of clique fights that characterized the formative nineteenth century. This pattern was not to be changed until the American occupation, and then only superficially. In spite of its long duration – 1915–34, that is, 20 years – the occupation left few positive traces. Admittedly, the Americans made an effort to clear up some of the worst abuses, for example, by purging government payrolls, getting rid of various types of 'zombie' employees that either did not exist or showed up only to collect the paycheck. However, as we found in the section on economic policy, the insistence on favoring the American bondholders above everything else starved Haiti of funds for economic development.

On the political level, this policy had its counterpart in the failure to develop democracy in Haiti.[59] It is not difficult to argue that the occupation forces missed a golden opportunity there. While they clearly saw the need for putting an end to the clique fights, they failed completely to provide a viable alternative, during two decades, or at least during one, if we start counting from 1922 when the occupation entered its allegedly 'constructive' phase. Elections and plebiscites were indeed held, on various occasions, up to 1929, but all of them had in common that they were controlled by the US Marines. It even seems as if genuine popular participation and democracy were seen as lost causes from the beginning, and when the so-called Forbes Commission appointed by President Hoover to make an evaluation of the occupation and look into the future US policy toward Haiti published its report, it concluded that the training given to the Haitians in matters of public administration and government had been insufficient and that no real foundations existed for democratic and representative government after the end of the occupation. One of the main reasons was the failure to provide education. We will come back to this below.

Instead of preparing Haiti for democratic government, the occupation paved the way for further kleptocratic rule.[60] In the same way as in Cuba, the Dominican Republic and Nicaragua, a Marine-trained constabulary mixing army and police functions – the *Garde d'Haïti* – was substituted for the old army, with the inevitable result that the new army became a decisive voice also in politics. On the predatory layer of the state was superimposed a praetorian one. It did not take long before the time-honored tendency to use political office for purely private purposes showed up again, and the post-occupation presidents holding office up to the beginning of the Duvalier dynasty in 1957 all attempted in various ways to extend their period in office beyond the constitutional one. Behind them, we find the army calling the shots.

Papa Doc changed all that.[61] He would presumably not have been elected without the consent of the army, and this he clearly realized. Hence, one of the first strategic decisions that he made was on the one hand to make certain that he – and nobody else – controlled it and on the other hand to set up a counterbalancing force that owed allegiance to nobody but the president. The high command of the armed forces was completely reshuffled in favor of newly promoted *Duvaliériste* officers and the dreaded paramilitary Gestapo-like *tonton macoutes* were created, recruited mainly from among the dreg at the bottom of Haitian society so as to make sure that they knew who was responsible for their advancement in life. This was complemented with the rural sheriffs, the *chefs de section*, the traditional wielders of power in the Haitian countryside, and the voodoo clergy who were made to accept Duvalier as their supreme leader. All other conceivable power structures were weeded out, until Haitian politics was completely dominated by a single man – the *Président à Vie*. The plunder could begin.

The foundations laid by the older Duvalier had an important drawback. They could not easily be transferred to his son and successor as president for life, because they all built on Papa Doc's person. Hence, Jean-Claude Duvalier had to opt for a different way of running the predatory state.[62] The more repulsive features – like the *tonton macoutes* – were pushed into the background, the young president began to associate himself more with traditional (and non-traditional) elite circles, and on the face of it, a more technocratically oriented government took over. In practice, this mattered little, because the state apparatus was still set for plunder, only that a 'fine tuning' phase had now begun, with more reliance being put on using the public administration and enterprises instead of resorting to the more direct and often clumsier methods that had characterized the 1957–71 period. The cumulative result was impressive. When Baby Doc fell from power in 1986, the wealth of the presidential family amounted to an estimated $1.6 billion.

Those who had hoped for a change once the Duvaliers had disappeared from the political scene were in for a great deception. The various military governments that succeeded Baby Doc from 1986 to 1994 had nothing but plunder in mind.[63] As could be expected, new links were added to the chain of predators extending back to the nineteenth century. We can just hope that this chain was broken in 1994 and that the break was a definite one, but we cannot yet be sure. In the past, the negative heritage of Haitian history has always taken over, and even people who are not necessarily corrupt from the beginning easily turn corrupt if the environment within which they are working give them bad incentives. The democracy that triumphed in the 1990 elections that made Aristide president is today an endangered species in Haiti, and the obverse of that coin is that whatever predatory tendencies that exist can all too easily make a come-back and push the country further into underdevelopment and backwardness.

Man versus man: The lack of social capital

To sum up our findings so far, Haiti's poverty during the twentieth century is due to a number of interrelated causes which all have their roots during the nineteenth century. The most fundamental one is the interplay between population growth and erosion that runs via the crop mix in agriculture. This over time tends to depress rural incomes. At the same time, it acts as a break on agricultural exports. Haiti never experienced any staples-led growth process, and it can even be argued that increasingly the country has been exporting land-intensive products in which it has a comparative disadvantage. However, the comparative advantage – cheap labor – increasingly revealed itself during the latter half of the twentieth century, and the labor-intensive products of the light assembly industry sector have now come to dominate exports.

The assembly industries, however, came close to being ruined by the politics of the predatory state in he 1990s, and the existence of a kleptocratic regime also lent a very heavy bias to economic policy. Economic development was never pursued, but policies were always made subservient to the selfish interests of the rulers. When Jean-Claude Duvalier fell from power in 1986, the history of unhampered plunder had thrown Haiti into a macroeconomic chaos from which the country has not yet emerged, due to the persistence of the 'old' political patterns.

Two more issues remain to be discussed: the lack of social capital and the deficient educational system. Both of these of course constitute important parts of the political–economic syndrome of Haitian underdevelopment, since they are consequences of the degeneration of politics. Here, however, we will deal with them in the context of development strategies. Would it have been possible to find a realistic counterfactual, based on honest government in politics and industrialization in the economy, that would have been able to lift Haiti out of the increasingly sad state that characterized in during the twentieth century, and will it be possible to do so in the future?

Let us begin with the issue of social capital. The rift between the government and the elite on the one hand and the masses on the other hand is one of the constant themes of Haitian history.[64] It was self-evident during the colonial period; Saint-Domingue was a society of slaves and slave-owners. The only reason for the existence of the former was their exploitation by the latter. After independence, this was expressed in the opposition between large plantations and small subsistence farms, a fight that the latter won.

The rulers did not give up that easy, however. Exploitation through more or less formalized and more or less legal taxation took the place of exploitation via land rents after 1809. During the rest of the nineteenth century, a society would develop that was so polarized that it even (mis)led James Leyburn to talk about castes rather than classes in the Haitian context.[65] The masses knew that when the ruling cliques expressed any interest in them, it was basically either as tax objects or as potential recruits for the army. Accordingly, they did their best to avoid the authorities. The character of the army has changed, as we have already seen, but the twentieth-century history of taxation remains one of paying without receiving very much in return.

The counterpart of the antagonistic positions of government and population is to be found in the relations between various groups in society, notably those who take part in the political game. Haitians are perfectly capable of cooperating for some common good, but given the political history of the country, cooperation has usually been limited both in scope and in time.[66] Nobody believes in the long run, but Haiti is a country where today easily dominates tomorrow – for obvious reasons. By the same token, striving for small but safe benefits is preferable to venturing into large-scale efforts involving many uncertain interests – not least a greedy state likely to intervene at any moment should things turn out well. Thus, no efficient larger social groupings or networks capable of handling long-run development efforts exist. Twentieth-century Haiti was a praetorian society, in the sense that most instances of life were politicized and that the groups involved faced each other in situations of direct and brutal confrontation where no institutionalized rules existed that could help to mitigate and solve conflicts.[67] There was no room for the losers, but the winners took everything. The Haitian political tradition has never been one which leaves any room for an organized opposition, but the only good opposition has been a crushed opposition without any power to interfere. The political contenders have behaved as mere sluggers, and the citizens have mistrusted them completely. This tradition is still very much alive – putting the frail flower of democracy in direct jeopardy. Unfortunately, it does not seem as if any change is imminent. The way Haitian politics developed during the 1990s leaves a lot to be desired. Politics continues to be an unabashed and unhampered game about power and money, and in the meantime, the economy continues its inexorable path toward ecological and human disaster.[68]

Rulers versus ruled: Education in Haiti

The second component of our counterfactual is education. At present, Haitian manufacturing is located on the lower rungs of the ladder of comparative advantage, on the level where cost advantages are a result of the existence of cheap labor with no special skills. This type of production results only in low incomes for those employed, and in the longer run, it is therefore desirable to move up the ladder, into production that is more skill-intensive. Could this have been achieved already during the twentieth century?

The answer to this question is no, not given the Haitian educational system.[69] At the beginning of the twentieth century, in 1906, the country had 594 public schools, a figure which in 1913 had shrunk to 465. These figures, however, were of little if any practical significance, because the tumultuous state of politics, with revolutions and uprisings constituting the order of the day, made it impossible to allocate funds to education. When the American occupation of Haiti began, the public school system was in a situation resembling 'total ruin'. The private school system had undergone exactly the same retrogression, from 82 schools in 1905 to 53 10 years later. The literacy rate in the country as a whole was well below 10 percent and in the countryside, virtually everybody was illiterate.

The American occupation attempted a restructuring of the Haitian school system. It was felt that the education that was offered was too 'impractical', deriving as it did from the French system, with emphasis on literature and classics. To this end, the Americans set up a more vocationally oriented system, with emphasis not least on farming, in *fermes-écoles*. These schools, however, never got off the ground, and by the time that the occupation began to be dismantled, in 1930, the farm school budget was cut drastically. As a result, once the Americans had left, the French-oriented system again took over. Then, however, the schools were in a dismal state, not least in rural areas, where in 1931, it was found that the typical school would hardly have any benches and possibly no blackboard, certainly no maps, the teacher would be illiterate and did not know the four simple arithmetical operations.

The following 15 years saw little change, especially in the countryside where grossly underpaid teachers had to teach 50 pupils each or more in deplorable material conditions. After the 1946 revolution that put Dumarsais Estimé into the presidency, the school system was reorganized. The rural schools, which in 1931 had been put under the control of the Department of Agriculture (together with some small-town schools) were brought under the same umbrella as urban education, and an adult alphabetization campaign was begun. In spite of this, the 1950 census revealed that the overall illiteracy rate was around 90 percent in the age groups over 15, with 93 percent in rural districts, some of which reached 97–98 percent – figures that are even likely to be underestimates.

These trends were to continue for the next 20 years. At the beginning of the 1970s, enrollment and illiteracy rates differed little from those prevailing two decades earlier in rural areas, whereas the illiteracy rate for the country as a whole had fallen to 80 percent. The public school system had suffered under Papa Doc, and a heavy burden fell on the private schools. At that time, the Haitian school system presented a number of negative 'filter' aspects. The medium of instruction was French – a foreign language for the majority of Haiti's children. Materials, buildings, and teachers were all usually of low quality. Strong emphasis was put on formal examination in each grade, which made many children, especially rural children, either repeat grades or drop out. This system made it virtually impossible to advance economically and socially through education for children who came from a disadvantaged background – that is, for the vast majority of children. Education, especially secondary and tertiary education, was reserved for the relatively well-to-do. In other words, a discriminatory system had been built up which helped to conserve the social structure of Haitian society. The representatives of the predatory state did not find it worthwhile to put money into something that did not yield immediate benefits for them. The rulers ensured that the educational system would help making the division between rulers and ruled a permanent one.

Since the beginning of the 1970s, it appears as if some progress has taken place. Presumably, the decision to use *kreyòl* as a medium of instruction in the schools has something to do with this, since it removed one of the major obstacles to learning how to read and write. Also, education received increased priority in the budget following the fall of Baby Doc in 1986, but much of this went into salary increases instead of investment. The private school system continues to be of supreme importance, even more so now than before, since the majority of all Haitian children now go to private schools: two-thirds on the primary level, over 80 percent on the secondary and about 50 percent on the tertiary. Enrollment has improved. No less than 90 percent of the children in school age also begin school, but less than 30 percent continue to the secondary level, where only 6 percent, however, finish, and a mere 4 percent go on to tertiary education.[70] If we are to believe official figures, literacy has increased considerably, to over 50 percent at the end of the 1990s, but as has already been pointed out, this figure appears to be too high.

Coming back to the issue of specific skills for the export industry, Haiti has a very long way to go before it can possibly compete in the production of goods with higher skill content than the one offered by the simple assembly industries. In 1995, no more than 5800 people were enrolled in technical education.[71] Whether we will see any expansion in this field is doubtful. A handful of years ago, 70 percent of all the technical schools were private. It remains for the government to profess more than a token interest in the upgrading of skills. The alternative is continued private expansion, but for this to work there must be a demand, and it is doubtful whether that exists. Traditionally, within the structure of the predatory state, it has paid much more handsomely to invest in the creation of contacts with the 'right' kind of people than in education,[72] that is, unless Haiti can break with its political past this situation will continue.

Education may present low returns for another reason as well.[73] One of the peculiarities of human capital is that it displays increasing returns to the already accumulated stock, that is, the higher the level of education, the easier it becomes to increase the stock. Assume that citizens derive utility not only from their own consumption, but also from the future consumption of their children. Assume furthermore that the consumption of the children increases with education and that parents in order to maximize their utility have to divide their time between the production of goods, child rearing, and education of the children. In Haiti, the existing stock of human capital is small. Thus the return to human capital creation should be low, there will be relatively much time available to simple child rearing, families will tend to be large and the rate of discount of the future (of the consumption of the children) high. No accumulation of human capital will then take place. A low-education, high-birth rate equilibrium trap will be created that is difficult to break out of. Unless more human capital is accumulated than what wears out the tendency will be for the stock of human capital to fall toward the zero level. Unless a jump or 'big push' in human capital formation is achieved, the economy may be stuck there.

The rate of return to skill accumulation may be kept down by competition in the world market for higher-skill manufactured goods.[74] These goods often require specialized inputs (intermediate goods) that have to be developed in close cooperation with the customers, that is, a *range* of such inputs (e.g., different services) may be needed. Unless there is a demand for the final product no inputs may be forthcoming, and the competition of already established, foreign low-cost producers in the final goods market could mean that the investment needed will never turn out to be profitable, and vice versa: the wider the range of inputs available, the lower the costs of the final-goods producers, but as long as intermediate production has not been developed, final goods production will be unprofitable: Catch 22.

In the worst case, the development of more skill-intensive production of manufactures may have undesirable side effects.[75] We may think of a three-sector economy, where agricultural goods are produced with the aid of land and unskilled labor, low-technology manufactures with the aid of unskilled labor and capital, and higher-tech manufactures with the aid of capital and skilled labor. The non-specific factors are assumed to be mobile between the two sectors that employ them. The income elasticity of demand for higher-tech manufactures is likely to be higher than that of simpler manufactured goods, in such a way as to make the relative price of the former rise over time as world income does. Let us, for the sake of simplicity, assume that the price of higher-tech goods rises while the prices of the other two goods remain constant. This will increase the return to both skilled labor and capital and hence pull capital out of simpler manufacturing and into the more advanced sector. Hence, the unskilled wage rate must fall (and the return to land increase, when unskilled labor is pushed back into agriculture). Thus, to the extent that capital can be transferred from one type of manufacturing to the other (the long run), 'trading up' in manufacturing may have undesirable side effects which makes it even more important to develop the educational system.

Conclusions

The relative position of Haiti in the Caribbean context does not come as any surprise. The country scores badly on all the dimensions that we have examined in this chapter. At the bottom of Haitian underdevelopment is a purely economic mechanism: the tendency for population growth to reduce per capita income via the process of soil erosion: a process which once it has been put in motion becomes self-sustained. Erosion feeds more erosion without any need for further population growth, and once it is taken into account that the population *does* continue to grow, the process becomes cumulative. This mechanism was operating during the entire twentieth century.

The soil destruction process is intimately related to the tendency created by population growth for labor-intensive food crops to be substituted for land-intensive export crops. Haitian agriculture has displayed a kind of an anti-export bias *sui generis*. Over time, it has become more and more difficult to export the traditional crops, and this tendency has been reinforced by political interventions of the most dubious kind. The fact that the export crops have been land-intensive, relatively speaking, has meant that as erosion has taken its toll whatever comparative advantage that Haiti may once have had in the production of these crops has been lost, and we have argued that after some point in time, the country may even have been exporting products in which, in fact, it has had a comparative *dis*advantage. Another indication of this is the rise of the small assembly manufacturing producers, who, however, also were badly hurt by the unfortunate state of Haitian politics. In spite of his, today Haiti is basically an exporter of manufactures, not of agricultural products, and this fact is completely central to all future discussions of development strategies.

Turning the attention to economic policy, we find that little has been done to facilitate development in Haiti. The first years of the twentieth century were chaotic, the American occupation was not helpful, at best a mere parenthesis between kleptocratic rulers, and after the end of the occupation policies were made to serve 'political' purposes. Predation culminated with the two Duvaliers, and thereafter three reform efforts have been made – efforts that have all failed due to political reasons.

Behind the failure of economic policy lies the degeneration of the Haitian state. This feature, which characterized the entire twentieth century, cannot be understood without going back to the nineteenth one, to the crucial year 1809, when the large-scale plantation system received a decisive blow from which it was never to recover. A nation of free peasants with access to free land could be made to yield a surplus to the government only through taxation. The presidential office turned into a prize which competing cliques were to fight over all the way up to the present. The only difference between the nineteenth and the twentieth centuries in this respect was the more important and more coordinated role played by the army until the latter was finally abolished after Aristide's return to Haiti in 1994.

A corollary of the degeneration of the state is to be found in the absence of social capital in Haiti. Since the citizens met the state only when they were to pay taxes or serve in the army, a wide gap between the people and the government opened during the turbulent nineteenth century, and this gap has never been healed. The Haitians still mistrust the authorities and the politicians. They have a clear understanding of why the latter are in the political game. The unfortunate heritage has in turn created a society that is very politicized on virtually all levels, where contending forces are facing each other, trying to wipe each other out and where constructive, cooperative, long-run solutions in the interest of the common good are conspicuous by their absence. This tradition is still very much alive in Haiti – with all the implications that his may have for the future.

Another corollary of the sad state of politics has been then failure to develop the educational system. As of today it is the private, not the public, schools that handle most of the pupils. During most of the twentieth century, the order of magnitudes was reversed, but this did not mean much in terms of success. In 1950, a minimum of 90 percent, and probably more, of all Haitians were illiterate, and the educational system that developed served more to put a brake on social mobility than to facilitate the accumulation of human capital. The situation toward the end of the century was somewhat better, among other things, because finally the language that all Haitians understand – *kreyòl* – was finally introduced as the means of instruction. Still, however, the kind of technical skills needed if Haiti is to raise its per capita income level are lacking.

This makes industrial development difficult, but demand factors may preclude industrialization at higher skill levels even if the decision is taken to do something about the educational system. Exports of skill-intensive goods cannot be developed in isolation. There are always foreign, low-cost, competitors to be reckoned with who may make it impossible to develop the necessary skills, and even if such skills should become available, they may have negative side effects on the majority of unskilled workers, which in turn will serve to put an even heavier strain on the educational system. It was never easy to be Haitian.

Acknowledgments

A preliminary version was presented at the conference explaining the Per Capita Income Gap among Countries in the Caribbean, St. James, Trinidad, May 14–15, 2001. I am grateful to the conference participants, in particular Lloyd Best, Compton Bourne, Victor Bulmer-Thomas and Eric Hershberg, for their constructive comments.

Notes

Published in *Integration and Trade*, No. 15, 2001, published by the Institute for the Integration of Latin America and the Caribbean, Buenos Aires. Reprinted by permission.

1. FAO (1995), p. 20, Catanese (1997).
2. IMF (2001), pp. 50–65.
3. IMF (1999), p. 3.
4. IMF (1995), p. 2.
5. Banque de la République d'Haïti (1995), p. 14. For other estimates, see Lundahl and Silié (2000).
6. According to both the IMF and the World Bank, at present, Nicaragua is worse off than Haiti. The IMF (2001, p. 52) figure for GDP per capita in Nicaragua is US$477 (1998), to be compared to US$524 for Haiti, and the latest World Bank (2001, pp. 274–75) figure for Nicaraguan GNP per capita (1999) is US$430 against US$460 for Haiti. To someone who has worked on

both Nicaragua and Haiti these figures, however, do not make sense. They simply raise severe doubts about the estimates for both Haiti and Nicaragua.

7. Lundahl (1997), pp. 3–4.
8. The poverty line is 'the local cost (at March 1996 prices) of reaching the FAO minimum nutritional standard of 2,240 calories daily per capita, with a diet that matches the food expenditure percentages of the average ... household [the indigency line] ... [plus] expenditure on non-food commodities, such that the percentage of food expenditure in total expenditure matches the average for poor rural households ....' The latter average is an 'average of the budgetary proportion spent on food for ... families for whom (a) total expenditure was in the vicinity of the indigency line and (b) food expenditure was in the vicinity of the indigency line' (Wiens and Sobrado, 1997, p. 3).
9. The human development index is an unweighted average of indices for life expectancy at birth, educational attainment and GDP per capita in US$ adjusted for purchasing power. The index for life expectancy takes 25 and 85 years as the minimum and maximum values and is computed as the difference between the actual value and the minimum value, divided by the difference between the maximum and minimum values. The educational attainment index is a weighted average of the combined gross primary, secondary and tertiary enrollment ratio (which may vary from 0 to 100 percent) (weight one-third) and the adult (above 15 years) literacy rate (between 0 and 100 percent) (weight two-thirds). These two indices are computed in the same way as the life expectancy index. The adjusted GDP per capita (PPP US$) index, finally, is obtained by first converting the GDP per capita figure into US$ using the purchasing power parity exchange rate (making one US$ have the same purchasing power over GDP as the US$ has over the US GDP), in order to correct for price level differences. The adjusted figure for GDP per capita is thereafter used to calculate the GDP per capita (PPP US$) index in the same way as the other indices (with PPP US$100 and 40,000 as the extreme values), but using the logarithms of the GDP per capita figures to account for the fact that there are diminishing returns to the ability of income to fulfill human needs (UNDP (2000), pp. 269, 278, 281).
10. Lundahl (1979), p. 110.
11. Ibid., p. 429.
12. Ibid.
13. IMF (2001), p. 56; Lundahl (1979), p. 478.
14. Leyburn (1941), Chapter 2.
15. Nicholls (1979), pp. 21–27.
16. Lundahl (1979), pp. 256–59.
17. Stoddard (1970), James (1963), Ott (1973), Fick (1990).
18. Lundahl (1992), Chapters 8–9.
19. Lundahl (1979), Chapter 6.
20. Thébaud (1967), pp. 73–74.
21. Lundahl (1992), pp. 233–36.
22. Domar (1970).
23. Lundahl (1979), pp. 326–34; Lundahl (1992), Chapter 11.
24. Heinl and Heinl (1978), p. 404.
25. Lundahl (1979), Chapter 5.

26. Ibid., Chapter 2.
27. Rybczynski (1955).
28. Lundahl (1979), p. 212.
29. Erlich et al. (1986), p. 36.
30. Adé and Monin (1998), p. 83.
31. ECMU (1994), p. 7.
32. Hilaire (1995).
33. Lundahl (1979), Chapter 5.
34. Ibid., p. 259.
35. Lundahl (1992), Chapter 5.
36. Lundahl (1993), pp. 192–93.
37. Ibid., p. 193.
38. Lundahl (1979), pp. 370–72, 266.
39. Lundahl (1993), p. 205.
40. Ibid., p. 209.
41. Ibid., pp. 210–12.
42. The following analysis of primary exports builds on Lundahl (1992), Chapter 5.
43. FAO (1996), p. 25.
44. Lundahl (1999), pp. 23–27.
45. Capital Consult (1995).
46. IMF (2001), p. 100.
47. IMF (2001), pp. 102, 100.
48. IMF (2001), p. 102; Lundahl (1992), p. 82.
49. IMF (2001), p. 100.
50. Johnson (1965).
51. Lundahl (1979), pp. 366–75.
52. Lundahl (1993), pp. 206–07.
53. IMF (2001), p. 210.
54. Ibid., pp. 212–13.
55. Lundahl (1992), Chapter 12.
56. Lundahl (1997).
57. Lundahl (1992), Chapters 14, 19.
58. Lundahl (1996), Lundahl and Silié (1998), (2005).
59. Lundahl (1979), pp. 463–67.
60. Lundahl (1992), Chapters 11, 13.
61. Ibid., Chapter 12.
62. Lundahl (1996), (1997), pp. 13–15.
63. Lundahl (1992), Chapter 14; Lundahl (1997), pp. 25–33.
64. Leyburn (1941).
65. Ibid. For a criticism of Leyburn on this point, see Price-Mars (1942).
66. Lundahl (1983), Chapter 12; Lundahl (1992), Chapters 17–18; White and Smucker (1997).
67. Lundahl (1992), Chapters 11–14.
68. Lundahl and Silié (1998), (2005).
69. Lundahl (1979), Chapter 10.
70. Mure-Ravaud and Rodd (1997), pp. 25–26, 3.
71. Silié and Hasbum (1996).

72. Cf. Baumol (1990).
73. Becker, Murphy, and Tamura (1990).
74. Pack and Westphal (1986), Rodrik (1995).
75. Jones and Marjit (2001).

References

Adé, Emmanuel and Monin, Emma (1998), 'La population et l'environnement', in: Paul Paryski et al. (eds), *La gestion de l'environnement en Haïti: Réalités et perspectives*. PNUD/UNOPS/HAI/92/001. Port-au-Prince: Programme des Nations Unies pour le Développement/United Nations Office for Project Services.

Banque de la République d'Haïti (1995), *Rapport annuel 1995*. Port-au-Prince.

Baumol, William (1990), 'Entrepreneurship: Productive, Unproductive, and Destructive', *Journal of Political Economy*, Vol. 98, 893–921.

Becker, Gary S., Murphy, Kevin M. and Tamura, Robert (1990), 'Human Capital, Fertility, and Economic Growth', *Journal of Political Economy*, Vol. 98, S12–S37.

Capital Consult (1995), *Compétitivité des industries d'Haïti*. Étude réalisée pour le compte de la Commission Présidentielle pour la Croissance et la Modernisation Économique. 12 December. Port-au-Prince.

Catanese, Anthony V. (1997), 'Priorities in the Economic Reconstruction of Rural Haiti', in: Robert I. Rotberg (ed.), *Haiti Renewed: Political and Economic Prospects*. Washington, DC: Brookings Institution Press.

Domar, Evsey D. (1970), 'The Causes of Slavery or Selfdom: A Hypothesis', *Journal of Economic History*, Vol. 30, 18–32.

ECMU (Unité de Coordination et de Suivi de l'Environnement), Programme des Nations Unies pour le Développement (1994), Haiti 1994: Indicateurs environnementaux de base: Étude préliminaire HAI/92/001. Port-au-Prince.

Erlich, Marko et al. (1986), *Haiti: Country Environment Profile: A Field Study*. Port-au-Prince: United States Agency for International Development.

FAO (Organisation des Nations Unies pour l'Alimentation et l'Agriculture) (1995), *Haïti: Analyse du sécteur agricole et identification de projets, Volume II. Rapport séctoriel*. 75/95 TCP-HAI 23-WP. Document de travail 3, *Cadre macro-économique*. 14 July. Rome.

FAO (Organisation des Nations Unies pour l'Alimentation et l'Agriculture) (1996), *Haïti: Analyse du sécteur agricole et identification de projets. Rapport sectoriel (final), Volume I: Rapport principal*. 75/95 TCP-HAI 23. 3 July. Rome.

Fick, Carolyn E. (1990), *The Making of Haiti: The Saint Domingue Revolution from Below*. Knoxville, TN: University of Tennessee Press.

Heinl, Robert Debs, Jr. and Heinl, Nancy Gordon (1978), *Written in Blood: The Story of the Haitian People 1492–1971*. Boston, MA: Houghton Mifflin.

Hilaire, Sébastien (1995), *Le prix d'une agriculture minière*. Port-au-Prince: Imprimerie Le Natal.

IMF (International Monetary Fund) (1995), *Haiti – Recent Economic Development*. SM/95/43. 1 March. Washington, DC: International Monetary Fund.

IMF (International Monetary Fund) (1999), *Haiti: Statistical Annex*. IMF Staff Country Report No. 99/118. Washington, DC: International Monetary Fund.

IMF (International Monetary Fund) (2001), *Haiti – Selected Issues*. IMF Staff Country Report No. 01/04. Washington, DC: International Monetary Fund.

James, C.L.R. (1963), *The Black Jacobins: Toussaint L'Ouverture and the San Domingo Revolution*. Second edition. Revised. New York: Vintage Books.

Johnson, Harry G. (1965), 'Optimal Trade Intervention in the Presence of Domestic Distortions', in: Richard E. Caves, Peter B. Kenen and Harry G. Johnson (eds), *Trade, Growth and the Balance of Payments: Essays in Honor of Gottfried Haberler*. Amsterdam: North Holland.

Jones, Ronald W. and Marjit, Sugata (2001), *Economic Development, Trade and Wages*. Mimeo, Department of Economics, University of Rochester.

Leyburn, James G. (1941), *The Haitian People*. New Haven, CT and London: Yale University Press.

Lundahl, Mats (1979), *Peasants and Poverty: A Study of Haiti*. London: Croom Helm.

Lundahl, Mats (1983), *The Haitian Economy: Man, Land and Markets*. London and Canberra: Croom Helm.

Lundahl, Mats (1992), *Politics or Markets? Essays on Haitian Underdevelopment*. London and New York: Routledge.

Lundahl, Mats (1993), *Kleptokrati, socialism och demokrati*. Stockholm: SNS Förlag.

Lundahl, Mats (1996), 'Problems of Policy Reform in Haiti', *Forum Empresarial*, Vol. 1, 32–52.

Lundahl, Mats (1997), *Towards the Abyss? The Political Economy of Emergency in Haiti*. UNU/WIDER, Research for Action 40. Helsinki: United Nations University/World Institute for Development Economics Research.

Lundahl, Mats (1999), 'Sustained Growth in Haiti: Pipe-Dream or Realistic Possibility?', *Iberoamericana*, Vol. 29, 13–42.

Lundahl, Mats and Silié, Rubén (1998), 'Economic Reform in Haiti: Past Failures and Future Success?', *Comparative Economic Studies*, Vol. 40, 43–71.

Lundahl, Mats and Silié, Rubén (2005), 'Haiti: Nothing but Crisis', in: Mats Lundahl and Michael L. Wyzan (eds), *The Political Economy of Policy Reform Failure*. London and New York: Routledge.

Mure-Ravaud, Georges and Rodd, Alistair (1997), *Éducation: Examen des dépenses publiques d'Haïti*. Note No. 7, March. Washington, DC: The World Bank.

Nicholls, David (1979), *From Dessalines to Duvalier: Race, Colour and National Independence in Haiti*. Cambridge: Cambridge University Press.

Ott, Thomas O. (1973), The Haitian Revolution 1789–1804. Knoxville, TN: University of Tennessee Press.

Pack, Howard and Westphal, Larry E. (1986), 'Industrial Strategy and Technological Change: Theory versus Reality', *Journal of Development Economics*, Vol. 22, 87–128.

Price-Mars, Jean (1942), 'Classe ou caste? Étude sur "The Haitian People" (Le peuple haïtien) de James G. Leyburn', *Revue de la Société d'Histoire et de Géographie d'Haïti*, Vol. 13, No. 46, 1–50.

Rodrik, Dani (1995), 'Getting Interventions Right: How South Korea and Taiwan Grew Rich', *Economic Policy*, No. 20, 55–107.

Rybczynski, T.M. (1955), 'Factor Endowment and Relative Commodity Prices', *Economica, N.S.*, Vol. 22, 336–41.

Silié, Ruben and Hasbum, Douglas (1996), *Situación de la enseñanza técnica y formación profesional de la República de Haití*. Consultant's Report. Santo Domingo: Organización de Estados Iberoamericanos (OEI).

Stoddard, T. Lothrop (1970), *The French Revolution in San Domingo*. Westport, CN: Negro Universities Press.

Thébaud, Schiller (1967), *L'évolution de la structure agraire d'Haïti de 1804 a nos jours*. Thèse pour le Doctorat ès Sciences Économiques. Université de Paris, Faculté de Droit et des Sciences Économiques.

UNDP (United Nations Development Programme) (2000), *Human Development Report 2000*. Oxford: Oxford University Press.

White, T. Anderson and Smucker, Glenn R. (1997). 'Social Capital and Governance in Haiti: Traditions and Trends', in: World Bank, *Haiti Poverty Assessment, Volume II: Technical Papers*. November. Washington, DC: The World Bank.

Wiens, Thomas and Sobrado, Carlos (1997), 'Rural Poverty in Haiti', in: World Bank, *Haiti Poverty Assessment. Volume II: Technical Papers*. November, Washington, DC: The World Bank.

World Bank (2001), World Development Report 2000/2001. Attacking Poverty. Oxford: Oxford University Press.

Part II
Contemporary Problems

Chapter 4, 'Economic and Political Forces in Haitian Underdevelopment', was published in 1996. The chapter sums up some of my views about what, in the past, has determined economic underdevelopment in Haiti. It is difficult not to interpret the available evidence with respect to the workings of the market mechanism to mean that markets are essentially competitive in Haiti. The main exceptions to this rule have been when political processes – usually of a highly dubious nature – have interfered with that mechanism.

The central elements in the underdevelopment equation are to be found instead in such structural forces as the interaction between population growth and erosion – a mechanism which inexorably drives per capita income toward ever lower levels in the countryside – the lack of technological progress and the dismal state of politics ever since the beginning of the history of Haiti as a sovereign nation. The first two elements will also continue to be present in country governed by democratic forces and a tremendous effort will be required if they are to be overcome. The likelihood of this happening is difficult to predict. The future may be gloomier than most observers realize.

Chapter 5, 'The Haitian Dilemma Reexamined: Lessons from the Past in the Light of Some New Economic Theory', was published in 1997. The chapter begins with a sketch of how the French colony of Saint-Domingue was created during the seventeenth and eighteenth centuries – a colony that rested on staple exports like sugar and coffee. Saint-Domingue was the richest French colony, but after independence, the new nation of Haiti underwent a process of retrogression which in the end would turn it into the poorest country in the Western Hemisphere. This fact is explained by resorting to a model of economic growth that has endogenous population growth as one of its main features and which allows for an equilibrium characterized by a low accumulation of human capital. Thereafter a 'Leviathan' model of the state, allowing for both productive and predatory features, is introduced.

This model is applied to the predatory state that developed in Haiti during the nineteenth century.

The third element of explanation is the interaction of population growth and soil destruction leading to lower peasant incomes. At some point, this is likely to require some kind of adjustment, and the chapter discusses the possible role of redistribution of consumption within the family, to the detriment of the children. Next, the protected import-competing industry sector is discussed and some modern trade theories are applied to it. The discussion shows that externalities that could generate growth have been absent and that the main explanation of the failure of the sector to develop is found in the protection of a sector operating for a market which was too small to allow for growth. The import-competing sector is contrasted with the dynamic assembly sector working directly for the world market, and the difficulty of the latter sector to develop beyond the labor-intensive, low-wage segment is discussed. Finally, the role of migration as a regulator of population growth is analyzed, also in a model context.

Chapter 6, 'Income and Land Distribution in Haiti: Some Remarks on the Available Statistics', was published in 1996. The chapter discusses the quality of available statistics on income and land distribution in Haiti. It is demonstrated that some of the most widely quoted figures do not stand up to methodological scrutiny. Hence, no serious discussion of redistribution, let alone practical measures, can be based on them.

Chapter 7, 'Some Economic Determinants of Haitian Migration to the Dominican Republic', was published in 2009. The chapter identifies some key economic factors behind the migration of Haitian agricultural workers to the Dominican Republic. Against the background of the deplorable working and living conditions facing the workers on their arrival, some economic theories of the migration decision are sketched, and the characteristics of the Haitian workers, as they emerge from field studies, are presented. Thereafter the most important information with respect to rural poverty in Haiti is summarized, an explanation that runs in terms of the interaction between population growth and soil erosion is presented and the life-cycle aspects of poverty are highlighted. The chapter concludes with an application of the Harris–Todaro model of migration to the empirical data.

4
Economic and Political Forces in Haitian Underdevelopment

Haiti's economic plight is well-known. The country is the poorest one in the Western Hemisphere, with a per capita income which by the time President Aristide returned in 1994 was estimated at US$250–260 per annum, perhaps even lower – certainly so in the countryside which is home to the majority of the population.[1] In addition, urban income is heavily concentrated in very few hands.[2] As a result, half, if not more than half, of the inhabitants of nation's capital are ultra-poor and have to spend at least 75 percent of their income to secure a daily intake of 1500 calories.[3]

Even though the absolute figures may not be entirely accurate,[4] virtually all observers agree about the basic facts of Haitian poverty. Haitians have extremely low incomes that do not suffice to provide them with an even minimally decent standard of living in terms of food, water, shelter, sewerage, clothing, and education. What is more, during the past few years, the standard of living has fallen dramatically as a result of kleptocratic military rule and the ensuing international sanctions. During the 1992–94 period GDP fell by an estimated 30 percent in real terms,[5] while the population continued to increase by an estimated 2.3 percent per annum:[6] a serious deterioration for the most vulnerable groups, namely those with incomes that were already considered inadequate before President Aristide was thrown out of the country in 1991.

While there is broad consensus about the facts of poverty, views regarding its causes differ widely. Essentially, there are two opposing schools of thought (although the dividing line is not always clear-cut). The first stresses the existence of market imperfections, and maintains that the Haitian masses – notably the peasants – are being exploited by a small minority of landowners, intermediaries, and urban-based merchants and industrialists.[7] The second contends that the market imperfections argument is an exaggeration, that markets in most cases tend to be competitive unless political forces intervene and that it is mainly these political forces coupled with structural factors such as population growth and soil erosion that are responsible for Haiti's underdevelopment.[8] The purpose of this chapter is to sum up some of my own views about the determinants of Haitian underdevelopment.[9] The discussion will focus on four different issues: population growth and erosion, the functioning of markets, the lack of technological progress, and the characteristics of the Haitian state.

Population growth and erosion

From a long-run perspective, Haiti's number one economic problem is the gradual destruction of the country's arable land area.[10] This destruction has reached alarming proportions – proportions that threaten the very survival of the country. Columbus, in 1492, found an island covered with dense, green forests which have disappeared as the trees have been felled for commercial purposes, for firewood and charcoal and for farming objectives. The exploitation of Haiti's precious woods (mahogany, logwood, and Brazil wood) began during the French period, and this practice continued until the supply was more or less exhausted, some time after World War II. Felling trees for fuel purposes, on the other hand, has continued to this very day. The Haitian peasant has no economic alternative to charcoal when it comes to energy and hence continues to cut.[11]

More important than the demand for energy, however, is the demand for food, this tends to grow *pari passu* with the population. As the latter increases, so does the man–land ratio, which, in turn, makes production increasingly labor-intensive in rural areas. This means that over time a given land area will undergo a transformation from forest to pasture to land-intensive crops. With each step in this sequence, the risk of erosion increases, since the soil becomes increasingly exposed to rains and wind as the permanent cover is removed and fallow periods are shortened.

What is worse is that this process tends to be cumulative and that no further population growth is needed to sustain it once it has been set in motion. What matters is simply the man–land ratio. A shrinking arable area with a given population works exactly as an increasing population on a given area, that is, it increases the labor intensity of production and changes the crop mix.[12] For several decades, ever more land has been taken out of the production of such perennial land-intensive crops as coffee (with its protective root system and foliage) to be used instead for food crop production, which requires the soil to be laid bare in order to be planted and sown precisely when the torrential rains come. The inevitable end result of this is soil destruction and declining per capita income in the countryside.[13]

The cumulative process of soil erosion is very difficult to stop since it involves considerable externalities. What one peasant does with his land affects not only him but other peasants as well, notably those below him on the hillsides. The situation is reminiscent of what in game theory is known as the prisoner's dilemma: a game where everybody can be better off provided that people cooperate, but where no incentives to cooperate exist. Unless all the peasants in a particular community or area undertake measures to combat erosion, those who do have no guarantees that their efforts will be successful. The magnitude of the problem increases with the number of peasants involved. Erosion control is also complicated by the fact that the costs in terms of labor effort and capital outlays arise in the present, while the benefits only accrue in future periods. Being as poor as he is, the Haitian peasant tends to value the present much higher that the future. Higher incomes later on are not terribly interesting if survival in the present period cannot be guaranteed.

The market economy: Good or bad?

That market imperfections may hamper economic development is a well-established fact. The extent to which such imperfections exist in Haiti and what their effects have been is a somewhat contentious issue, as pointed out in the introductory section. What does the available evidence look like?

The Haitian economy is a market economy *par excellence*. When the researchers of the Inter-American Institute of Agricultural Sciences mapped the system of marketplaces in the mid-1970s, they found more than 500 with a minimum of 50 sellers and buyers active on a normal market day.[14] In these markets, through which the food crops produced in Haiti move, competition is strong indeed.[15] There are few barriers to entry on the lowest retail level and the profit level there appears to be 'normal', but on average, it is so low that what the retailers earn is a wage for their labor effort rather than a profit in the economic sense of the word. From the retail level, in turn, the more successful *revandèz* move into wholesale operations whenever the market situation so permits, handling larger volumes of goods. In this system, prices are determined in what very much resembles the 'textbook' fashion, with procedures like haggling coming into the picture to compensate for uneven qualities and irregular or heterogeneous measures.

Export crops move via a different network, with *spekilatè* and their representatives buying mainly coffee from the peasants and selling it, in turn, to a limited number of exporters. In other words, the coffee market is oligopsonistic, and this introduces the possibility of exploitation of the producers by the middlemen, notably the exporters. The debate has swung back and forth, with strong positions being assumed both by those claiming that coffee marketing is an essentially competitive activity in spite of the low number of actors involved and those who argue that collusion is the rule.[16] What has emerged, I believe, is a mixed picture – with periods of organized collusion alternating with intense competition for market shares in a branch where ultimately the price fetched by the exporters is determined by the conditions prevailing in the world market. This appears to have been the situation at least from the beginning of the 1950s to the mid-1980s.[17]

Turning to the factor side, the land market is of central importance, because imperfections in that market easily create imperfections in the markets for credit and labor as well.[18] The problem in the Haitian case is that, formally speaking, property rights in land are chaotic. No cadastral survey has been taken which clearly establishes who owns that and with what rights. This opens the field for more or less well-founded speculation. Again, as pointed out initially, we find two opposing camps, one contending that Haiti shares the strong land concentration pattern which is typical of most Latin American countries, and the other arguing that most of those living in the countryside have access to land in a manner which does not subject them to exploitation by a landowner class.

The best way to approach the Haitian land problem is to employ a comparative perspective, and the obvious comparison of course is the neighboring country: the Dominican Republic.[19] Once this comparison is made, it becomes fairly clear that placing Haiti in the same category of land concentration as most of the South and Central American states[20] makes little sense. Haiti and the Dominican Republic represent two very different patterns of development of land ownership and the decisive events here, of course, are the establishment of the slave-based French colony of Saint-Domingue and the slave rebellion of 1791 that was to create the independent nation of Haiti. Once the plantation economy collapsed for lack of capital, labor, and markets, Haiti embarked on a course that ultimately led to the creation of a nation of smallholders: one which later efforts to reintroduce large-scale agriculture and take over peasant landholdings have not been able to change. This, of course does not exclude local abuse, but it would be absurd to claim that Haiti has a land concentration problem on the *national* level.

Another difficult market to analyze is the credit market.[21] In most cases, credit comes from informal credit markets, where the most important sources are traders, friends, family, rotating credit associations, and so on. In the Third World, rural informal credit markets in particular tend to display high effective rates of interest.[22] These rates, however, seldom lend themselves to simple, direct interpretations. In principle, the rate of interest is determined by four factors: the opportunity cost of the funds lent, the transaction costs of each loan, the risk of borrower default, and, finally, the possible presence of monopoly elements. The relative importance of each one of these factors is an exclusively empirical matter. One must be careful not to jump to any conclusions, judging from the rates alone. There is little evidence to suggest that monopolistic or semi-monopolistic conditions prevail systematically in the Haitian informal credit markets.

In the Haitian case, the high rates appear to stem from the other three components. Transaction costs and risk are likely to be important determinants. The typical loans are short-term. The peasants borrow to carry them over the dead season before, for example, the coffee harvest brings in cash. Longer loans are riskier and hence carry high interest. Risk is seldom absent from short-term loans either, and the Haitian peasants seldom possess good collateral which may be used to secure repayment. Transaction costs play a role as well, since the alternative to taking a loan could be to sell an asset and repurchase it (or its equivalent) at a later stage. Such transactions, however, have their costs which, in turn, make loans at what *a priori* may seem high interest rates an attractive economic proposition.

What is even more striking is that the opportunity cost of money appears to be very high. As Simon Fass has demonstrated, in the highly labor-intensive environment of Port-au-Prince, it is not difficult to find credit uses that are profitable enough to make borrowers willing to pay 25–50 percent per month (the latter for unsecured loans).[23] The credit market is fragmented, and the rate of time preference (the extent to which additions to present income are preferred to additions to future income) is high.

The extent to which Fass' finding applies to rural Haiti as well is not known. Presumably, it is harder to find investments in the same profitability range as that encountered by Fass. Nevertheless, the urban and rural markets for credit are likely to be interconnected to some extent. Coffee exporters and *spekilatè* who are based in urban districts have diversified their activities to encompass urban pursuits as well, and it would be strange if this diversification did not include urban lending as well as an alternative to advancing credit to the peasants from whom they buy agricultural produce. The same is likely to be the case with female wholesale agricultural traders.[24]

Thus, summing up the role of markets in Haitian underdevelopment, our knowledge is far from perfect, but, by and large, the available evidence seems to suggest that market imperfections are of comparatively minor importance in the equation of Haitian underdevelopment. The overall importance of monopolies (monopsonies) or collusive oligopolies as the cause of the country's economic underdevelopment has been limited – and definitely much more limited than the defenders of market imperfections would have us believe.

The absence of technological progress

One of the most conspicuous features of the Haitian economy is its low technological level, especially in the agricultural sector.[25] The Haitian peasant works his land with the aid of a few hand tools and some circulating capital in the form of seeds and plants only. The methods employed are very labor-intensive.

The most astonishing part of all this is that during the French colonial period, a plantation system which made use of some of the most technologically advanced practices of its day had developed. However, during the wars of liberation (1791–1803) and during the first decades of independence, this sophistication gave way to simpler techniques that can still be observed today. Haiti underwent a technological retrogression from which the country has never been able to recover.

This retrogression is not difficult to explain. During the wars, the entire educated labor force disappeared with the French and so did much of the capital stock. This shock sent the Haitian economy into a low-technology deadlock which requires considerable human capital formation to break. The problem, however, is that education, or accumulation of knowledge in general, is an activity which tends to display increasing returns to the already accumulated stock. The higher the educational standard of a country, the easier it becomes to learn more. Conversely, in an economy where the stock of human capital is more or less nonexistent, it will not pay for the individuals to educate themselves. The returns to education become too low to make it worthwhile.[26] The lack of human capital in Haiti also stems for the failure of the state to build an educational system which does not discriminate against the masses.[27] This supply failure has in the past interacted with the lack of demand in a cumulative fashion. The lack of a supply of education has discouraged the demand for it, and the demand for it has made it unattractive to expand supply. In addition, there is the unwillingness of the predatory Haitian rulers to spend on measures that enhance the productivity of the citizens.

Other factors also make it difficult to foster technological change. For example, it is well known from studies of the Green Revolution that many agricultural innovations are profitable only in situations where material production factors, including capital, are cheap, relatively speaking, since these innovations tend to be capital-using. In Haiti, the opposite situation has applied in the factor markets. Labor is abundant and cheap, whereas capital, as we found in the discussion of the credit market, tends to be expensive. Thus, the peasant does not adopt some otherwise superior techniques.

The factor price problem is often compounded by the fact that some innovations contain indivisibilities. A case in point is the plow, or the plow plus a draft animal. The plow is essentially a labor-saving device and if the purchase of this tool is to pay off, the peasant must have a farm which is of a certain 'threshold' size. If he does not have enough hectares to plow it makes no sense to make the acquisition.

Innovation in agriculture has also been hampered by risk. The peasants cannot afford to experiment with techniques which may increase the variance of output or which introduce crops that are subject to large price fluctuations even if they promise higher expected returns than what they already grow. Since their incomes are close to subsistence level, the peasants are likely to 'play it safe' attempting to minimize the probability of falling below this level instead of maximizing expected profits.

The politics of kleptocracy

One of the perennial issues in the discussion of economic policy is whether government failures have a more negative impact on living standards than market failures. In the Haitian case, the answer is easy. Along with erosion, political degeneration is the most important determinant of mass poverty.[28]

Degeneration was present in Haiti from the very beginning of its existence as a sovereign state. The French colonial system had built on the exploitation of the masses of slaves by their masters. The ideas inherent in this system were taken over by the early rulers of the new country.[29] The problem they faced was exactly the same as the one faced by the French: how to generate an income without working the land themselves. In a situation where the ex-slaves were free and in addition had unlimited supplies of land at their disposal, this could not be accomplished unless one or both of these freedoms were abolished. To this end, the masses were put back on the plantations, to work under strict military supervision. The surplus thus generated was partly employed for procuring arms and ammunition that could be used to prevent the French from reconquering the colony they had lost, but the remainder was pocketed by the new elite.

In 1809, after what amounted to the first land reform in Latin America, the plantation system broke down for good in Haiti. This presented the new elite with a dilemma. The masses could no longer be restricted either in terms of personal freedom or with respect to access to land. New methods for appropriating a surplus had to be devised. Not least, taxation had to be resorted to. The peasants could always be deprived of some of their product by means of quasi-legal tax measures imposed by those wielding the political power. In this way, politics in Haiti turned into a race for income and other perquisites of office during the second half of the nineteenth century, up to the beginning of the American occupation in 1915.

All the presidents that held office in Haiti from 1843 to 1915 were kleptocrats, pure and simple. During this period, the predatory state reached full maturity in Haiti. The political process degenerated into a mere competition for the spoils of the presidential office. Private income became the quintessence of governance and most presidents concentrated on income to the detriment of their security with the result that they did not last very long in office. In the main, they created polities (administrations) that were too small to prevent them from being overthrown by rival outside contenders for power.[30] Of the 22 heads of state between 1843 and 1915, all except 5 were overthrown in a more or less violent manner and 11 lasted for less than a year. Coup succeeded coup and uprising succeeded uprising during these tumultuous years, and most of the time the national treasury was either empty or about to be emptied.

The American occupation of Haiti (1915–34) put a temporary end to predation, but as soon as the Americans pulled out, the time-honored practices of plunder made a comeback. Unfortunately, the most lasting achievement of the occupation was the substitution of a modern, relatively efficient constabulary for the old army: a measure which made it possible for the post-occupation presidents to concentrate more on plunder and less on security. The army simply had the last word when it came to deciding when time was up for the sitting ruler.

This state of affairs lasted until the election which put François Duvalier in the presidency in 1957. Duvalier had observed the fate of his predecessors and was determined not to share it. To this end, he set out to break the power of the army and substituted a completely new power structure for it, one which built exclusively on allegiance to his own person.[31] The Duvalier *père* years constituted the beginning of the apogee of kleptocracy in Haiti. His son was to build on the foundations that he laid. By making unhampered use of the entire state apparatus – not least the state monopoly enterprises – Jean-Claude Duvalier brought what his father began to its logical culmination,[32] with the Duvalier Family pocketing between US$1.5 and 2 billion between 1957 and 1986.

The consequences of predation

Predation, which continued under the military regimes after the fall of Baby Doc in 1986, has had enormous consequences for Haiti. There is virtually no limit to the damage that small cliques such as those governing Haiti from its inception as a sovereign nation to the present day are prepared to inflict on the economy in order to redistribute income in their favor. Redistribution in the predatory state typically entails the creation of rents through government regulations of some kind, for example, the establishment of monopolistic state enterprises: rents which are appropriated by the ruling clique. These regulations distort resource allocation and hold back growth, that is, they reduce the gross domestic product to a level below the one which would have prevailed in an economy without predation. Of course, the ruling clique itself may also suffer the consequences of GDP reduction – but only to an extent which is more or less proportional to its share of GDP, and since this share tends to be small, or negligible, at least for cliques that have not been in power for very long, it means that these cliques are prepared to go to extremes. A clique controlling 1 percent of GDP can in principle afford a total GDP reduction of 100 times the gain it makes by redistributing before it decides that redistribution is not worthwhile.

Since effective kleptocracy presupposes the use of the state apparatus for predatory purposes, corruption will characterize the public administration – on all levels. In Haiti, corruption has always stemmed from the top of the administrative pyramid, and from there it has trickled down to the lower layers. To be able to extract rents from the population, a corrupt government needs an administration, and this administration will function according to more or less the same principles as the government itself. As long as the top layer receives that, it deems to be a satisfactory income through the administration it will not bother to punish its agents for behaving in a manner for which the ruling clique itself has set the precedent.

The behavior of the private sector is also affected. A predatory government and a corrupt public administration require special attention if the damage inflicted on private undertakings is to be minimized. This, in turn, diverts resources from the production of goods and services. (The same is true with respect to the regulations enforced by the government for purely redistributive purposes. Both types of activities reduce the allocative efficiency of economy.)

Investment is also held back by the existence of a predatory state, and if it is not held back – usually because it benefits the political actors – it will not be very productive. Private entrepreneurs are not likely to expand their activities unless they can obtain guarantees that they will also be in a position to reap what they sow, which of course is highly unlikely in a country where the fingers of the rulers are sticky. A common pattern is that of collaboration between more or less obscure 'entrepreneurs' and the government. The former are given some kind of business privilege, which can be used to create and appropriate rents, by the latter in return for kickbacks. Also, whatever government investment that is undertaken is not likely to be of the kind that enhances productivity in the economy – for example, in education – but rather of the variety that serves to generate income for those in power in a distortionary manner.

Another consequence of predation is the creation of macroeconomic imbalances. Perhaps the best example of this in Haiti is the beginning of the 1980s, when the fiscal deficits that resulted from the unabashed activities of Jean-Claude Duvalier led to money creation, inflation, increased import demand, reduced exports, and balance of payments problems.[33]

Conclusions

This chapter sums up some of my views about what, in the past, has determined economic underdevelopment in Haiti. It is difficult not to interpret the available evidence with respect to the workings of the market mechanism to mean that markets are essentially competitive in Haiti. The main exceptions to this rule have been when political processes – usually of a highly dubious nature – have interfered with that mechanism.

The central elements in the underdevelopment equation are to be found instead in such structural forces as the interaction between population growth and erosion – a mechanism which inexorably drives per capita income toward ever lower levels in the countryside – the lack of technological progress and the dismal state of politics ever since the beginning of the history of Haiti as a sovereign nation. The first two elements will also continue to be present in country governed by democratic forces, and a tremendous effort will be required if they are to be overcome. The likelihood that this should happen is difficult to predict. The future may be gloomier than most observers realize.[34] However, provided that Haiti has finally been put on the road to democracy and popular influence – which may in the worst case also be a dubious proposition[35] – at least a starting point for future development is now available.

Notes

Published in Laënnec Hurbon (ed.), *Les transitions démocratiques* (French version), Paris: Syros, 1996.

1. International Monetary Fund (1995), p. 2; Inter-American Development Bank (1995), p. 28. PNUD (1995), p. 12, gives a GDP per capita figure of US$212.
2. World Bank (1981), pp. 6–7; Fass (1988), pp. 89–95.
3. Fass (1988), pp. 89–95.
4. Cf., for example, the remarks of Catanese (1997), pp. 191–92.
5. Inter-American Development Bank (1995), p. 3; International Monetary Fund (1995), p. 2.
6. PNUD (1995), p. 12.
7. Cf., for example, Pierre-Charles (1965), Brisson (1968), Luc (1976), Caprio (1979), Joachim (1979), Girault (1981), Trouillot (1986), and Dupuy (1989a), (1989b).
8. See, for example, Rotberg and Clague (1971), Zuvekas (1978), Lundahl (1979), (1983), (1992), (1997), World Bank (1988), Banque Mondiale (1985), Fass (1988), Barthélemy (1989), Catanese and Perlack (1993), Latortue (1995), but also Trouillot (1986), as far as the political part is concerned.
9. Most of the work is available in Lundahl (1979), (1983), and (1992).
10. See Lundahl (1979), Chapter 5, for details.
11. During the 1991–94 international sanctions episode, woodcutting accelerated, since the relative price of charcoal fell when the oil price increased dramatically.
12. This follows from application of the Rybczynski theorem (Rybczynski [1955]) which states that in an economy with two goods (presently export crops and

domestic food crops) produced with the aid of two factors (land and labor), with linearly homogeneous production functions (no economies of scale), if the endowment of one of the factors (population and labor) grows while the endowment of the other factor (land) remains constant, at constant relative commodity prices, the production of the good using the growing factor intensively (food crops) will increase while the production of the other good (export crops) will decrease. The same effect is produced when the available land area shrinks as a result of erosion (the Rybczynski theorem 'in reverse'). Thus, erosion leads to increased production of precisely those goods prone to create more erosion. In the Haitian case, the process has also been accelerated by a secular decline in the relative price of export goods.

13. The present environmental situation is summed up in Erlich et al. (1986).
14. LaGra, Fanfan, and Charleston (1975).
15. See Lundahl (1979), Chapter 4, for a summary of the available evidence.
16. See ibid., Girault (1981); Lundahl (1983), Chapter 10; Lundahl (1992); and Bourdet and Lundahl (1989), for the main discussion.
17. This finding is also confirmed by and large by later investigations. See Lopez and Dorsainvil (1990) and Lopez and You (1993a), (1993b).
18. Cf., for example, Griffin (1969), Chapter 1.
19. Lundahl and Vedovato (1991).
20. Cf., for example, Griffin (1969), p. 72.
21. See Lundahl (1979), Chapter 11; Smucker (1983); and Fass (1988), Chapter 7.
22. Cf., for example, Tun Wai (1957).
23. Fass (1988), Chapter 7.
24. The labor market is competitive. In the countryside, the most common form of work is on the family farm, and in urban districts, the labor market is basically completely unregulated, in spite of existing minimum wage regulations.
25. Lundahl (1979), Chapter 12; Lundahl (1983), Chapters 13–14; Lundahl (1997).
26. Lundahl (1997).
27. Lundahl (1979), Chapter 10.
28. Lundahl (1979), Chapters 7–12; Lundahl (1992); Lundahl (1997).
29. Lundahl (1992), Chapters 8–9.
30. Ibid., Chapter 11.
31. Ibid., Chapter 12.
32. See, for example, Maingot (1986–87) and Danielson and Lundahl (1994).
33. Lundahl (1992), Chapter 19.
34. Cf. Lundahl (1997).
35. Cf. Fatton (1997).

References

Banque Mondiale (1985), *Haïti Étude du secteur agricole. Volume I: Rapport principal.* Rapport No. 5375-HA, June 14. Washington, DC.

Barthélemy, Gérard (1989), *Le Pays en dehors. Éssai sur l'univers rural haïtien.* Second edition. Port-au-Prince: Éditions Henri Deschamps.

Bourdet, Yves and Lundahl, Mats (1989), 'Una reevaluación del mercadeo del café haitiano', in: Mats Lundahl and Wim Pelupessy (eds), *Crisis económica en Centroamérica y el Caribe*. San José, CA: Editorial DEI.

Brisson, Gerald (1968), *Les relations agraires dans l'Haïti contemporaine.*, México, DF: Mimeo.

Caprio, Giovanni (1979), *Haïti – wirtschaftliche Entwicklung und periphere Gesellschaftsformation*. Frankfurt/Main: Haag + Herchen Verlag.

Catanese, Anthony V. (1997), 'Focal Points in the Economics Reconstruction of Haiti', in: Robert I. Rotberg (ed.), *Haiti Renewed: Political and Economic Prospects*. Washington, DC: Brookings Institution Press.

Catanese, Anthony V. and Perlack, Robert (1993), 'Reforestation in Haiti', *Canadian Journal of Development Studies*, Vol. 14, 59–72.

Danielson, Anders and Lundahl, Mats (1994), 'Endogenous Policy Formation and the Principle of Optimal Obfuscation: Theory and Some Evidence from Haiti and Jamaica', *Comparative Economic Studies*, Vol. 36, 51–78.

Dupuy, Alex (1989a), *Haïti in the World Economy, Class, Race and Underdevelopment Since 1700*. Boulder, CO and London: Westview Press.

Dupuy, Alex (1989b), 'Peasant Poverty in Haïti', *Latin American Research Review*, Vol. 24, 259–71.

Erlich, Marko et al. (1986), *Haiti: Country Environmental Profile. A Field Study*. Port-au-Prince: United States Agency for International Development.

Fass, Simon (1988), *Political Economy in Haïti: The Drama of Survival*. New Brunswick, NJ and Oxford: Transaction Books.

Fatton, Robert, Jr. (1997), 'The Rise, Fall, and Resurrection of President Aristide', in: Robert I. Rotberg (ed.), *Haiti Renewed: Political and Economic Prospects*. Washington, DC: Brookings Institution Press.

Girault, Christian (1981), *Le Commerce du café en Haïti (habitants, spéculateurs et exportateurs)*. Paris: Éditions du Centre National de la Recherche Scientifique.

Griffin, Keith (1969), *Underdevelopment in Spanish America, An Interpretation*. London: George Allen and Unwin.

Inter-American Development Bank (1995), *Emergency Economic Recovery Program. Haiti*. Report of the Joint Mission (November 7–20, 1994), January 3. Washington, DC: Inter-American Development Bank.

International Monetary Fund (1995), *Haiti – Recent Economic Developments*. SM/95/43. March 1. Washington, DC: International Monetary Fund.

Joachim, Benoît (1979), *Le Racines du sous-développement en Haïti*. Port-au-Prince: Éditions Henri Deschamps.

LaGra, Jerry, Fanfan, Guy and Charleston, Wesner (1975) *Les marchés publics d'Haïti*. Mimeo. Institut Interamericain des Sciences Agricoles (IICA), Port-au-Prince: IICA.

Latortue, Paul (1995), 'Toward a Viable Economic Structure in Haiti'. Paper presented at the conference Dialogue for Development in Haiti, University of Puerto Rico, Mayagüez campus, Mayagüez September 20–24.

Lopez, Rigoberto A. and Dorsainvil, Daniel (1990), 'An Analysis of Pricing in the Haitian Coffee Market', *Journal of Developing Areas*, Vol. 25, 93–106.

Lopez, Rigoberto A. and You, Zhikang (1993a), 'Determinants of Oligopsony Power', *Journal of Development Economics*, Vol. 41, 275–84.

Lopez, Rigoberto A. and You, Zhikang (1993b), 'The Impact of Oligopsony and Taxation on the Haitian Coffee Economy', *World Development*, Vol. 21, 465–73.

Luc, Jean (1976), *Structures économiques et lutte nationale populaire en Haïti*. Montréal: Éditions Nouvelle Optique.

Lundahl, Mats (1979), *Peasants and Poverty: A Study of Haiti*. London: Croom Helm.

Lundahl, Mats (1983), *The Haitian Economy: Man, Land and Markets*. London and Canberra: Croom Helm.

Lundahl, Mats (1992), 'Social Security in Haiti: Informal Initiative in a Welfare Less State', in: Christopher Abel and Colin M. Lewis (eds), *Welfare, Equity and Development in Latin America*. London and Basingstoke: Palgrave Macmillan.

Lundahl, Mats (1997), 'The Haitian Dilemma Reexamined: Lessons from the Past in the Light of Some New Economic Theory', in: Robert I. Rotberg (ed.), *Haiti Renewed: Political and Economic Progress*. Washington, DC: Brookings Institute Press.

Lundahl, Mats and Vedovato, Claudio (1991), 'The Structure of Landownership in Haiti and the Dominican Republic: Causes and Consequences', in: Magnus Mörner and Thommy Svensson (eds), *The Transformation of Rural Society in the Third World*. London and New York: Routledge.

Maingot, Anthony (1986–87), 'Haiti: Problems of Transition to Democracy in an Authoritarian Soft State', *Journal of Interamerican Studies and World Affairs*, Vol. 28, 75–102.

Pierre-Charles, Gérard (1965), *La economía haitiana y su vía de desarrollo*. México, DF: Cuadernos Americanos.

PNUD (Programme des Nations Unies pour le Développement), Unité de Coordination et de Suivi de l'Environnement (ECMU) (1995), *Haïti 1994. Indicateurs environnementaux de base, Étude préliminaire*. Port-au-Prince: PNUD.

Rotberg, Robert I. and Clague, Christopher K. (1971), *Haiti: The Politics of Squalor*. Boston, MA: Houghton Mifflin Company.

Rybczynski, T.M. (1955), 'Factor Endowment and Relative Commodity Prices', *Economica, N.S.*, Vol. 22, 336–41.

Smucker, Glenn R. (1983), *L'offre de crédit au paysan haïtien*. Mimeo. Washington DC: Development Alternatives Inc.

Trouillot, Michel-Rolph (1986), *Les racines historiques de l'état duvaliérien*. Port-au-Prince: Éditions Deschamps.

Tun Wai, U. (1957), 'Interest Rates Outside the Organized Money Markets of Underdeveloped Countries', *Staff Papers – International Monetary Fund*, Vol. 6, 80–142.

World Bank (1981), *Haiti's Economic Memorandum. Recent Economic, Industrial and Sector Development*. Report No. 3079-HA, February 17. Washington, DC.

World Bank (1988), *Economic Recovery in Haiti: Performance, Issues and Prospects*. Report No. 7469-HA, December 23. Washington, DC.

Zuvekas, Clarence, Jr. (1978), *Agricultural Development in Haiti: An Assessment of Sector Problems, Policies and Prospects Under Conditions of Severe Soil Erosion*. Mimeo. Washington DC: USAID.

5

The Haitian Dilemma Reexamined: Lessons from the Past in the Light of Some New Economic Theory

A good part of our knowledge of how economies develop can be attributed to historical observation, and only the historical 'laboratory' is large enough to offer the development economist the variety required for generalization and construction of theories of wide applicability.[1] Unfortunately, the economics profession has often failed to recognize this reality, and has proceeded instead in an armchair fashion.

Economists are not only ones to blame, however. Economic historians often do a poor job interpreting their data for lack of an appropriate theory. Their historical analyses frequently take place in a theory-less vacuum or overemphasize the historically specific circumstances of a particular phenomenon while overlooking important general aspects that may be brought to bear on a wider range of situations.

The present chapter constitutes an attempt to make use of both economic theory and historical observation. It deals with economic and political lessons from Haiti's past as they emerge from the application mainly of some of the most recent strands of growth theory and political economy to the historical material. The intent is to offer insights with respect to the obstacles that must be overcome if Haiti is to break out of its present low-income equilibrium.

The rise of Saint-Domingue: A staples episode

A series of critical events was responsible for shaping the course of Haiti's economic history.[2] One was the creation of the French colony of Saint-Domingue during the seventeenth and eighteenth centuries. Let us begin by highlighting some of the salient characteristics of the colonial economy with the aid of the staples theory of economic growth.[3]

A staple is defined as a product with a large natural resource content, the production of which, in some sense, must take place on the spot, and which furthermore does not require any elaborate processing demanding special skills or large amounts of capital. It is valuable enough to bear transport costs, and it is in international demand.[4] Typically, staples are either minerals or agricultural products, and they enter international trade either because a natural resource has been discovered, because the capital or knowledge, or both, necessary for the exploitation of a known but hitherto unexploited resource is made available, or because the demand for the resource in question increases enough to make its production worthwhile.

If we limit our attention to agricultural produce, staples episodes – notably the opening of the economy to international trade – tend to conform to a pattern. Historically, this has been the case with the regions of recent settlement, like Canada, United States, Australia, and Argentina; with plantation economies, like Malaya or Costa Rica; as well as with peasant export economies, like the Gold Coast or Burma.[5] Saint-Domingue is another case in point: a plantation economy *par excellence*. The common features are rising international prices and expanding markets, the existence of a land frontier – that is, uncultivated land that has to be cleared at a cost in terms of labor and capital – and the generation of a demand for labor a capital that has to be satisfied, at least in part, by foreign sources.

The most important staple of Saint-Domingue was sugar (with coffee following close behind at the end of the colonial period).[6] Sugar had been introduced by the Spaniards already at the beginning of the sixteenth century. It had been considered a luxury item in medieval Europe, but with the Spanish and Portuguese conquest of the Atlantic islands, larger quantities could be made available at a lower price, and its consumption spread to ever wider circles of European society. By the early eighteenth century, a strong international demand had been established.

The colony of Saint-Domingue was in an excellent position to respond to this demand. The climate was ideal for sugar production. Moreover, Saint-Domingue had a land frontier. The Spaniards had first destroyed the indigenous population and thereafter, from the early seventeenth century, left the western third of Hispaniola virtually uninhabited. The French moved into this vacuum, and in time a sugar economy was established. During most of the eighteenth century, sugar plantations remained an attractive investment in the colony, with French sugar driving its English competitor out of the continental European market between 1720 and 1740. In 1783, the sugar production of Saint-Domingue was almost equal to that of all the British Caribbean colonies combined. The capital required for establishing the plantations and their crushing mills came from France, and the necessary labor was imported from Africa.

Other plantation crops were introduced as well, following the staples pattern: coffee, indigo, cocoa, and cotton, all requiring less capital and less labor. Saint-Domingue never became a monoculture economy, and toward the end of the colonial period, the value of coffee exports was almost as high as that of sugar exports.[7] In 1789, Saint-Domingue was producing as much as 60 percent of the world's coffee.[8] This coffee was produced with the aid of the best technology of its day. By the eve of the slave uprising that triggered the wars of liberation in 1791, the French planters of Saint-Domingue had already pioneered new techniques of coffee cultivation (pruning, drying, and cleaning) which had established a reputation for quality second to none in the world. French planter society possessed some unique skills that were used to excellent effect in coffee production.[9]

The sugar story is slightly different. The main characteristic of sugar technology was the indivisibility of the crushing mill that made for both the (relatively large) optimum size of the plantation and the corresponding optimum size of the slave labor force needed to cut the cane and bring it to mill.[10] Whether the technology employed by the French in Saint-Domingue was superior to that used by their competitors elsewhere is somewhat of a moot point. Robert Rotberg and Christopher Clague offer the following summary:

> Whether the competitive edge of Saint-Domingue over the British islands was due to the superior fertility of its soil or to the skill and industry of the French is a matter on which the British and the French disagreed. Edwards estimated the sugar yields per acre to be two-thirds greater in Saint-Domingue than in Jamaica, but he attributes this to the better irrigational possibilities and superior soils in Saint-Domingue. Vernault de Charmilly asserts that the French planters were more innovative and industrious, in part because absenteeism was less prevalent than in Jamaica.
>
> Ragatz, who is very critical of the entrepreneurial failings of the British planters, indicates that the French might have been more enterprising. He attributes inertia in large measure to absenteeism. Perhaps one reason for the industry and enterprise of the

> Saint-Domingue planters was the migration there in the seventeenth century of French Protestants.
>
> Saint-Domingue also had the benefit of a somewhat more enlightened colonial policy than that applied to the British islands.... Still, that Saint-Domingue was more prosperous was not solely a function of differences in colonial policy vis-à-vis the British-held islands. Saint-Domingue's soils were fertile and extensive, and her French owners had put their talents and their savings to work to create an impressive and efficient economic machine.[11]

At any rate, there seems to be no evidence to suggest that the techniques employed in Saint-Domingue were any less advanced than those used elsewhere, even though few people were involved in the high-level technical and managerial operations.[12]

When the wars of liberation broke out in 1791, Saint-Domingue was a plantation economy that in many ways was at the technological forefront of plantation agriculture. During the course of these wars, and during the decades that followed, the country underwent a technological retrogression.[13] It can even be argued that the agricultural technology that prevailed during the last decades of the colonial period was superior to the practices available to present-day peasants.

During the nineteenth century, the unit value of Haitian coffee sold abroad declined relative to that of the produce of other coffee-exporting countries. Apparently, this was the result of the adoption not only of less labor-intensive techniques but also of inferior technology. Elaborate French practices could no longer be maintained when the small peasant family farm replaced the large colonial plantation.

Since then, little progress has been made. Today's agricultural technology has much more in common with nineteenth- than with eighteenth-century practices. Attempts undertaken during the American occupation (1915–34) to upgrade the technological level of agriculture by way of education failed completely, as did attempts to introduce new varieties of some of the most important crops. Later efforts fared no better. The Haitian peasant continues to work his land with the aid of techniques selected from a technological spectrum that is far from the efficiency frontier. In fact, it is difficult to find examples of successful innovations in the Haitian countryside.

The obvious question at this stage is: What caused this technological retrogression with consequences that continue to have an impact to this day? To answer this question, I will make use of an approach to knowledge and economic growth that incorporates endogenous population growth as one of its main feature. The purpose is to demonstrate how Haiti may have turned from a high-knowledge, or high-technology, economy, where population growth was no problem, into a low-knowledge, low-technology economy with a rate of population growth that perpetuates such a low-level equilibrium.

Children versus education

In a model that incorporates both endogenous fertility and accumulation of human capital, Gary Becker, Kevin Murphy, and Robert Tamura point to the conflict between having more children and educating the ones you already have and explore the implications for economic growth.[14] The model is one of overlapping generations with parents who, to a varying degree, are altruistic with respect to their children. These parents derive utility from their own consumption in the present but also from the utility their children obtain in the future, when they themselves are no longer around. The latter is discounted with an altruism factor that is lower the larger the family.

Child rearing requires both material (consumption) goods and time (care). If, in addition, the children are to accumulate human capital, they must be taught, and how much they accumulate depends, on the one hand, on how much time the parents' generation devotes to teaching them and, on the other, on the parents' endowment of human capital. The parents may also choose to produce consumption goods, which requires both time and human capital.

Two problems face the parental generation. First, it must decide how many children to have, given that children require both time and consumption goods and hence compete with the parents' own consumption. Second, it must decide how to divide its time between simple child rearing, education of the children, and production of consumption goods. These two decisions are interdependent. (The problem may be simplified by assuming that the time and material goods required per child for simple child-rearing are both constant.)

How many children will then be born, and how much human capital will be accumulated? The answer to these questions is that two steady states are possible.[15] To see how this works, assume that society has no human capital as all. This means that the return to accumulating such capital is likely to be very low. Human capital has a special feature in that it displays increasing returns to the already accumulated stock. The better educated a society, the easier it is to accumulate more human capital, at least up to some point where 'it becomes increasingly difficult to absorb more knowledge'.[16] Possibly, accumulation can go on indefinitely without reaching this point.

This means that in a society with no human capital, relatively more time is available for rearing children, that families will be large as a consequence, and that the value the parents attach to each child's future utility will be low. The rate at which the future is being discounted is then likely to be higher than the rate of return on human capital, and no accumulation of human capital will take place. The economy is stuck in an undeveloped or underdeveloped state with high birth rates and no education.

The low-level equilibrium is locally stable. Small additions to human capital will be of no avail. The economy simply returns to the original steady state. To break the deadlock, human capital formation is required that is large enough to raise the rate of return to the point where it is higher than the rate of discount on future consumption. Unless more human capital is being accumulated in each period than that which wears out, the economy will always fall back to the zero-human-capital position.

For a breakthrough to be possible, exogenous forces must come into play. Individual, marginal decisions do not suffice. A jump or big push is necessary. Once this jump has been achieved, however, increasing returns to human capital formation in combination with increasing costs of rearing children will guarantee that accumulation will proceed, either indefinitely, at an eventually constant level, or until a high-level human capital stock is reached in a steady state where the return to further accumulation equals the discount rate, which has fallen as the average family size has decreased. The high-level state corresponds to the developed economy, with a large stock of human capital, low birth rates, and small families.

Whether an economy ends up in the low-level or the high-level state very much depends on where it started. One of the most prominent features of the model is that it displays path dependence. Thus major exogenous shocks are required to make the economy move from one type of steady state to another.

The Haitian economy has been exposed to at least one such shock: the wars of liberation of 1791–1803. The French had managed to build the most prosperous colony in the world in Saint-Domingue with the aid of an agricultural technology that was both elaborate and intricate. The wars of liberation destroyed both physical and human capital, and, what is more important in the present context, virtually eradicated the entire educated labor force of the colony. Those with technical and administrative expertise either emigrated or were killed off.[17] This result drastically altered the human capital situation in Haiti. In terms of the Becker–Murphy–Tamura (BMT) model, the economy received a shock, 'as when a conqueror kills off the educated class' that propelled it toward stagnation.[18]

Subsequently, exactly as the model predicts, Haitians remained uneducated.[19] King Henry Christophe and Presidents Alexandre Pétion and Jean-Pierre Boyer showed some interest in education, but little came of their efforts. As it seems, the demand for education remained weak throughout the entire nineteenth century. Even the private school system stagnated. When the American occupation began in 1915, literacy rates in the countryside were close to zero.[20] American efforts to change the schooling system failed, and the return to a domestic administration again brought little progress. Today, the situation is much the same. Haiti continues to have the lowest enrollment and literacy rates in the Western Hemisphere. Less than 50 percent of the children between 5 and 11 years attend school, and between 65 and 80 percent of the Haitian population is believed to be illiterate.[21]

Elsewhere I have analyzed at some length the reluctance of Haitian governments to address the education problem, and the next section will shed some more light on government action (and inaction).[22] The lack of education stands out not only as a supply problem, but as one of insufficient demand that is linked to insufficient supply through increasing returns to human capital formation. It is a version of Say's law in reverse: The lack of supply holds demand back as well. Or, to put it slightly differently, a cumulative process has already run its course. The lack of supply has made for low returns on investment in human capital, and, hence, for a weak demand for education. This, in turn, has held back supply, and so forth, in a cumulative fashion until a low-level steady state has been reached.[23]

The demand trend may recently have been broken, however. Household expenditure figures show that, on average, urban households in 1994–95 spent between 1300 and 6700 gourdes on education, either directly or indirectly, and rural households somewhere between 1300 and 3200 gourdes. Insofar as these figures are representative of the overall situation in Haiti, they indicate that households spend approximately 15 percent of their income (12 percent of GDP) on education.[24]

Assuming that the figures are reasonably correct and therefore that a substantial demand for education actually exists in Haiti, it becomes important to investigate the causes of this demand and their economic implications. The 'simplest' interpretation is that Haitians are envisaging a better future in the wake of the recent political changes and hence are willing to undertake long-term educational investments. There may be a grain of truth in this explanation, but it is not likely to provide us with more than part of the picture. Another, at least complementary, and presumably more plausible, hypothesis is that education is demanded with emigration in mind. The return to human capital formation may be too low inside Haiti to warrant substantial investment, but once the possibility of settling elsewhere is taken into account, the benefit-cost ratio may be much higher for the individual – but not for Haitian society as a whole.

The predatory state: Too small and yet too large

As Sidney Mintz points out, the nineteenth century was crucial for Haiti.[25] Not least, it determined the political course followed to the present day. Between independence in 1804 and the beginning of the American occupation in 1915, a predatory state evolved, one that has continued to plague the country until very recently. The rise and logic of the predatory state is a topic examined as some length elsewhere.[26] A central feature is the modeling of ruler behavior in a situation where a balance has to be struck between concerns for income and security. Given that the ruler derives satisfaction from both these elements, he selects the size of polity or governing clique that maximizes his utility in a situation where increased income can only be obtained at the cost of an increased probability of being deposed by outside revolutions or inside palace coups. The consequences of this behavior have been distorted resource allocation, reduced national product, and highly unequal distribution of wealth and income. One aspect that has not been addressed, however, is the extent to which the predatory state has also displayed productive features, that is, whether government was an unqualified evil or its behavior contained any redeeming features. Was there anything about the logic of the predatory state that also allowed for productive behavior, and if so, what conclusions can be drawn?

Ronald Findlay and John Wilson have constructed a model of the state that incorporates both the predatory and the productive aspects of government behavior.[27] Their model contains two sectors: a private one that produces goods and services (national income) with the aid of labor and capital, and a government sector that, using only labor, contributes to the social and physical infrastructure in a way that increases private productivity. Government activities are subject to diminishing returns. Increasing the size of the public sector also has a negative effect on private production, one that has to be weighed against the positive contribution to productivity, since it takes labor away from work in the private sector. National income is maximized when the influences of these two forces balance each other at the margin.

The ruler in the Findlay–Wilson model taxes his citizens by retaining a fixed percentage of their incomes. This assumption means that gross tax revenue is maximized at the same size of public employment as the national income, declining thereafter as the value of private production decreases. Tax revenues may be used for financing public employment, that is, for wage payments in the government sector and for consumption and wealth accumulation by the ruler. Government expenditure increases monotonically as the size of the public sector increases. The reason is that wages will increase, first, because when the public sector bids away labor from private activities, it can do so only at an increasing wage, and, second, because increasing the public sector increases the overall productivity level of the private sector.

The optimal level of taxation in the Findlay–Wilson model is that which maximizes national income. The ruler already knows the optimal size of the public sector. He also knows the wage required to arrive at precisely that size. Equipped with this knowledge, he can calculate the optimal tax level. The optimal tax is that which suffices to finance optimum employment in the public sector, and nothing else. A benevolent ruler with the good of his people in mind will choose that level. But will a predatory ruler do so too?

If he does, the distributional implications will be different. A benevolent ruler would use taxes just for his wage bill. The predator instead aims at maximizing his own income. If he is free to set the tax level, he will choose the optimum size of the public sector, because this maximizes national income, that is, it gives him the largest possible cake upon which to feast. Findlay and Wilson suggest that the citizens will get only as much as they would if there were no public sector at all. Wages and capital income will both be taxed until they are no larger than their level in this 'state of nature'. So long as this is the case, the incentive to topple the ruler will be weak. It is only when the people become worse off as a result of state action that they are likely to rise up.

The ruler may, however, choose not to expand the public sector to its optimum size. Paradoxical as it may seem, this case is likely to arise when the ruler is subject to some degree of control by the population. For example, he may be allowed to set the tax at a level just sufficient to pay for optimal public employment, because this maximizes national income. If so, he will, however, *not*, choose this public employment level because he will then be left without any net income for himself. With the assumptions made by Findlay and Wilson, given the optimum tax rate, the expenditure curve will cut the tax revenue curve from below at the size of the public sector that maximizes national income. At that level, all government revenue is spent on wage payments. The ruler will therefore stop short of this point, at the size of the public sector that makes his marginal tax revenue equal to his marginal wage expenditure, since that is where the difference between revenue and expenditure, the surplus accruing to the ruler himself, is maximized. The size of the public sector thus becomes smaller than optimal.

What Findlay and Wilson have shown is that with a predatory government, the state either becomes too small or it reaches its optimum size but leaves the citizens no better off than the Hobbesian state of nature – without any government at all. What are the implications for Haiti?

In principle, Haiti has been a predatory state ever since its birth as a sovereign nation. The first rulers had to satisfy both their own demands for income and those of the coalitions that backed them and extract sufficient government revenue in foreign currency to be able to purchase the arms required to prevent a French return. To this end, the Haitian population was taxed through a crop-share tax of one-fourth of agricultural output and through levies on exports and imports. (Pétion abolished the crop-share tax, but the duties on exports and imports had come to Haiti to stay.)[28]

It may very well be that the taxes imposed were those that maximized national income in the Findlay–Wilson fashion during the early years of independence. The early governments did make a contribution *sui generis* to private productivity by placing agricultural laborers under military supervision, and perhaps what the rulers did to defend the country belongs to the productivity-raising category of outlays as well, freeing the private citizens from the responsibility of handling this problem themselves.[29] However, it is also clear that the policy of Toussaint Louverture, Jean Jacques Dessalines, and Christophe was one of maximizing the surplus of public revenue over public expenditure in the sense of Findlay and Wilson (that is, expenditure that increased private productivity). The situation may not have been that different from the one in which the ruler maximizes national income but only leaves to the citizens what they would have received in the absence of any productivity-raising state intervention. Dessalines, in particular, was known to have been extraordinarily greedy, something that no doubt contributed to his eventual downfall, since his greed was instrumental in keeping down both the wages of workers and soldiers and the income of the estate owners.[30]

The early rulers represented only the beginning of the predatory state in Haiti. The nineteenth century was to witness a rapid succession of kleptocratic rulers especially after the fall of Boyer in 1843, who viewed the presidency as no more than a source of private income. Their other main concern was how to remain in power so as to be able to continue their plunder of the Haitian population. This continued until the beginning of the American occupation in 1915. The pursuit of income resulted in a neglect of security with the result that the period in office of the majority of shoes presidents was short-lived, and those who lasted for longer periods made special efforts to increase security.[31]

What insights does the Findlay–Wilson model offer with respect to the turbulent period of Haitian history from 1843 to 1915? Hardly any of these rulers did anything to stimulate private production, that is, agriculture. It is hence unlikely that national income ever increased above the level that it would have reached in the absence of a Haitian government, if that state of events can be imagined. Still, there was taxation, mainly of foreign trade.[32] There was government expenditure as well, but not on productivity-enhancing activities. The bulk of it consisted of repayment of a foreign debt that, among other things, had been created to stuff the pockets of the rulers and was accumulating rapidly during the last quarter of the nineteenth century, and of payment to the army and the police to increase ruler security.[33]

Nineteenth century governments made national income decrease in Haiti because they absorbed and wasted resources that could have been used for the production of goods and services for the citizens instead, simply for redistributive purposes.[34] In terms of the Findlay–Wilson model, the latter half of the nineteenth century and the first 15 years of the twentieth represent a 'corner solution', with next to no resources devoted to boosting production, but with taxation and with expenditures of an unproductive kind, with national income below that of the 'no-government state' and with a disastrously skewed income distribution.

A strict interpretation of Findlay and Wilson suggests that the state was too small because it had a public sector that was too small to allow maximum national income to be reached. In another sense, however, the state was far too large, because it served no purpose. The vast majority of the government employees were people who worked the extractive machinery or who were employed to share the spoils of office or both. The distinction between productive and unproductive bureaucrats is of supreme importance when one attempts to understand Haiti's plight.

The predation of the governments of Haiti on the population did not end with the American occupation. The occupational forces made some half-hearted attempts to create a functioning physical and social infrastructure, along the lines depicted in the Findlay–Wilson model, but taxed much of the productivity gains away via forced repayment of the country's foreign debt.[35] At any rate, the occupation was nothing but a parenthesis in Haiti's history. Once it was over, the predators were back in the nation's driver's seat.[36]

Predation escalated dramatically during the 1940s and the 1950s, reaching an all-time high during the era of the two Duvaliers.[37] It cannot be denied that presidents Sténio Vincent (1930–41), Elie Lescot (1941–46), Dumarsais Estimé (1946–50), and Paul Magloire (1950–56) made some efforts to develop the country's productivity-increasing infrastructure.[38] However, none put national income before plunder. What this means, simply, is that the size of the productive public sector remained too small from the end of the occupation to the coming of François ('Papa Doc') Duvalier in 1957. During this period, the Haitian governments were in the 'intermediate' position of the Findlay–Wilson model. Tax rates were more or less determined by the precedent that had already been established, and the rulers concentrated on maximizing the surplus of government revenue over expenditure on the productive bureaucracy, preferring to keep that net revenue for themselves or distributing it to the unproductive parts of the public administration.

With the Duvaliers, the situation changed again, this time for the worse. Despite the promises delivered during the election campaign of 1957, Papa Doc did next to nothing to boost productivity in the economy. Instead, he concentrated on devising different ways of preying on the citizens. The new president was an innovator in the predatory state.[39] When his son succeeded him in 1971, it appeared for a while as if the worst features of Duvalierism were gone, with technocrats taking over the ministerial portfolios from the *tonton macoute* dinosaurs that had served under Duvalier *père*. This change, however, was purely cosmetic. If anything, predation escalated and became more refined than ever. Haiti entered what Anthony Maingot aptly termed 'the fine tuning or modernization' phase of predation, where the main private access to government funds was via the public enterprises.[40] Basically, the economy was back to the Findlay–Wilson corner solution, with next to no productive state action but plenty of predatory activities, a situation that remained virtually unaltered during the politically turbulent years of military government that followed.

The sketch of Haiti drawn with the aid of the Findlay–Wilson framework should of course not be taken literally. Still, from the application of this model, it is possible to gain some fairly robust insights. In most instances, the state in Haiti has been both too small and too large at the same time: too small in the sense that it has failed to create a policy environment conducive to productivity and growth, and too large if one takes into account the number of public sector employees who have been taken into the service of kleptocrats to assist in the creation of private ruler income or have served solely as recipients of public funds without performing any duties other than backing a ruler politically.

The policy conclusions are very clear. In some circles, Presidents Aristide and Préval have been accused of being the errand boys of 'neoliberals' and 'big business' because of their cutbacks of public administration. This hardly provides an accurate picture of what is going on. Transition in an economy must always involve an element of what might be termed constructive destruction. This is evident from the experiences of the former communist countries of Eastern Europe. The reform process has had great problems in taking off where the implementation is still dominated by the old *nomenklatura* or, for that matter, by bureaucrats who stood to gain from the now discarded system. Haiti constitutes an exact parallel. It would be utterly naïve to believe that the old structures built with predation in mind could suddenly turn productive in the way described by the Findlay and Wilson model. These structures have to be put aside before new and better ones can be put in place. Attempting to impose the latter with the former still in place leads nowhere.

Attempting to institute new structures while the old structures are still in place is, in fact, dangerous. Corruption tends to breed corruption.[41] A public employee is always faced with the choice of remaining honest or becoming corrupt. The factors involved in this decision are (1) his salary; (2) the incidence of corruption among other bureaucrats; (3) the probability of detection; (4) the size of payments received for rendering corrupt services; and (5) the rate at which future income is being discounted when compared with present income. The salary determines what he stands to lose in the future if he is caught and dismissed for being corrupt. The discount rate determines how much he values his future salary in comparison to an addition to income in the present by being corrupt. The size of the bribe determines how much he can add to his salary by being corrupt. The probability of being detected influences his possibility of getting away with illicit practice. Finally, if he is caught by a colleague who is also corrupt, he will presumably not lose his job, but simply have to share some of his illicit income with the latter.

The crucial element in the Haitian context is the overall incidence of corruption in the public administration. Other things being equal, if most of his colleagues are corrupt, the probability of any given bureaucrat following suit is high, since the chances of being caught and punished tend to be low. Through this mechanism, an administration that is basically corrupt also tends to corrupt new employees. Graft and inefficiency become self-perpetuating, and it becomes impossible to create a developmental state. Short of brainwashing, or milder forms of ideological retraining, which all face an incentive problem, the only way out of this high-corruption deadlock is to reduce the old public sector in principle to zero before starting to set up a bureaucracy that has something to contribute to productivity and welfare.[42]

Alone against nature: The Haitian peasant

Following the land reform policies initiated by Pétion in 1809, plantation agriculture gradually disappeared in Haiti. During the course of the nineteenth century, a peasant economy based on the family farm evolved. This economy has displayed remarkable resistance to attacks from outside forces, notably those attempting to reintroduce large-scale agriculture to the detriment of the peasants.[43] That conclusion does not mean, however, that the Haitian peasant is without problems. Equipped with little technology and little, if any, education, he is at a clear disadvantage when it comes to eking out a living. The *otorite* (authorities) have not cared too much about him, except in his capacity as a generator of revenue. His dilemma is further compounded by population growth, which tends to make it increasingly difficult to reduce poverty with every passing year. The relationship between population growth and rural per capita income constitutes one of the main themes of my book *Peasants and Poverty*.[44]

The most serious problem facing the Haitian peasant is that population growth and soil destruction interact in a cumulative way to depress rural incomes over time. This insight can be reached with the aid of one of the standard theorems of international trade: the Rybczynski theorem.[45] It states that in a setting where two goods are produced with the aid of the same two factors, and neither of the two lines of production displays any increasing returns to scale, and one of the factors grows while the endowment of the other factor remains constant, at constant commodity prices, the output of the good employing the growing factor intensively increases while that of the other good contracts in absolute terms.

Translated into the Haitian setting, peasants produce land-intensive export goods on the one hand, and labor intensive food crops on the other. As the population and the labor force grow, this practice, at constant prices (given, for example, by the level prevailing in the world market), makes the production of food crops increase while coffee production, for example, shrinks. Coffee is a perennial crop with a root system that binds and protects the soil, while the cultivation of food crops makes it necessary to lay the soil bare for planting when the rains come, which increases the risk of erosion, given Haiti's topography.

In other words, the available land shrinks, and this, in terms of the Rybczynski theorem, means that once more, the man–land ratio is altered. Again, population pressure on the land increases, more food crops are produced, and so on. Even without further population growth, the process will continue in a self-sustaining and cumulative fashion. Once set in motion, erosion will keep feeding on itself, and sooner or later per capita income will decline in the Haitian countryside, as it has for at least half a century, and presumably for much longer. It should also be noted that the Rybczynski theorem only requires constant relative commodity prices but in Haiti, the cumulative process has received further impetus from a decline in the relative price of export crops, notably coffee.[46]

This process is extremely serious, since it threatens the very base of peasant existence, and more so every year. The question is: How much longer will it continue? Socioeconomic systems as a rule do not have truly explosive features, that is, cumulative processes do not go on forever. Sooner or later, they lose their momentum. In the Haitian case, one may think of three different brakes: slowed population growth, employment outside the agricultural sector, or emigration of the agrarian population.

The BMT model provides some idea as to whether population growth can be expected to slow. In the low-level steady state prevailing in Haiti, very few efforts have been made to increase the human capital stock. In practice, the available time is devoted either to production or to child rearing. In this model, the simplest way to interpret the erosion process is as a reduction of the efficiency of the production of consumption goods. To do so leaves four adjustment options: Adult consumption of goods decreases, fewer children are born, the time devoted to child rearing decreases, or the amount of consumption goods devoted to each child decreases. The choice among these different adjustment mechanisms is an open one. The outcome is not necessarily slowed population growth, because the opportunity cost of a large family is not simply lower adult consumption. It could easily be that instead children suffer a reduction of their standard of living, either in terms of consumption or in terms of care.

Unfortunately, the latter possibility appears realistic, judging from past evidence. In a survey of nutrition research in Haiti up to the late 1960s, Kendall King concluded it was 'clear that the present national food resources preclude the possibility of really well nourished nation. On the other hand, the resources that are presently available are enough that no one need to starve to death. In spite of this, thousands of Haitian infants do not get their fair share of calories and protein from the family pot.'[47] With falling per capita income reduced altruism over time is a realistic possibility. This result also follows from traditional capital theory, as expounded by Irving Fisher.[48] In this theory, the rate of time preference (the opposite of altruism in the BMT model) – that is, the extent to which at the present time an addition to present income is preferred to which at the present time an addition to present income is preferred to and addition to future income – is determined mainly by three factors: the size of income, its distribution over time, and its probability or uncertainty (but not by family size alone as in the BMT case).

People with low incomes are likely to value the present very highly. This is most apparent at very low income levels. Staying alive today is an absolute prerequisite for being able to enjoy any income whatsoever in the future. Thus, looking at income size alone, one should expect in Haitian peasant to be strongly in favor of present over future income, and even more so the closer he is to the subsistence level.[49] This argument could be even more valid when future income will be enjoyed not by the peasant himself but by his offspring.

The second factor, time distribution, presumably works in the opposite direction. The erosion process is cumulative, which means that incomes should decline faster and faster over time, making additions to future income relatively more attractive. Again, however, the matter is complicated by the fact that future income accrues to future generations. This effect may then easily be swamped by the size effect.

Finally, there is the question of uncertainty. Reduced probability of receiving a given income in synonymous with impoverishment in the eyes of the income earner. Also, most people would tend to regard their immediate incomes as more certain than their future incomes, since information about the present is better than information about more distant time periods. This speaks in favor of additions to future income, but again, these additions accrue to someone else.

Thus, population growth tends to depress per capita income over time in a cumulative fashion through its interaction with erosion. Possibly, in due course, this growth will be reduced as households have to adjust their size to counteract the falling standard of living, but not necessarily. The adjustment mechanism may very well be one of redistribution within the family, to the detriment of the most vulnerable members: the children.

The failure of import substitution

The second possible remedy to falling incomes is employment outside agriculture. Historically, the road to higher living standards has almost always involved some degree of industrialization.

The first and largest industrial sector to be created in Haiti was the import-substituting segment. This enjoyed substantial protection from 1949 to 1986.[50] According to traditional trade theory, which analyzes competitive situations, import substitution should have led to an inefficient allocation of resources and welfare losses in the economy. However, a new approach to international trade centers on the existence of markets dominated by imperfect competition.[51] In this context, the optimality of free trade from a welfare point of view has been called into question. That, of course, raises the question of whether this bears on the Haitian case as well, that is, of whether import substitution behind tariff walls constitutes an efficient way of boosting non-agricultural employment.

The call for intervention in international trade has basically centered on two cases.[52] The first focuses explicitly on the possibility of stimulating technological change. The argument is the following: Certain industries are intensive in research and development activities, that is, they generate new knowledge. Knowledge, in turn, is a public good. It is non-rivalrous because the fact that one firm uses it does not preclude another from doing so. It is also, to a large extent, non-excludable in the sense that once the knowledge is spread, the firm that originated it cannot prevent other firms from making use of it. With imperfect patent legislation, knowledge spills over from those who developed it to their competitors.

Hence, especially in cases where the investment needed to produce the knowledge is high, firms may tend to underinvest in research and development activities. Then, one way of ensuring that innovating firms that contribute to growth by creating positive knowledge externalities are allowed to capture at least some of the profits that arise from being able to sell in a non-competitive environment is to give them monopoly status in the domestic market, behind protective tariff walls.

The argument is dubious, however, and especially so in the case of Haiti. In the first place, the argument has mainly been advanced in the context of economies with large domestic market, such as Japan or the United States, and not for small countries with a severely limited purchasing power. In Haiti this erroneous argument could easily lead to the creation of small firms that never reach large enough scale economies to make their efforts profitable. Second, domestic customers will suffer, exactly as in the competitive case, since tariff (or quota) protection will increase the prices that they have to pay. Third and most important, in the Haitian case, externalities have never existed. The industries that received protection were mainly of the simple consumer goods type: soap, detergents, shoes, cement, plastic and metal housewares, steel rods and corrugated sheets, textiles, paper products, cooking oil, flour, milk, matches, tomato paste, cigarettes, soft drinks, beer, and so forth, which do not rely heavily on continuous technological development.[53]

The second argument for strategic intervention in international trade refers to the case in which a foreign firm captures large rents in an imperfectly competitive industry that could be transferred to domestic producers, consumers, or the government. (These rents would show up either as high profits or as high factor rewards – for example, wages.) The typical case would be that of a foreign monopolist who exports to a domestic market where either there are no domestic producers at all or where domestic production takes place under competitive conditions but the domestic producers are not efficient enough to outcompete the foreign monopolist completely.[54]

The problem is one of making the monopolist supply his product at cost, not at cost plus monopoly profit. The remedy is to impose a price ceiling on imports. With imports coming from a monopolistic supplier, the marginal import cost always exceeds the marginal cost for the monopolist of producing the good in question, provided that the latter cost is rising. As more units are imported, the import price increases, not only on additional imports, but also on inframarginal imports. The price of imported goods to the domestic consumer should thus be put equal to the marginal import cost, while the foreign seller should receive only his marginal cost of production times the imported quantity. The difference may be collected as a tariff.

The foreign monopoly case is hardly representative of the Haitian reality either. Tariffs on manufactures have never been imposed to maximize the sum of consumer surplus, domestic producer surplus, and government revenues. The Haitian story is an altogether different one. No monopolies have threatened domestic producers. On the contrary, the products that received tariff protection could all be obtained at a given, competitive, price in the world market. Thus, one simply has the traditional case of import substitution behind tariff walls. Instead of using tariffs in combination with import price ceilings, domestic monopoly or near-monopoly firms were created in a number of consumer goods industries. According to Simon Fass, 'Under industrial development policies established and modified from 1949 onwards, any substitution industry that could produce enough to supply a substantial share of the local market was protected from import competition by stiff tariffs or outright import bans and from competition from other local producers by their inability to obtain operating licenses after one or a few firms took over the market.'[55]

So long as domestic demand was not saturated, the output of import substituting industries grew rapidly, in some instances up to the 1970s. Thereafter, however, the rate of expansion slowed down, being determined by rising incomes. The growth impulse provided by tariff protection had faded.

As Fass explains, the basis of import substitution was unsound from the very beginning:

> The cost of cornering the market, given that equipment and supplies could be had duty-free, was low. An individual with initiative, resources, and the necessary kinds of connections to assure that government would provide the operating license and then impose and maintain the protective clauses of policy could take control of supplying most or all of local demand. The first investor into a market therefore claimed the profits of other importers and of pre-existing local producers too small to benefit from policy, and monopoly rents from consumers. The only marketing skill required was that of selling the idea to the right people in the right places, not a difficult thing to do by definition if someone already had sufficient resources in hand.[56]

The situation became even more aggravated between the end of the 1970s and the mid-1980s, when the Haitian government established direct ownership of five major firms in soybean oil, wheat flour, cement, and sugar (two factories). Inefficiency became endemic in the public import-competing sector. None of the companies created or taken over by the government was ever allowed to function according to conventional business management principles. They were all turned into vehicles for grinding out illegal incomes for the presidential family. None ever became economically viable. The sugar and flour operations were, in addition, undercut by illegal imports that formed part of a smuggling racket presumably organized by Ernest Bennett, the president's father-in-law.[57]

In 1986, when the Duvalier dictatorship fell, import-competing manufacturing in Haiti displayed high rates of both nominal and effective protection. The former rates could be as high as 200 percent and the latter 100 percent on average, being the result not only of tariffs but also of quantitative import restrictions. Some 10 percent of the industrial output value enjoyed an effective protection of more than 300 percent.[58] This protection was harmful because it made consumers pay more than they would have under conditions of free trade, and it misallocated resources in the domestic economy to the production of goods in which the country has a comparative *dis*advantage.

From the point of view of technological change as well, tariffs under the traditional assumption of competitive markets are likely to do more harm than good. As is well known from comparative studies of manufacturing in developing countries, excessive tariff protection tends to breed inefficiency and low capacity utilization.[59] The lack of exposure to international competition means that import-substituting industries are not forced to think of means of cutting their costs, for example, by innovating processes, inputs, or products. They make profits and stay in business because tariffs make for high prices of their output and because tariffs on imported inputs are usually low.

The Haitian government that took over in February 1986 set out to reduce protection levels so as to lower the average effective rate of protection to less than 40 percent, closed one of the sugar factories and the soybean oil factory, and revoked the monopoly concessions of the cement and flour operations. Import-competing industries entered a difficult period of adjustment to market-like conditions, a period that was to be further aggravated by the political turmoil of the 1990s and the subsequent international embargo, and that is not yet over.[60]

Haiti has a long way to go before domestic producers in general are in a position to compete efficiently with imported goods without government support. Indeed, the effects of protection in the Haitian case closely mirror the situation described by traditional trade theory, compounded by predatory manipulations of those in political power. Clearly, this situation had very little to do with the potentially (but not necessarily) favorable sequence of events envisaged by more recent approaches of trade theory. The import-substituting segment of Haitian manufacturing never became economically sound. Protectionism is not the way to gainful employment. The costs it imposes on the economy are too high, a lesson that is as relevant for the future.

The assembly export sector

The fact that import substitution behind high tariff walls was not a proper industrial strategy or employment strategy was also borne out by the experience of the export-oriented assembly industries. These industries constituted a dynamic and fast-growing segment of the Haitian economy during the 1970s and the 1980s. Between 1966 and 1984, the share of manufactures in exports increased from a mere 4 percent to 66 percent. By the latter date, employment in the sector amounted to about 30,000, a figure that was to increase to 46,000 in 1990.[61]

The growth of the assembly sector did not take place in splendid isolation. On the contrary, the government intervened in a number of ways. Some of those ways were dubious, such as preventing labor unionism under the two Duvaliers, which positively served to strengthen Haiti's comparative advantage in the form of low wages.[62] Others were more legitimate: exemption of import duties on inputs and export duties on outputs, and income and license taxes for determined periods, as well as the provision of infrastructure.[63] Against these gains, however, must be set the fact that the anti-export bias created by the protection of the import-substituting industries was not removed until 1986.

Furthermore, a long list of obstacles connected with the general underdevelopment of Haiti had to be overcome. Simon Fass has listed the various complaints that were voiced at one time or another between 1949 and the late 1980s:

> ...inadequate numbers of qualified government workers, entrepreneurs, managers, supervisors, and skilled workers; inadequate or overpriced infrastructure services; insufficient investment, promotion, training, or credit; haphazard and arbitrary application of regulations concerning taxes, investment incentives, tariffs and labor; inappropriate legislation with respect to these issues; inadequate coordination among government agencies, among businesses, and between government and businesses; insufficient data or research;

> inappropriate or irrelevant advice from foreign technical assistants; insufficient coordination among foreign-assistance agencies; too many foreign economists without business knowledge; too many local investors without sufficient economics; poor quality control; absence of clear or rational planning in either the public or private sector; excessive tax evasion by the private sector and graft in the public sector; minimum wages too high for international competitiveness or too low to maintain worker productivity, purchasing power, and stability; and always, there was the inadequacy of the general investment 'climate'.[64]

In spite of all these obstacles, Haiti developed into an exporter of labor-intensive assembly products. 'The accomplishment was in fact remarkable', concludes Fass.[65]

The assembly sector survived the increased organization of factory workers that came in the wake of the fall of Jean-Claude Duvalier in 1986. The upward pressure on the wage level that resulted could be accommodated.[66] Far less easy to handle were the political disturbances that resulted when the 1987 elections approached.[67] When the military regime was subjected to external pressure through increasingly tight sanctions after the coup against Aristide in 1991, the goose that had laid the golden egg was all but killed by the representatives of the predatory state. Value added in the assembly sector fell from US$4 million in September 1991 to US$0.06 million in January 1992.[68] The number of firms in the sector fell from 252 in 1990 and 145 in 1991 to less than 30 in early 1994, with employment being reduced from more than 40,000 to about 6000 to 8000 over approximately the same period. Toward the end of 1994, operations in this sector had virtually come to a standstill.[69]

Notwithstanding the difficulties faced by the assembly sector over the past 4 or 5 years, it can presumably be rebuilt substantially over the course of the next few years, provided the political temperature remains within tolerable limits. The comparative advantage remains the same – low wages – and so do, for that matter, many of the obstacles the sector has to overcome.

If Haiti enters a phase of political stability, assembly production, with all its problems, will provide an alternative to agriculture in terms of employment – in fact, one of the few outside the informal sector and the public administration. In the long run, however, other problems have to be tackled. The main complaints lodged against the assembly sector have to do with low wages and weak linkages with the rest of the economy.[70] To the extent that these complaints are true, the assembly sector only constitutes a marginal advance on traditional pursuits. The question then is whether better alternatives may be available in the future.

One of the facts of economic development is that developing countries specializing in the production of relatively capital-intensive modern manufactures tend to have higher national incomes per capita than countries specializing in traditional, labor-intensive products (manufactures or agricultural goods). The prime examples are the so-called Asian tigers of the Pacific Rim.

Using this observation as a starting point, Dani Rodrik has constructed a model that focuses on when countries begin to develop a modern sector and become exporters of non-traditional goods.[71] The Rodrik model contains two tradable final goods: a labor-intensive, 'traditional' one, produced with the aid of labor and capital, and a 'modern' good produced with capital and a range of intermediate goods that are imperfect substitutes for each other, both produced under constant returns to scale. The intermediates may be thought of as producer services ('skilled and specialized workmanship') or specialized inputs or technologies.[72] For example, extensive communication may be needed between the producers of modern goods and the suppliers of intermediaries before arriving at specifications that fit the supplier. 'A salient aspect of these exchanges is the dependence of the outcome on extensive interaction between suppliers and users in iteratively changing both process and product characteristics.'[73] Thus, both geographical proximity and variety matter. The wider the range of specialized intermediates available to the final-goods producers, the lower the unit costs of the firm in the modern sector.

The proximity requirement makes the intermediates nontradables. They are produced with the aid of skilled labor alone and under increasing returns to scale, because of the fixed costs that are required to develop the specialized skills – that is, under conditions of monopolistic competition (each intermediate being produced by a single firm). The higher the skill level, the lower the unit cost of the intermediate in question.

This creates a Catch-22 situation. The profitability of the modern sector depends on the range of intermediates available, but the viability of intermediate production simultaneously depends on the existence of a demand from the modern sector. Thus, in an economy that specializes in the production of traditional goods, neither the intermediate sector nor the modern one will be established, since it does not pay for individual producers of intermediates to establish themselves, for lack of demand.[74] It would take a coordinated movement of resources into modern and intermediate production to break away from specialization in traditional goods, but this in turn presupposes the existence of both a sufficiently well educated labor force and a large enough capital stock.

Should the Rodrik model constitute a good approximation of reality, countries such as Haiti are caught in a double trap. The lack of education not only produces a high rate of population growth, as in the BMT framework, but it also puts the economy in a traditional-goods deadlock that cannot be broken by gradual change, that is, by marginal efforts of individual producers. In the worst case, the political situation remains turbulent and the assembly sector fails to recover, with investors going elsewhere inside or outside the Caribbean. If so, Haiti is back to a traditional economy in which agriculture and informal urban pursuits constitute the only alternatives – a gloomy situation, indeed.[75]

Migration

The retrogression to a purely traditional economy leaves only the third alternative when it comes to slowing population growth: emigration. This is already the main adjustment mechanism. The erosion process triggers migration via the reduction of incomes.

One recent model that focuses on this feature in a growth context has been developed by Juan Braun.[76] At the center of Braun's analysis is the existence of some natural resource that is in fixed supply and becomes congested as the population grows. This resource could be thought of as land in the Haitian context. It imposes diminishing returns to scale for labor and capital. It also makes the wage earned in the domestic economy a function of how much of this resource is available on a per capita basis: The more there is, the higher the wage. The production function of the economy also contains a standard efficiency or technology parameter, which may be interpreted, as in the Findlay–Wilson model, to depend on government policies. This parameter influences the wage rate in basically the same way: The higher the level of the technology, the higher the domestic wage.

The migration decision in the Braun model depends only on the wage differential between the rest of the world and the domestic economy, since capital is taken to be completely mobile across national boundaries and a single rate of return prevails everywhere in the world. In the case of Haiti, of course, there is a low availability of land per capita as well as a low level of technology. Hence, the prevailing wage rate can be expected to be low from an international perspective, which is also the case empirically. Haiti then becomes a country with net emigration, even in the absence of population growth.

The Braun model, however, may also be linked to the BMT model. This explains the low technological level as a result of conscious decision-making. It also makes for endogenous population growth that in turn influences the domestic wage level. In the Braun model, as people move out of the country, land gets less congested and the wage rate tends to rise. As long as the economy stays in the BMT low-level equilibrium with high population growth, however, one should not expect wages to rise. Wage rates will remain low; land will continue to be congested; and people will continue to leave Haiti. Wage rates will not be equalized between Haiti and the rest of the world, and the incentive to migrate will remain.

Conclusions

The French colony of Saint-Domingue was the richest of its kind in the world. Present-day Haiti is the poorest country in the Western Hemisphere. The shock received when the country lost its skilled labor force during the wars of liberation heralded an end to the staples-led economic expansion in the nineteenth century. Haiti became a low-technology economy that failed to create an educational system that could put an end to retrogression. Low returns to human capital formation coupled with government passivity concerning educational matters threw the country into mass illiteracy. Secular stagnation gradually set in with diminishing returns to labor, soil erosion in agriculture, and political degeneration. The peasantry was squeezed between a rock and a hard place, between the relentless forces of nature and a relentless state.

Import substitution in the industrial sector has failed, both for economic and political reasons. It never made any sense in the first place to foster high-cost ventures producing for a small domestic market, and once that sector became a playground for kleptocratic political interests, it virtually collapsed.

Today, the Haitian economy may be in the worst place of its history. Per capita income has declined to a level of US$250–260 or less.[77] The only sector displaying any dynamism over the past two decades – assembly manufacturing for export – received a terrible blow as a result of political turmoil and international sanctions. At the same time, agricultural exports have become increasingly difficult, as the interplay between population growth and erosion pushes the rural economy more and more toward the production of domestic crops. The country's economic structure may be locked into a low-level equilibrium that offers no easy way out. This equilibrium is characterized by high population growth and a very small stock of human capital that tends not to expand.

As Uli Locher has pointed out, traditional agriculture hardly has any future: 'There is a pervasively pessimistic undercurrent in virtually every recent assessment of Haiti's likely future. I think it is time to face up to the facts and realize that rural Haiti as we know it is doomed.'[78] In 1950, the arable land area per capita was 0.38 hectares. With the trends that prevailed at the time Locher made his assessment in 1988, it would appear that the population in the year 2000 would amount to 7.5 million and that the arable area per capita would be reduced to 0.16 hectares. Food production would be lower than ever, and aid-financed food imports would reach an all-time high.[79]

Locher is right, and what is worse, as of 1997 there are no viable alternatives, with the possible exception of a revitalized assembly sector. Assembly production may not be able to do very much, either. It is a low-wage sector and has a virtually unlimited supply of labor (in the sense of Lewis) on which to draw.[80] Without a substantial stock of solid human capital, it is impossible to move into high-growth industries with more advanced technologies, but human capital formation may be locked into a low-level trap. Even with a larger stock of human capital, 'trading up' may be difficult in the context of an internationalized economy. As Pranab Bardhan has observed, 'trade may reduce the profitability of R&D in the poor country as it places local entrepreneurs in competition with a rapidly expanding set of imported, differentiated products and may drive the country to specialize in traditional, possibly stagnant, industries which use its relatively plentiful supply of unskilled worker.'[81]

This is already the case in Haiti.

The future looks gloomy. Demographic pressure is exhausting the available soil at an increasing pace. The assembly sector is down to less than 10,000 jobs. Per capita income is falling and would fall even quicker were it not for emigration. Moreover, emigration takes place under exceedingly difficult circumstances.

The old, or traditional, aggregate neoclassical theory of economic growth reduced long-run growth of per capita income to a matter of population growth on the one hand and technological change on the other, both exogenously derived.[82] The new theory of economic growth escapes the determinism of the old growth models. Most importantly, it endogenizes technological change.[83] What it does *not* tell us is how to bring about this change. In this chapter, the new growth theory explains important parts of Haiti's economic reality. But that is also where the story ends. As pointed out by Paul Krugman, 'New growth theory has been preoccupied with a different question than high development theory [of the 1950s and 1960s]: how to explain the persistence of growth rather than how to get it started.... So while the philosophy of new growth theory is in essence a rediscovery of high development theory, it has not returned to the same questions.'[84]

Unfortunately, it is precisely in this area that development practitioners must concentrate their efforts, finding ways of breaking out of the interlocking traps that have been exposed in this chapter. It is clearly not an easy undertaking. In the worst case, it is an impossible one. Still, it must be attempted.

At least, the unwilling government that was previously the constraint dominating all other constraints has been removed. This fact, however, creates not just new opportunities but also new problems. This chapter has dealt only with nonconvexities and externalities relating to the production of goods and services and not with the 'massive costs of collective action in building new economic institutions and political coalitions and in breaking the deadlock of incumbent interests threatened by new technologies'.[85] Even well-intentioned governments with a purged, honest, bureaucracy have a Herculean task in this respect. It would be unrealistic to expect any miracles.

Acknowledgments

Thanks are due to Clive Gong, Paul Latortue, Robert Maguire, Fairauld Maignon, Robert Rotberg, and Charles Tardieu for constructive criticism of the original version.

Notes

Published in Robert I. Rotberg (ed.), *Haiti Renewed: Political and Economic Prospects*. Washington, DC: Brookings Institute Press, 1997, published for the World Peace Foundation by the Brookings Institution Press. Reprinted by permission.

1. Schultz (1977), pp. 245–53.
2. Lundahl (1995–96).
3. Lundahl (1991), pp. 66–68; Findlay and Lundahl (1994), pp. 68–93, and the references cited there, for an overview and formalization of the theory.

4. Helleiner (1972), pp. 15–16.
5. Findlay and Lundahl (1994).
6. The following builds on Lundahl (1979), pp. 256–59.
7. Rotberg and Clague (1971), p. 28.
8. Ibid., p. 29.
9. Lundahl (1979), pp. 563–66.
10. Ibid., 257–58.
11. Rotberg and Clague (1971), pp. 30–31.
12. A summary description of the sugar production techniques employed in Saint-Domingue, and their evolution is offered in SACAD and FAMV (1993), pp. 70–75; Baldwin (1956), pp. 161–79.
13. Lundahl (1977), pp. 69–85; Lundahl (1979); Lundahl (1983b), pp. 61–93.
14. Becker, Murphy, and Tamura (1990), pp. 512–37.
15. A steady state is defined as a situation in which the various quantities grow as constant rates.
16. Becker, Murphy, and Tamura (1990), p. 516.
17. Lacerte (1974–75), pp. 78–79; Rotberg and Clague (1971), p. 48.
18. Becker, Murphy, and Tamura (1990), p. 532.
19. Lundahl (1979), pp. 453–501; Tardieu (1990).
20. Lundahl (1979), p. 463.
21. Academy for Educational Development (1995), pp. 3, 5, Annexe onze.
22. Lundahl (1979).
23. Quite likely, many households in Haiti are also facing a liquidity constraint, which makes it impossible to finance education to the extent desired (Academy for Educational Development [1995]). As demonstrated by Barham et al. (1995), pp. 1257–75, this could produce a poverty trap: 'Once a member of a family decides not to invest in education, all of that individual's descendants will be uneducated also' (ibid., p. 1267).
24. Academy for Educational Development (1995).
25. Mintz (1966), p. 5.
26. See Lundahl (1979), (1983a), and (1992a).
27. Findlay and Wilson (1987), pp. 289–304. See also Findlay and Wellisz (1988), pp. 59–80.
28. Lundahl (1979), p. 392. The economic systems of Toussaint and Dessalines are analyzed in Lundahl (1985a) and (1984a).
29. Hedlund et al. (1989), pp. 45–71, analyze the agricultural system of the early rulers as one of short-run extraction rather than one aiming for production in the long run. A similar view is presented in Barthélemy (1989).
30. See Lundahl (1984a), for details.
31. Lundahl (1985b), pp. 175–218.
32. Lundahl (1979), p. 393.
33. Ibid., pp. 366–70, 375–79.
34. The activities of the nineteenth-century governments were mainly directly unproductive profit-seeking activities undertaken simply to redistribute income from the population in favor of the various governing cliques without producing anything wanted by the citizens. See Bhagwati (1982), pp. 988–1002.
35. See Schmidt (1971) and Castor (1971), for the detailed picture.
36. Lundahl (1985b).

37. Lundahl (1984b), pp. 39–78; Danielson and Lundahl (1994), pp. 51–78.
38. See Lundahl (1979), pp. 302–08; Lundahl (1993), pp. 177–259.
39. Lundahl (1984b) gives the details.
40. Maingot (1986–87), p. 83. Cf. Abbott (1988), p. 250.
41. See Andvig and Moene (1990), pp. 63–76.
42. It should be stressed that I am not arguing for a minimal public sector. That should be a transitory state of affairs. The 'new' bureaucracy should be of the size that is optimal in the Findlay–Wilson sense, that is, the size that maximizes national income.
43. See Murray (1977); Lundahl (1979), pp. 255–95; and Barthélemy (1989), for an analysis of the causes of this strength and the mechanisms employed to defend peasant property.
44. Lundahl (1979), pp. 187–254.
45. Rybczynski (1955), pp. 336–41.
46. See Lundahl (1979), pp. 187–254; Bourdet and Lundahl (1991); and International Monetary Fund (1995), p. 3.
47. King (1969), p. 187.
48. Notably Fisher (1930). This theory is applied to Haiti in Lundahl (1979), pp. 503–55.
49. See Lundahl (1979), pp. 226–27, 514–15.
50. Lundahl (1992b), pp. 5–32.
51. See, for example, Helpman and Krugman (1985), (1989); Krugman (1986), (1990); and Grossman and Helpman (1991). Helpman (1990), pp. 193–216, gives an introduction to the field.
52. These are discussed extensively in the articles contained in Krugman (1986).
53. Fass (1988), p. 33.
54. See Helpman and Krugman (1986) for a formal analysis of this case.
55. Fass (1988), p. 33.
56. Ibid.
57. Lundahl (1983a), pp. 5–32.
58. World Bank (1989), p. 5.
59. Notably Little et al. (1970), Bhagwati (1978), Krueger (1978), Michaely et al. (1991).
60. Lundahl (1992a), pp. 416–17.
61. Lundahl (1992b), p. 16; Inter-American Development Bank (1995), p. 4.
62. Lundahl (1988), pp. 88–119.
63. Lundahl (1983a), pp. 15–16.
64. Fass (1988), p. 39.
65. Ibid., 43.
66. Ibid., 44–45.
67. World Bank (1988), pp. 14–15.
68. Verret (1992).
69. Inter-American Development Bank (1995), p. 36; International Monetary Fund (1995), p. 3.
70. Fass (1988), p. 41; Grunwald et al. (1984), pp. 231–52.
71. Rodrik (1995), pp. 55–107.
72. Ibid., p. 80.
73. Pack and Westphal (1986), p. 110, quoted in Rodrik (1995), p. 81.

74. This argument applies not only to specialized intermediates. It is easy to envisage a similar situation in the case of infrastructure. Building roads, railroads, or power stations is typically associated with a large fixed cost and may hence not take place unless there are many industrial units using these facilities (Murphy, Shleifer, and Vishny (1989), pp. 1003–26). Without industrialization, there is no pressure to build the kind of infrastructure analyzed by Findlay and Wilson (1987), and without infrastructure there may be no industrialization.
75. These are examined in detail in Fass (1988).
76. Braun (1993). Here, I discuss one of his models as presented by Barro and Sala-i-Martin (1995), pp. 300–8.
77. International Monetary Fund (1995), p. 2; Inter-American Development Bank (1995), p. 28.
78. Locher (1988), p. 16.
79. Ibid., pp. 15–16.
80. Lewis (1954), pp. 139–91.
81. Bardhan (1993), p. 24; Bardhan (1995), p. 2987.
82. Notably, Solow (1956), pp. 65–94, and the literature derived from this work.
83. See, for example, Romer (1986), pp. 1002–37; Romer (1990), p. 71; and Lucas (1988), pp. 3–42, as well as the works cited in this chapter.
84. Krugman (1993), p. 31. See also Bardhan (1995), p. 2992.
85. Bardhan (1995), p. 2995.

References

Abbott, Elisabeth (1988), *Haiti: The Duvaliers and Their Legacy*. New York: McGraw-Hill.

Academy for Educational Development EDUCAT, *Diagnostic technique du secteur éducatif haïtien* (1995), Version provisoire. August 14. Port-au-Prince: EDUCAT.

Andvig, Jens Christopher and Moene, Karl-Ove (1990), 'How Corruption May Corrupt', *Journal of Economic Behavior and Organization*, Vol. 13, 63–76.

Baldwin, Robert E. (1956), 'Patterns of Development in Newly Settled Regions', *Manchester School of Economic and Social Studies*, Vol. 24, 161–79.

Bardhan, Pranab (1993), 'The New Growth Theory, Trade and Development: Some Brief Reflections', in: Göte Hansson (ed.), *Trade, Growth and Development: The Role of Politics and Institutions*. London and New York: Routledge.

Bardhan, Pranab (1995), 'The Contributions of Endogenous Growth Theory to the Analysis of Development Problems: An Assessment', in: Jere Behrman and T.N. Srinivasan (eds), *Handbook of Development Economics*. Amsterdam: North-Holland.

Barham, Vicky, et al. (1995), 'Education and the Poverty Trap', *European Economic Review*, Vol. 39, 1257–75.

Barthélemy, Gérard (1989), *Le pays en dehors. Essai sur l'univers rural haïtien*. Port-au-Prince: Éditions Henri Deschamps.

Barro, Robert J. and Sala-i-Martin, Xavier (1995), *Economic Growth*. New York: McGraw-Hill.

Becker, Gary S., Murphy, Kevin M. and Tamura, Robert (1990), 'Human Capital, Fertility, and Economic Growth', *Journal of Political Economy*, Vol. 98, 512–37.

Bhagwati, Jagdish N. (1978), *Foreign Trade Regimes and Economic Development: Anatomy and Consequences of Exchange Control Regimes*. New York: National Bureau of Economic Research.

Bhagwati, Jagdish (1982), 'Directly Unproductive, Profit-Seeking (DUP) Activities', *Journal of Political Economy*, Vol. 90, 988–1002.

Bourdet, Yves and Lundahl, Mats (1991), 'Patterns and Prospects of Haitian Primary Exports', *Latin American Issues*, No. 9, A Monograph Series on Contemporary Latin American and Caribbean Affairs, Allegheny College, Meadville, PA and University of Akron, OH.

Braun, Juan (1993), 'Essays on Economic Growth and Migration'. PhD dissertation, Harvard University.

Castor, Suzy (1971), *La ocupación norteamericana de Haití y sus consecuencias (1915–1934)*. México DF: Siglo Veintiuno.

Danielson, Anders and Lundahl, Mats (1994), 'Endogenous Policy Formation and the principle of Optimal Obfuscation: Theory and Some Evidence from Haiti and Jamaica', *Comparative Economic Studies*, Vol. 36, 51–78.

Fass, Simon M. (1988), *Political Economy in Haiti: The Drama of Survival*. New Brunswick, NJ and Oxford: Transaction Books.

Findlay, Ronald and Lundahl, Mats (1994), 'Natural Resources, "Vent-for-Surplus," and the Staples Theory', in: Gerald M. Meier (ed.), *From Classical Economics to Development Economics*. New York: St. Martin's Press.

Findlay, Ronald and Wellisz, Stanislaw (1988), 'The State and the Invisible Hand', *World Bank Research Observer*, Vol. 3, 59–80.

Findlay, Ronald and Wilson, John D. (1987), 'The Political Economy of Leviathan', in: Assaf Razin and Efraim Sadka (eds), *Economic Policy in Theory and Practice*. London: Macmillan.

Fisher, Irving (1930), *The Theory of Interest*. New York: The Macmillan Company.

Grossman, Gene M. and Helpman, Elhanan (1991), *Innovation and Growth in the Global Economy*. Cambridge, MA and London: MIT Press.

Grunwald, Joseph, Delatour, Leslie and Voltaire, Karl (1984), 'Offshore Assembly in Haiti', in: Charles R. Foster and Albert Valdman (eds), *Haiti – Today and Tomorrow: An Interdisciplinary Study*. Lanham, MD: University Press of America.

Hedlund, Stefan, Lundahl, Mats and Lyttkens, Carl-Hampus (1989), 'The Attraction of Extraction: Three Cases of State versus Peasantry', *Scandia*, Vol. 55, 45–71.

Helleiner, Gerald K. (1972), *International Trade and Economic Development*. Harmondsworth: Penguin.

Helpman, Elhanan (1990), 'The Noncompetitive Theory of International Trade and Trade Policy', *Proceedings of the World Bank Annual Conference on Development Economics 1989*. Washington, DC: The World Bank.

Helpman, Elhanan and Krugman, Paul R. (1985), *Market Structure and Foreign Trade: Increasing Returns, Imperfect Competition, and the International Economy*. Cambridge, MA and London: MIT Press.

Helpman, Elhanan and Krugman, Paul R. (1989), *Trade Policy and Market Structure*. Cambridge, MA and London: MIT Press.

Inter-American Development Bank (1995), *Emergency Economic Recovery Program: Haiti*, Report of the Joint Mission (November 7–20, 1994), January 3. Washington, DC: Inter-American Development Bank.

International Monetary Fund (1995), *Haiti – Recent Economic Developments*, SM/95/43, March 1. Washington, DC: International Monetary Fund.

King, Kendall W. (1969), 'Nutrition Research in Haiti', in: Richard P. Schaedel (ed.), *Research and Resources of Haiti: Papers of the Conference on Research and Resources of Haiti*. New York: Research Institute for the Study of Man.

Krueger, Anne O. (1978), *Foreign Trade Regimes and Economic Development: Liberalization Attempts and Consequences*. New York: National Bureau of Economic Research.

Krugman, Paul R. (ed.) (1986), *Strategic Trade Policy and the New International Economics*. Cambridge, MA and London: MIT Press.

Krugman, Paul R. (1990), *Rethinking International Trade*. Cambridge, MA and London: MIT Press.

Krugman, Paul R. (1993), 'Towards a Counter-Counterrevolution in Development Theory', *Proceedings of the World Bank Annual Conference on Development Economics 1992*. Washington, DC: The World Bank.

Lacerte, Robert (1974–75), 'The First Land Reform in Latin America: The Reforms of Alexander Pétion, 1809–1814', *Inter-American Economic Affairs*, Vol. 28, 77–85.

Lewis, W. Arthur (1954), 'Economic Development with Unlimited Supplies of Labour', *Manchester School of Economic and Social Studies*, Vol. 22, 139–91.

Little, Ian, Scitovsky, Tibor and Scott, Maurice (1970), *Industry and Trade in Some Developing Countries*. London: Oxford University Press.

Locher, Uli (1988), 'Land Distribution, Land Tenure and Land Erosion in Haiti', paper prepared for the Twelfth Annual Conference of the Society for Caribbean Studies, Hoddesdon, Herfortshire, July 12–14.

Lucas, Robert E., Jr. (1988), 'On the Mechanics of Economic Development', *Journal of Monetary Economics*, Vol. 22, 3–42.

Lundahl, Mats (1977), 'Les obstacles au changement technologique dans l'agriculture traditionelle haïtienne', *Conjonction*, No. 135, 69–85.

Lundahl, Mats (1979), *Peasants and Poverty: A Study of Haiti*. London: Croom Helm.

Lundahl, Mats (1983a), *The Haitian Economy: Man, Land and Markets*. London: Croom Helm.

Lundahl, Mats (1983b), 'Peasants, Government and Technological Change in Haitian Agriculture', in: Hans F. Illy (ed.), *Politics, Public Administration and Rural Development in the Caribbean*. Munich: Weltforum.

Lundahl, Mats (1984a), 'Defense and Distribution: Agricultural Policy in Haiti during the Reign of Jean-Jaques Dessalines, 1804–1906', *Scandinavian Economic History Review*, Vol. 32, 77–103.

Lundahl, Mats (1984b), 'Papa Doc: Innovator in the Predatory State', *Scandia*, Vol. 50, 39–78.

Lundahl, Mats (1985a), 'Toussaint L'Ouverture and the War Economy of Saint-Domingue, 1796–1802', *Slavery and Abolition*, Vol. 6, 122–38.

Lundahl, Mats (1985b), 'Government and Inefficiency in the Haitian Economy: The Nineteenth Century Legacy', in: Michael B. Connolly and John McDermott (eds), *The Economics of the Caribbean Basin*. New York.

Lundahl, Mats (1988), 'The Rise and Fall of the Haitian Labour Movement', in: Malcolm Cross and Gad Heuman (eds), *Labour in the Caribbean: From Emancipation to Independence*. London and Basingstoke: Macmillan.

Lundahl, Mats (1991), 'Staples Trade and Economic Development', *EFI Yearbook 1991*, Stockholm: Stockholm School of Economics.

Lundahl, Mats (1992a), *Politics or Markets? Essays on Haitian Underdevelopment*. London and New York: Routledge.

Lundahl, Mats, (1992b), 'The Haitian Economy Facing the 1990s', *Canadian Journal of Latin American and Caribbean Studies*, Vol. 17, 5–32.

Lundahl, Mats (1993), *Kleptokrati, socialism och demokrati*. Stockholm: SNS Förlag.

Lundahl, Mats (1995–96), 'Five Decisive Events in the Economic History of Haiti', *Historia y Sociedad*, Vol. 8, 7–28.

Maingot, Anthony P. (1986–87), 'Haiti: Problems of Transition to Democracy in an Authoritarian Soft State', *Journal of Interamerican Studies and World Affairs*, Vol. 28, 75–102.

Michaely, Michael; Papageorgiou, Demetris and Choksi, Armeane M. (1991), *Liberalizing Foreign Trade: Lessons of Experience in the Developing World*. Cambridge, MA and Oxford: Basil Blackwell.

Mintz, Sidney W. (1966), 'Introduction', in: James G. Leyburn, *The Haitian People*. Revised ed. New Haven, CT and London: Yale University Press.

Murphy, Kevin M., Shleifer, Andrei and Vishny, Robert (1989), 'Industrialization and the Big Push', *Journal of Political Economy*, Vol. 97, 1003–26.

Murray, Gerald Francis (1977), *The Evolution of Haitian Peasant Land Tenure: A Case Study in Agrarian Adaptation to Population Growth*. PhD dissertation. New York: Columbia University.

Pack, Howard and Westphal, Larry E. (1986), 'Industrial Strategy and Technological Change: Theory versus Reality', *Journal of Development Economics*, Vol. 22, 87–128.

Rodrik, Dani (1995), 'Getting Interventions Right: How South Korea and Taiwan Grew Rich', *Economic Policy*, Vol. 20, 55–107.

Romer, Paul M. (1986), 'Increasing Returns and Long-Run Growth', *Journal of Political Economy*, Vol. 94, 1002–37.

Romer, Paul M. (1990), 'Endogenous Technological Change', *Journal of Political Economy*, Vol. 98, S71–S102.

Rotberg, Robert I. with Christopher K. Clague (1971), *Haiti: The Politics of Squalor*. Boston, MA: Houghton Mifflin Company.

Rybczynski, T.M. (1955), 'Factor Endowment and Relative Commodity Prices', *Economica, N.S.*, Vol. 22, 336–41.

SACAD (Systèmes Agraires Caribéens et Alternatives de Développement) and FAMV (Faculté d'Agronomie et de Médecine Vétérinaire) (1993), *Paysans, systèmes et crise. Travaux sur l'agraire haïtien. Tome 1: Histoire agraire et développement*. Clamecy: Université des Antilles et de la Guyane and Université d'État d'Haïti.

Schmidt, Hans (1971), *The United States Occupation of Haiti, 1915–1934*. New Brunswick, NJ: Rutgers University Press.

Schultz, Theodore W. (1977), 'On Economic History in Extending Economics', in: Manning Nash (ed.), *Essays on Economic Development and Cultural Change in Honor of Bert F. Hoselitz*. Supplement to *Economic Development and Cultural Change*, Vol. 25, 245–53.

Solow, Robert M. (1956), 'A Contribution to the Theory of Economic Growth', *Quarterly Journal of Economics*, Vol. 70, 65–94.

Tardieu, Charles (1990), *L'éducation en Haïti de la période coloniale à nos jours (1980)*. Port-au-Prince: Imprimerie Henri Deschamps.

Verret, Gabriel (1992), *Haiti – Financial Update*. Port-au-Prince: Mimeo.
World Bank (1988), *Economic Recovery in Haiti: Performance, Issues and Prospects*, Report No. 7469-HA, December 23. Washington, DC: The World Bank.
World Bank (1989), *Haiti: Staff Appraisal Report. Industrial Restructuring and Development Project*, June 20. Washington, DC: The World Bank.

6
Income and Land Distribution in Haiti: Some Remarks on Available Statistics

The logical starting point for an investigation on distributional issues in Haiti is James Leyburn's 1941 classic, *The Haitian People*,[1] which divides the Haitian population into two distinct classes: the elite and the peasant masses. This division cannot be based on any single scale of measurement; several criteria must be employed. According to Leyburn,[2] the following are the most important distinctions: the elite do not perform manual labor, are educated, speak French, live in towns, are formally married, practice Roman Catholicism, and are (predominantly but not necessarily) light-skinned. The peasants, on the other hand, are manual workers, illiterate speak nothing but Creole, live in the countryside, practice common-law marriage and voodoo, and are black. More importantly, especially as concerns the focus of the present work, the two groups differ dramatically in economic terms:

> Since the maintenance of a high standard of living is costly, it is obvious that another source of caste[3] distinction lies in the inequalities of wealth and property. Wealth is a relative term, however, and the Haitian peasant is so poor that by contrast a few hundred dollars' income a year will seem like riches. The elite live economically by American standards, yet even parsimonious spending of many may, when governed by a consciousness of social distinctions, make the peak of aristocracy unassailable.[4]

Even though Leyburn was exaggerating the extent of the cleavage between Haitian societies by referring to a 'caste system'[5] he was, nevertheless, pointing out a fundamental economic fact: the separation of the rich from the poor. Haiti had a patent problem with income distribution.

The extent of this income distribution problem is largely unknown, even to this very day. Many conjectures and guesses have been made, but, by and large, hard facts are lacking. The first statistics on national income were computed in the early 1960s and were based on guesswork and approximations, rather than on solid empirical knowledge.[6] Censuses, when taken, have been notoriously weak, usually among the worst in Latin America. Surveys of varying quality have been available from time to time. Still, data continue to be unreliable, to the point where one of the economists who participated in a recent conference on Haiti found it necessary to make the following statement:

> Data about Haiti's real *per capita* income must be believable and accurate because there is no better way to know if Haiti is improving economically. Most human development indicators reflect Haitians' inability to buy goods and services, but not as unambiguously as their wretched *per capita* income. Specifically, we must know the average purchasing power for Haitians and the variation around that average. We need to know those numbers for rural Haiti, particularly by Department and Section, for which they do not exist.[7]

This chapter takes a critical look at the most important data available on income and land distribution in Haiti in order to demonstrate that our knowledge of the subject is both scanty and piecemeal, and that some of the figures most commonly quoted have been calculated by means of methodological procedures which are so highly deficient that their conclusions are, by and large, based on almost sheer assumptions. Some policy implications are also derived from our findings.

Labor income figures for 1970

The first systematic attempt to calculate income distribution in Haiti was undertaken in 1976 by a mission from the World Bank.[8] The computations were based on a survey that had been conducted previously by the Institut Haïtien de Statistique in April 1970 (the *Enquête socio-économique*) and covered only the income derived from labor. Above all, the findings pointed to significant differences between rural and urban areas, as shown in Table 1.

Poverty proved much more pronounced in the countryside than in the urban districts. In the rural areas over 90 percent earned less than 1200 gourdes (US$240) *per annum*, while the corresponding figures were that fewer than 60 percent earned under that amount in all urban areas,

Table 1 Distribution of labor income, 1970 (percent of total*)

	Country total		Rural areas		Urban areas (including Port-au-Prince)		Port-au-Prince	
	E	LI	E	LI	E	LI	E	LI
Low incomes								
< 1200 gourdes	86.9	55.8	92.0	72.1	58.0	18.4	53.8	14.8
Medium incomes								
1,200–3,600	10.9	28.0	7.4	23.3	30.6	38.8	31.5	34.6
3,601–6,000	1.3	6.9	0.4	2.3	6.9	17.5	8.2	18.1
6,001–10,800	0.6	4.5	0.1	1.2	2.9	12.2	3.9	14.1
High incomes								
10,801–13,000	0.1	1.4	0.1	0.2	0.7	4.3	1.1	6.1
13,201–20,400	0.1**	2.1	0.3	0.6	0.6	5.3	1.0	7.6
> 20, 400	0.1**	1.3	0.1	0.3	0.2	3.4	0.4	4.6
Total	100.0	100.0	100.0	100.0	100.0	100.0	100.0	100.0

E = employment, LI = labor income.
* = The figures are rounded and therefore do not always add up to 100.0.
** = Figure corrected due to a misprint in the original table.
Source: World Bank (1976b), Table 1.4.

and fewer than 55 percent earned less than that amount in the capital. On the other hand, high-income wage and salary earners accounted for far more of the total income from labor in the urban districts, namely 13 percent (over 18 percent in Port-au-Prince) compared to a mere 1 percent in the countryside.

Thus, poverty appeared to be spread more evenly outside the urban agglomerations than inside: seemingly a statistical confirmation of the concentration of the elite in the cities.

On a nationwide scale, the poorest 87 percent of all labor-income earners received almost 56 percent of the total income derived from labor, while the richest 1 percent (less than 12,000 people) received just a little over 9 percent of the total,[9] an 'inequality in the distribution of incomes [which], while it exists, is much less glaring than in most countries'.[10] The average income *per employee* amounted to 765 gourdes in the countryside and 1892 gourdes in the cities (rising to 2185 in Port-au-Prince), which, if converted to labor income *per capita* of all inhabitants in the respective areas yields 277 and 448 (459) gourdes.[11]

Thus, the 1970 figures for income from labor, provided they are reasonably accurate,[12] do not point to an extremely skewed distribution of income in Haiti. However, their limitations must be recognized. At the time, labor income accounted for approximately 70 percent of the Haitian gross national product (GNP), and capital depreciation accounted for another estimated 20 percent, leaving the final 10 percent for profits.[13] The question then arises as to how profits ought to be distributed across the different labor income groups. As is well known from other countries, profits are not a homogeneous income category.[14] They include everything from profits made by large organized companies and state enterprises to the incomes of the self-employed in the informal sector. Thus, it cannot automatically be assumed that all profits accrued solely to high-income earners. An unknown share was actually labor income (much of which went to low-income earners) and should therefore be treated as such. The profit category also hides land rents and some of these accrued to the peasants, most of whom belonged to the lowest income category of Table 1. Thus, adding non-labor income to the picture that emerges from that table probably would not have dramatically altered the impression conveyed by the latter.

Still, the picture was bad enough as it was. The World Bank mission also calculated *per capita* consumption of three types of items: (1) basic consumption items (food, rent and fuel, medical care, and clothing); (2) regular consumption items (lighting, toiletries and detergents, education, transport, recreation and culture, and 'other'); and, finally, (3) occasional consumption items (furniture, luxury items, home repairs, and 'other').[15] The result of this exercise was that consumption averaged 398 gourdes for rural areas 712 gourdes for urban areas, when all three items were included – and 382 gourdes and 686 gourdes, respectively, when only necessities (defined as the first two categories) were included. This meant that, even on average, labor incomes alone did not suffice to cover the necessary outlays of Haitian households in 1970, let alone the income of the poor majority, where the average income from labor was 600 gourdes, to be shared by an estimated three persons.

Total income distribution in 1976

In 1976, the Institut Haïtien de Statistique conducted another survey,[16] which was also used by a World Bank mission – this time to calculate the distribution of *total* national income.[17] The results of this calculation were widely quoted,[18] and their significance was noted. As one of the surveys of Haiti's problems in the 1980s concludes:

> These figures set the dimensions of the income distribution problem which the government refuses to admit exists.... social justice and equity are not part of the official vocabulary, even for purposes of rhetoric.[19]

Unfortunately, however, the calculations upon which statements such as this are based are grossly deficient from a methodological standpoint. The 1976 survey covered 10,000 people all over the country, and, like its 1970 predecessor, its data on income dealt only with that which derived from labor, while no effort was made to cover the non-labor component of the national income, which was estimated, at that time, to be 39 percent (compared to just 30 percent a mere 5 years earlier). Even the data on labor income were sorely incomplete, with gaps amounting to 16.5 percent of the employed population in Port-au-Prince, 49.1 percent in other towns, and no less than 77.5 percent (i.e., the vast majority) in rural districts. With 10.8 percent, 9.2 percent, and 79.9 percent, respectively, of the Haitian population belonging to these three categories, more than 68 percent of the total employed population was left outside the survey, plus 100 percent of the total non-labor income.[20] Thus, there is a definite risk that the World Bank estimates were made from a base that covered only a minor part of the national income.

In order to be able to employ a data set that was so incomplete as that produced by the 1976 survey, the World Bank mission had to make some heroic assumptions – that are so arbitrary as to render the results more or less worthless.[21] Beginning with the survey data, it was assumed that everyone in a certain income bracket (as specified by the survey) was earning the mean income of that particular bracket. For the highest bracket, an average of 30,000 gourdes was assumed, 'which is in line with information obtained from the tax administration'[22] – not a very accurate source in Jean-Claude Duvalier's Haiti.

The survey reported a mix of incomes of persons employed on a daily, weekly, half-monthly, and monthly basis, all of which had to be converted into figures for the year. In this context, totally arbitrary assumptions were made which suggested that urban labor income earners worked 250 days per year while their rural counterparts only worked 175 days, without any empirical evidence whatsoever to substantiate these claims.

The third problem which the mission had to solve was what to assume about those who could not, or would not, report their income, namely, two-thirds of all labor income earners covered by the survey. It was then assumed that this category, in the towns, consisted of two – but only two – groups: those in the lowest brackets, who '[did] not know', and those in the highest bracket, who '[did] not want to reveal'. The non-respondents were then separated into one or the other of these categories in proportion to what was presumed to be the number of respondents in that category ('the number of people in the lowest and highest income brackets' in the words of the World Bank).[23] This procedure introduced two types of biases. First, by omitting all of the middle categories, it increased the bimodality of the labor income distribution. Second, it implicitly assumed that the proportion of respondents in the low-income bracket to those in the high-income bracket was also representative of the proportion of non-respondents. However, this is an invalid assumption in a situation where one should, rather, suspect that the proportion of respondents to non-respondents among the high-income earners should probably differ considerably from that same proportion in the low-income category precisely because the two categories would logically have differed in the main reasons for their failure to respond.[24]

In the rural areas, where not only had more than three-fourths failed to respond but also a subsistence component entered the picture, even more Herculean efforts were required. First, total agricultural income from *labor* was estimated to be 70 percent of the agricultural sector's net value added, which was, in turn, taken to be 90 percent of the gross figure. Labor income was then distributed between the different income brackets 'on the basis of average incomes calculated for persons specified by the survey',[25] that is, once again those who had reported income from labor were also presumed to be representative of those who had not. This is a procedure which is highly dubious, particularly in a situation where it could be that labor incomes related to agriculture are, in the main, relatively evenly distributed because the land is, while those reporting an income are likely to have been either specialized workers, with relatively high earnings, or casual day laborers who may be suspected of earning very little.[26]

The above procedure allowed a table to be constructed showing the distribution of income from labor.[27] However, the World Bank team did not stop there but continued to calculate the distribution of total national income as well. This required further assumptions. Thus, the 39 percent of national income not accruing to labor was assumed to be 'income from entrepreneurship and property' and was attributed exclusively to the highest income bracket in urban areas, because 'rural areas in Haiti are little attractive, and the urban sector comprises even communities with a population of little more than 1000 inhabitants'.[28]

This is in no way an innocent assumption, since it suggests that all income accruing to land (assumed to be 30 percent of the total) goes to absentee landowners, and again, that is hardly the case in a country where landownership is very widespread and where, furthermore, the system of tenure is exceedingly complicated, with the same person usually cultivating both his own land plus land leased from others while, at the same time, leasing out land to other people.[29] Nor is the assumption that the returns to entrepreneurship and capital accrue only to the highest income bracket an innocent one. The same critique applies here as to the 1970 data referred to above.

Finally, it should be noted that at least two important sources of income are presumably missing: (1) remittances from Haitians abroad and (2) the incomes of sugar-cane cutters migrating to the Dominican Republic, since these tend not to figure in the balance of payments statistics.[30]

The main result of this chamber of horrors of assumptions was that 43.5 percent of national income was concentrated in the hands of less than 0.4 percent of the employed population, while the poorest 68 percent of the employed earned less than 20 percent of the total – a positively arbitrary result.[31]

The land tenure issue

One of the main determinants of income distribution in Haiti is the distribution of landownership. Haiti is an eminently agrarian country. The majority of the population have been peasants ever since the early nineteenth century, and today it is estimated that more than 70 percent of the population still live in rural households.[32]

Unfortunately, no cadastral survey exists, and nothing came of the efforts undertaken during the US occupation (1915–34) using aerial photography, since the building where the photos were stored burned down under 'unexplained' circumstances.[33] Instead, the first systematic data concerning land tenure in Haiti derive from the 1950 census. These figures, which covered only four of the five geographic departments in existence at the time, are shown in Table 2, together with figures from the 1971 and 1982 censuses. This table represents, by and large, the conventional wisdom with respect to the distribution of landownership in Haiti.

The main finding was that the distribution of land was relatively even. This was later confirmed by the 1971 and 1982 census figures.[34] In the main, the land in Haiti is owned by small peasant farmers.

Table 2 Land distribution by number of farms and size, according to the 1950, 1971, and 1982 censuses (percent)

Farm size (carreaux)**	1950*		1971	
	Farms	Area	Farms	Area
< 1	39.4	11.0	71.0	32.5
1.0–1.99	30.3	22.7	17.9	26.1
2.0–4.99	24.2	36.9	9.3	27.1
5.0–	6.1	29.4	1.8	14.3
	1982***			
	Farms	Area		
< 0.5	20.9	3.8		
0.5–1.49	54.2	35.9		
1.5–4.99	21.9	41.5		
5.0–9.99	2.4	10.9		
10.0–	0.6	7.9		

*Covers four departments (of five).
**1 carreau = 1.29 hectares.
***Covers two departments (of nine).
Source: Locher (1988), p. 3.

This argument has not gone unchallenged, however. On the contrary, from time to time the case of strong concentration has been presented, most recently in an ambitious study of Haitian peasant agriculture.[35] This case derives mainly from a pamphlet written by Gérald Brisson which attempts to prove that the 1950 census figures constitute a gross misrepresentation of the Haitian reality, and that, in fact, Haiti is just another example of the typical Latin American *latifundio–minifundio* problem.[36] Brisson's conclusions are summarized in Table 3.

Table 3 Land distribution in 1950 according to Gérald Brisson (percent*)

Farm size (carreaux)	Farms	Land
< 2	69.3	10.2
2–10	29.5	23.2
> 10	1.2	66.6

*Covers four departments.
Source: Brisson (1968), Table 6.

Brisson argues that the census figures misleadingly draw on the fact that 85 percent own *some* land to imply that the land is also evenly distributed, and then proceeds to recalculate the distribution. In order to do so, he first calculates the area that he considers to be arable, that is, that which may be used for cultivation and/or animal husbandry, by adding Food and Agriculture Organization (FAO) estimates of arable land and grazing land. This gives a total of 1.6 million hectares, which turns out to be a figure that is, comparatively speaking, very high[37] – and forms a crucial determinant of the final results. From this, a figure for the Département du Sud must be deduced, since the census covered only the other four departments. This leaves the total arable area of the Sud.

Brisson then calculates the area actually cultivated within each of the categories for farm size employed in the census by multiplying the number of farms in each category by the corresponding midpoint figure for that particular interval, obtaining the figure for the highest category as the residual. Third, after regrouping the farms into the three categories based on size shown in Table 3, he introduces another crucial assumption: that, for the small- and medium-sized categories, there is no difference between the land that is owned and land that is cultivated. Consequently, the total areas for the two small-size categories are obtained, and what is left – including the *entire* area classified as grazing land: 45 percent of the total – is simply imputed to *'la grande propriété foncière'*.[38] Finally, the percentages for each category are calculated.[39]

Again, we are faced with calculations that are not only totally arbitrary, but are founded on assumptions that are far from innocent. In fact, they constitute what is perhaps the best example of what David Nicholls has called the 'need to force Haitian reality into a Procrustean bed built at the British Museum in the nineteenth century and recently reconstructed in the Bois de Vincennes'.[40] Whatever may be the real distribution of land in Haiti, it is definitely more likely to resemble the one indicated by the three censuses rather than the one calculated – or, perhaps one should say, assumed – by Brisson.

The criticism that may be advanced against Brisson does not mean, however, that the census data are completely reliable. On the contrary, they are known to have a number of defects as well. The 1950 census is known to have been of very poor quality as far as the demographic aspects are concerned.[41] Not least, there was a tendency for men between 15 and 39 years to evade the census since they feared that the findings might be used for taxation or conscription purposes.[42] It would be strange indeed if the same type of considerations did not lead to an under-reporting of landownership.

The main defect of the official census figures is that these tend to omit large properties. The most important landowner of all is the state. In 1809, Haiti experienced the first land reform in Latin America, one which consisted, by and large, of the redistribution of government land.[43] Despite this redistribution, the state continues to own substantial areas of Haitian territory. In the mid-1980s, it owned close to 60,000 hectares in the Northeast, the Plateau Central, the Artibonite Valley, and some of the smaller plains. In addition, around the same time, large plantations were known to exploit an area much the same size, if not larger.[44] What is more, the census data do not provide any estimates of the number of agricultural workers who were landless.[45]

The impression that landownership is a great deal less concentrated in Haiti than in the rest of Latin America is also borne out, however, by local surveys. Twelve studies of specific communities and regions from the 1970s report that 58–100 percent of all peasants own at least part of their land,[46] while 4 more studies from the 1970s and 1980s confirm this impression.[47] Uli Locher summarizes the evidence as of 1988:

> 1. Land distribution is much more egalitarian than has been found elsewhere in Latin America. Large estates are virtually absent in these communities, though they are known to exist elsewhere in the country.
> 2. Most farmers own at least some land but the amount owned is very small. Average farm size is said to be somewhere between 1.0 and 1.5 hectares. [...]
>
> The most important result... is the extremely small size of most Haitian landholdings.[48]

Unfortunately, not very much is known about the development of landownership over time. In general, the absence of legal deeds in rural Haiti has served to invite the takeover of peasant lands by outsiders, a practice to which Haitian history has borne witness at various points in time.[49] Locher points out that there is some evidence that there has been an increasing concentration of landholdings in some areas, notably places where the land is irrigated. Irrigation tends to accelerate the sale of land from smallholders to richer farmers.[50] The evidence, however, is not very systematic.

There are also mechanisms that tend to counteract the tendency to concentration. Locher himself reports that, following the fall of Jean-Claude Duvalier in 1986, peasants in the Artibonite Valley proceeded to destroy the rather complete records of landownership in the area – which had accumulated over time, as Duvalier supporters took possession of land from the peasants – so as to make it more difficult (for the *tonton macoutes* in particular) to prove the 'legality' of their claims and acquisitions.[51]

Gerald Murray points to three other mechanisms which serve as guardians of peasant rights. Often the *gran pyès* (i.e., the original deed to an undivided family estate of some generations back) still exists, and this can be used to trace later changes in land tenure, acting, in its turn, as a further check on takeover attempts.[52] In his in-depth study of the Thomazeau area, Murray also found that the main threat to peasant landholdings came, not from outright outsiders, but from the heirs of people who had left the area one or more generations previously and had thus, in practice, forfeited their right to ownership. These, however, were considered to be especially vulnerable to sorcery from those who were actually using the land.[53]

Gérard Barthélemy has suggested that the complexity of the land tenure system, including the very lack of written deeds, may serve more as an instrument of defense for the peasants than as an invitation to abuse by outsiders.[54] As Murray has shown, the same person may often cultivate not only his/her own land, under a more or less secure title, but also land leased from other peasants (usually as part of a sharecropping contract).[55] At the same time, the owner may lease out some of his/her own land to others. The complexity of these arrangements can so confuse the situation that it makes it difficult for outsiders to intrude and alienate peasant land. The main accumulation that takes place in this system is a life-cycle phenomenon. The rich peasant is usually an old peasant, and accumulation is limited to one lifetime. If nothing else, whatever savings a peasant may have are frequently eaten up by funeral expenses.

This mechanism forms part of a broader pattern that is not confined to land issues alone, and which serves to protect the peasant and what belongs to him. Barthélemy points to a number of devices that Haitian peasants employ to create confusion and uncertainty among people who do not belong to the local community.[56] The equilibrium of peasant society has always been threatened by outside forces, most notably by a state that has not protected the interests of the peasant but has tended to prey on its rural inhabitants instead.[57] Hence, the need for special defense mechanisms. These are at work at every conceivable level. The Haitian peasant is well-known for the ability to ingratiate him or herself with outsiders. In so doing, many basic facts of rural life may be deliberately concealed. Thus, it is never quite clear to the potential intruder just where the real centers of authority and power lie. The importance of voodoo is consciously downplayed, and the inner workings of the secret societies are not revealed. Technical advisers who attempt to enter into a dialogue with the peasants may find themselves suddenly dealing with all kinds of committees, apparently organized spontaneously, in which it is difficult to ascertain just who is really exerting authority, so that development projects are often left to decay as soon as outside experts have left the scene. Finally, when intrusion threatens to take place, verbal skills (dissuasion, mockery, and the like) are mobilized and brought to bear, and, if need be, violence as well. Thus, to conclude, for a concentration of land to take place, a number of obstacles – most of deliberate design – have to be overcome.[58]

Conclusions

Our knowledge with respect to the distribution of income landownership and wealth in Haiti is indeed incomplete. Perhaps the best way of summarizing the situation is to state that we suspect that the distribution of land is more equal in Haiti than in Latin America in general, and that available data tend to support that view. The question is, rather, what is missing in these data. We know that they understate the degree of concentration of ownership, but not by how much, and the 'calculations' that have been attempted to make up for this inaccuracy are grossly misleading due to the methods employed. The only way to arrive at an accurate picture is by means of a cadastral survey, although, as has been pointed out, the design, implementation, and interpretation of such a survey are fraught with what seem to be almost insurmountable obstacles.

The lack of a clear picture of landownership means that it becomes impossible to calculate the distribution of national income with any degree of accuracy. (The World Bank's attempt to do so does not stand up to serious scrutiny.) Calculations based on 'labor incomes' are difficult to employ in estimating the differences in rural income. An implicit wage then has to be found in a society where the vast majority are owner-cultivators and, thereafter, the non-wage component has to be estimated, which is, of course, impossible as long as there is no clear picture of the distribution of land, let alone the quality of the different plots. It should also be added that peasant households in Haiti, as elsewhere in the Third World, derive their incomes from a variety of sources, which include not only agriculture but also sales activities and remittances from family members working outside agriculture (including those working abroad). The only reliable way to arrive at any reasonably correct figures for income, therefore, is to resort to direct interviews which cover all sources.

These conclusions have clear implications for policy. In the current Haitian political debate, redistribution is often advocated as a way to help resolve the country's economic woes – sometimes even as a panacea. Given the lack of statistical information, however, we must first ask ourselves: Redistribution of what? From whom? And to whom? There are undoubtedly some very wealthy people in Haiti, but the more interesting question is *how much* of the national income is concentrated in their hands, that is, how much could be gained from a redistribution? (On top of this, there is the difficult problem of how redistribution would affect entrepreneurship and production.) Unless we can arrive at a picture of the existing distribution of wealth and income, it will be impossible to effect any real distribution, other than one that would be completely arbitrary, which, of course, should hardly be the aim of a democratic society. The question of the desirability of redistribution in Haiti is fundamentally an empirical one. There is simply no way around the painstaking labor required to gather the necessary, and relevant, knowledge.

Postscript

Since this chapter was published, our knowledge of income and wealth distribution in Haiti has improved substantially, mainly through a major project jointly carried out by the Institut Haïtien de Statistique et d'Informatique and the Norwegian research organization FAFO Institute for Applied International Studies.[59] The findings reported therein by and large confirm that the suspicion of large income and wealth differences is correct.[60] Thus, the Gini coefficient for Haiti that emerged was 0.65, one of the highest ever recorded in the world.[61]

Notes

Published in the *Journal of Interamerican Studies and World Affairs*, Vol. 38, No. 2–3 (Summer-Fall) 1996, published for the Graduate School of International Studies, University of Miami, by North-South Center Press, Miami. Reprinted by permission.

1. Leyburn (1941).
2. Ibid., Chapter 1.
3. Leyburn erroneously maintained that the separation of the two classes in Haiti was so rigid as to warrant the label 'caste system'. For an immediate criticism of this thesis, see Price-Mars (1942).

4. Leyburn (1941), p. 6.
5. Nicholls refers to use of the term of 'caste system' as 'a gross misrepresentation of the situation' (1979), p. 38.
6. OEA–CEPAL–BID, (1962).
7. Catanese (1997).
8. Gow (1976), p. 16 provides an unsystematic estimate of the income distribution among rural families that is based on 243 farmers in 4 villages located in the Northwest. However, Gow's figures overestimate the degree of rural income concentration (cf. Zuvekas (1978), p. 64; World Bank (1976a), pp. 7–10; and World Bank (1976b), Table 1.4).
9. World Bank (1976b), Table 1.4.
10. World Bank (1976a), p. 8.
11. World Bank (1976b), Table 1.4.
12. They may not be. Cf. below, the discussion of rural labor income.
13. World Bank (1976a), p. 9.
14. On Chile, for example, see Mamalakis (1976), pp. 232–33.
15. World Bank (1976b), Table 1.5.
16. The so-called *Enquête à buts multiples*.
17. World Bank (1978a), (1978b).
18. Cf., for example, Weinstein and Segal (1984), p. 138; Fass (1988), pp. 89–90; Dupuy (1989a), p. 184; and Trouillot (1990), p. 182.
19. Weinstein and Segal (1984), p. 138.
20. Greene (1979).
21. World Bank (1978b), pp. 24–26.
22. Ibid., p. 24.
23. Ibid.
24. On the other hand, I cannot see any good reason why the failure to report among low-income earners in Haiti, where *leta* (the state) has such a bad reputation for abusing the poor, should not be due, at least in part, to reluctance rather than mere ignorance.
25. World Bank (1978b), p. 25.
26. Greene (1979), p. 4.
27. World Bank (1978b), p. 23.
28. Ibid., p. 25.
29. For a thorough discussion of the complicated land tenure system in Haiti, see Murray (1977).
30. Greene (1979), p. 5.
31. Figures are also available in condensed from the World Bank (1978a, p. 61). The figures in these two tables do not coincide, and no explanations are provided for these discrepancies (World Bank, 1978b, p. 27).
32. IDB (1995), p. 32.
33. Schmidt (1971), p. 179.
34. The 1982 figures only cover two departments: Sud and Grande-Anse.
35. SACAD (1993), pp. 11–15, for another attempt, see also Dupuy (1989b).
36. The figures given by Brisson (1968) are also reproduced and employed by Pierre-Charles (1969, pp. 132–33), Jean (1974, pp. 32–34), and Trouillot (1990, p. 77), while Casimir (1964) claims that more than half of the acreage consists of holdings larger than 20 *carreaux* (see also Pierre-Charles (1965), pp. 83–101).

37. Brisson (1968), p. 14. Other estimates, for different years between 1957 and 1975, ranging from 637,000 to 1,407,800 hectares, are presented in Lundahl (1979), p. 59.
38. Brisson (1968), p. 18.
39. Actually, with only one exception, the figures for land distribution, shown in Table 3, are incorrect. Brisson's own assumptions yield 12.2 percent for the lowest category and 64.6 percent for the highest.
40. Nicholls (1979), p. 243.
41. Cf. Saint Surin (1962), pp. 4–5.
42. Brand (1965), p. 20.
43. For details, see Lundahl (1979), Chapter 6.
44. World Bank (1985), p. 85, see also Zuvekas (1978), pp. 25, 27 and Lundahl (1979), p. 52.
45. Zuvekas (1978), p. 10.
46. Summarized in ibid., pp. 12–15.
47. Summarized by Locher (1988), pp. 3–4.
48. Ibid., pp. 3, 5.
49. Lundahl (1979), pp. 603–04.
50. Ibid., pp. 5–6.
51. Locher (1988), note 6, p. 5.
52. Murray (1977), pp. 310–11, 353–54.
53. Ibid., pp. 320–22. The discussion in Murray (1978) and Thome (1978) is also of interest in this context, although Palmer (1976, p. 149) reports exactly the opposite: that those remaining in the countryside do not dare to touch the land left idle by those who leave for the cities.
54. However, the pattern is not a generalized one, with the main exceptions being the north and the Artibonite Valley. Where it does work, which is mainly in the more isolated parts of the southern peninsula and the Plateau Central, it ensures, according to Barthélemy, that around 80 percent of the land is also cultivated by its owner (Barthélemy (1989), pp. 51–53).
55. Murray (1977).
56. Barthélemy (1989), *Première partie*.
57. Lundahl (1992), passim; Lundahl (1979), Chapters 7–12.
58. Nevertheless, it should be noted that these mechanisms have been rendered less effective over time. As the number and intensity of the contacts between peasant and outside society have increased, it renders more difficult the employment of traditional peasant weapons and undercuts their efficacy.
59. See, for example, République d'Haïti (2004), Egset and Sletten (2003), Sletten and Egset (2004), (2006), and World Bank (2007).
60. Cf. also Boccanfuso and Siméon (2006).
61. Egset and Sletten (2003).

References

Barthélemy, Gérard (1989), *Le pays en dehors: Essai sur l'univers rural haïtien*. Second edition. Port-au-Prince: Éditions Henri Deschamps.

Boccanfuso, Dorothée and Siméon, Alex (2006), Pauvreté, croissance et redistribution en Haïti, Cahier de recherche 06–17, Groupe de Recherche en Économie et Déveleoppement International, Université de Sherbrooke, Sherbrooke.

Brand, Willem (1965), *Impressions of Haiti*. The Hague: Mouton & Co.

Brisson, Gérald (1968), *Las relations agraires dans l'Haïti contemporaine*. México, DF: Mimeo.

Casimir, Jean (1964), 'Aperçu sur la structure économique d'Haïti', *América Latina*, Vol. 7, 37–56.

Catanese, Anthony V. (1997), 'Priorities in the Economic Reconstruction of Rural Haiti', in: Robert I. Rotberg (ed.), *Haiti Renewed. Political and Economic Prospects*. Washington, DC: Brookings Institution Press.

Dupuy, Alex (1989a), *Haiti in the World Economy: Class, Race, and Underdevelopment since 1700*. Boulder, CO: Westview Press.

Dupuy, Alex (1989b), 'Peasant Poverty in Haiti', *Latin American Research Review*, Vol. 24, 259–71.

Egset, Willy and Sletten, Pål (2003), *La pauvreté en Haïti: Un profil de la pauvreté en Haïti à partir des données de l'Enquête ECVH*. Oslo: FAFO Institute for Applied International Studies.

Fass, Simon F. (1988), *Political Economy in Haiti: The Drama of Survival*. New Brunswick, NJ: Transaction Books.

Gow, David D. (1976), *Report on the Establishment of a Baseline Data-Gathering System for HACHO* (August 16). Port-au-Prince: US Agency for International Development.

Greene, Richard (1979), Analysis of World Bank Income Distribution Estimates for Haiti 1976 (memorandum from Richard Greene to William Rhoads, March 2). N.p.

Inter-American Development Bank (IDB) (1995), *Emergency Economic Recovery Program. Haiti*. Report of the Joint Mission (November 7–20, 1994). Washington, DC.

Jean, Rodrigue (1974), *Classes sociales et sous-développement en Haïti*. Ville St-Laurent: Editions Québecoises.

Leyburn, James G. (1941), *The Haitian People*. New Haven, CT: Yale University Press.

Locher, Uli (1988), 'Land Distribution, Land Tenure and Land Erosion in Haiti'. Paper presented at the 12th Annual Conference of the Society for Caribbean Studies, July 12–14. (Mimeo, Department of Sociology, McGill University, Montreal). High Leigh Conference Centre, Hoddesdon, Hertfordshire.

Lundahl, Mats (1979), *Peasants and Poverty: A Study of Haiti*. London: Croom Helm.

Lundahl, Mats (1992), *Politics or Markets? Essays on Haitian Underdevelopment*. London and New York: Routledge.

Mamalakis, M.J. (1976), *The Growth and Structure of the Chilean Economy*. New Haven, CT: Yale University Press.

Murray, Gerald F. (1977), *The Evolution of Haitian Peasant Land Tenure: A Case Study in Agrarian Adaptation to Population Growth*. PhD dissertation. Columbia University, New York.

Murray, Gerald F. (1978), 'Land Tenure, Land Insecurity, and Planned Agricultural Development among Haitian Peasants'. (Mimeo, August 25.) Port-au-Prince: US Agency for International Development.

Nicholls, David (1979), *From Dessalines to Duvalier: Race, Colour and National Independence in Haiti*. Cambridge: Cambridge University Press.

Organización de Estados Americanos/Comisión Económica para América Latina/ Banco Inter-Americano de Desarrollo (OEA-CEPAL-BID) (1962), Mission Conjointe OEA-CEPAL-BID en Haïti, *Rapport general présenté au Gouvernement de la République d'Haïti* (December). Washington, DC: Organization of American States.

Palmer, Ernest Charles (1976), *Land Use and Landscape Change Along the Dominican-Haitian Border*. PhD dissertation. University of Florida at Gainesville.

Pierre-Charles, Gérard (1965), *La economía haítiana y su vía de desarrollo*. México, DF: Cuadernos Americanos.

Pierre-Charles, Gérard (1969), *Radiografía de una dictadura, Haíti bajo el régimen del doctor Duvalier*. México, DF: Editorial Nuestro Tiempo.

Price-Mars, Jean (1942), 'Classe ou caste? Étude sur "The Haitian People" (Le peuple haïtien) de James G. Leyburn, New Haven, Yale University Press 1941.' *Revue de la Société d'Histoire et de Géographie d'Haïti*, Vol. 13, No. 46, 1–50.

République d'Haïti, Ministère de l'Économie et des Finances, Institut Haïtien de Statistique et d'Informatique (2004), *Enquête sur les conditions de vie en Haití (ECVH-2001), Volume I*. Port-au-Prince: Imprimerie Henri Deschamps.

SACAD (Systèmes Agraires Caribéens et Alternatives de Développement) and FAMV (Faculté d'Agronomie et de Médecine Vétérinaire) (1993), *Paysans, systèmes et crise. Travaux sur l'agraire haïtien. Tome 1: Histoire agraire et développement*. Clamecy: Université des Antilles et de la Guyane and Université d'État d'Haïti.

Saint Surin, Jacques (1962), *Indices démographiques et perspectives de la population d'Haïti de 1950 à 1980*. Port-au-Prince: Imprimerie de l'Ètat.

Schmidt, Hans (1971), *The United States Occupation of Haiti, 1915–1934*. New Brunswick, NJ: Rutgers University Press.

Sletten, Pål and Egset, Willy (2004), 'Poverty in Haiti'. FAFO Paper 2004:31. Oslo: FAFO Institute for Applied International Sudies.

Sletten, Pål and Egset, Willy (2006), 'Poverty in Haiti', *Iberoameriana*, Vol. 36, 41–59.

Thome, Joseph R. (1978), *Land Insecurity in Haiti* (Mimeo June 26). Port-au-Prince: US Agency for International Development (USAID).

Trouillot, Michel-Rolph, (1990), *Haiti: State Against Nation; The Origins and Legacy of Duvalierism*. New York: Monthly Review Press.

Weinstein, Brian and Segal, Aaron (1984), *Haiti: Political Failures, Cultural Successes*. New York: Praeger.

World Bank (1976a), *Current Economic Position and Prospects of Haiti, Vol. I: Main Report*. Report No. 1243-HA; December 7. Washington, DC: The World Bank.

World Bank (1976b), *Current Economic Position and Prospects of Haiti, Vol. II: Statistical Appendix*. Report No. 1243-HA; December 7. Washington, DC: The World Bank.

World Bank (1978a), *Current Economic Position and Prospects of Haiti, Vol. I: Main Report*. Report No. 2165-HA; December 22. Washington, DC: The World Bank.

World Bank (1978b), *Current Economic Position and Prospects of Haiti, Vol. II: Statistical Appendix*. Report No. 2165-HA; December 22. Washington, DC: The World Bank.

World Bank (1985), *Haiti: Agricultural Sector Study, Vol. II. Annexes A-F*. Report No. 5375-HA; June 14. Washington, DC: The World Bank.

World Bank (2007), *Social Resilience and State Fragility in Haiti: A World Bank Country Study*. Washington, DC: The World Bank.

Zuvekas Jr., Clarence (1978), *Land Tenure, Income and Employment in Rural Haiti: A Survey*. Washington, DC: Rural Development Division, Bureau for Latin America, US Agency for International Development (AID).

7

Some Economic Determinants of Haitian Migration to the Dominican Republic

Nobody knows with any degree of accuracy how many Haitians there are at any given time in the Dominican Republic. Estimates range between a few hundred thousand and two million. Presumably, the truth is closer to the former than to the latter, but we do not know.[1] No exhaustive survey has ever been undertaken and it is not even clear who should count as 'Haitian'. Thousands have lived in the Dominican Republic for many years without any kind of identity documents. Many 'Haitians' were born on the Dominican side of the border and have never visited their 'home country'.

While the number of Haitians in the Dominican Republic is a matter of considerable dispute, their place in the economic and social hierarchy is not. It is at the very bottom. Haitians perform work that the Dominicans refuse. In particular, the environment in which they work and live on the Dominican sugar plantations has become a matter of notoriety during the past 30 years.[2] The publication of such documents as *Migrant Workers in the Dominican Republic*, by the Anti-Slavery Society for the Protection of Human Rights, in 1979,[3] *'Sold Like Cattle': Haitian Workers in the Dominican Republic*, by the World Council of Churches in 1980,[4] *Sucre amer: Esclaves aujourd'hui dans les Caraïbes*, by Maurice Lemoine, the following year,[5] the *Report of Commission of Inquiry* of the ILO, in 1983,[6] the two books by Dominican lawyer Ramón Antonio Veras, *Inmigración-haitianos-esclavitud* (1983)[7] and *Migración caribeña y un capítulo haitiano* (1985),[8] the massive *El Batey* (1986), by a team headed by Frank Moya Pons,[9] Roger Plant's *Sugar and Modern Slavery: A Tale of Two Countries* (1987),[10] and *Haitian Sugar Cane Cutters in the Dominican Republic*, published jointly in 1989 by Americas Watch, National Coalition for Haitian Refugees and Caribbean

Rights,[11] all contributed to exposing slavery-like conditions on the plantations: undernourishment, tremendous overcrowding, lack of water, absence of sanitary facilities, lack of medical attention, extremely long working days, military discipline, arbitrary treatment by overseers, physical abuse, restricted freedom of movement, extremely low wages, cheating with payments, deprivation of human rights, and so on.

The indignation of the international community upon learning the fate of the Haitians was not diminished when, in addition, it was revealed that the legal part of the temporary migration was organized as a money-making racket by the Haitian and Dominican governments.[12] The Dominican president, Rafael Trujillo, had instigated a major massacre on Haitians in 1937,[13] but as he gradually took an interest in sugar production, after World War II, he also needed workers, and in 1952 the Dominican government signed an agreement with its Haitian counterpart with respect to the seasonal migration of sugar cane cutters. This agreement was renewed in 1959 and 1966, and in 1971, the first of a series of contracts between the Dominican Consejo Estatal del Azúcar (CEA) and the Haitian government was signed. These contracts were not discontinued until the fall of Jean-Claude Duvalier in 1986. The agreements quickly degenerated into a vehicle for money-making for the various Haitian governments. Not only were the latter paid a sum to set up recruitment centers in Haiti, but part of the wages of the migrants was withheld as well, officially to be paid to the workers at the end of their stay, but in practice, it was sent to Haiti, where it ended up in the pockets of the governing *Duvaliériste* clique.[14]

The appalling conditions facing the Haitians in the Dominican Republic immediately leads to the question of why the workers emigrate there in the first place. In this chapter, we will make an attempt to provide at least a partial answer to this question. As we will demonstrate, the migration from Haiti to the Dominican Republic, as it emerges from field studies, is essentially an economic phenomenon and hence amenable to analysis with the aid of economic theory. In the next section, we will briefly survey some of the main theories of migration in the Third World.[15] This will be followed by an examination of the characteristics of Haitian migrants, as these emerge from the most important field surveys. Next, we will pay attention to some 'push' factors. The fact that the conditions that the Haitians meet on the other side of the border are extremely bad is an indication that the situation prevailing in Haiti itself may be an important part of the explanation. We will then present some statistics describing poverty in rural areas and provide an explanation of why poverty seems to be increasing. On the basis of this, we will, finally, apply some simple economic principles to shed light on the migration decision. Throughout the chapter, the emphasis will be on the 'traditional' type of Haitian migrant to the Dominican Republic: the agricultural worker who sooner or later returns to Haiti. We will deal only marginally with those who stay permanently and not at all with the recent phenomenon of migration to urban areas across the border.[16]

Economic theories of migration

Migration from one rural area in the Third World to another is a phenomenon which has attracted only a fraction of the interest that has for several decades pertained to rural-urban flows of people. However, this does not mean that intra-rural migration is an insignificant phenomenon. On the contrary, according to a recent survey of migration in developing countries: 'Where analysis proves possible, the rate of rural-rural migration typically proves far higher than of rural-urban migration...'[17] In Haiti, we find both types of migration, both inside the country and out of it. This chapter will not make any attempt to determine the relative importance of the two types of currents. Its scope is far more limited. We will deal only with the part that takes Haitians across the border, into the neighboring Dominican Republic, mainly, but not exclusively, on a temporary – seasonal – basis as cane cutters during the *zafra* [sugar harvest].

That most of the available analyses deal with the movement from country to town is due partly to a lack of data, partly to a lack of interest, but partly also to the fact that

> ...intra-rural migration may have many properties in common with rural-urban migration: it can enhance income opportunities, may involve a transition from family to wage labor, may involve a shift from one line of production to another (between subsistence and cash crops, or simply between crop types), and may offer many opportunities for faily risk-spreading, no less than does rural-urban migration...[18]

Here, we are forced to concentrate on the literature on rural–urban migration. We will then, however, emphasize precisely those aspects that appear to be relevant also for the case of rural–rural labor migration from Haiti to the Dominican Republic. The discussion will also be selective in the sense that it will deal mainly with the determinants of migration and not with the consequences.[19]

One of the earliest attempts to explain migration is based on the gravitation theory, a direct analogy with physics,[20] where migration is a positive function of the population in the areas of origin and destination and a negative function of the distance between them. This theory, however, fails to specify the elements that govern the decision to migrate. It is altogether devoid of behavior. In contrast, in most modern theories of migration that include explicit modeling of the decision to migrate (made either by individuals or families) income differences between the point of origin and the point of destination play the central role.[21] The simplest way to model this is to regard migration as a form of investment.[22] The individual compares the present value of earnings if he moves with what he would earn if he stays where he is, and, if the difference is positive, subtracts the costs of moving. Possibly, psychic benefits and costs enter the picture as well.

It is, however, often not the case that the prospective migrants know with certainty what they will earn if they move to a new location. They simply have some kind of notion of the probable earnings, based, for example, on the going wage rate and the probability of getting a job.[23] Hence, information matters and individuals may migrate even if they will not obtain employment immediately. The search for jobs is easier to carry out at the new location than at the place of origin,[24] and the probability of being employed may increase with the number of periods of residence at the new location. Possibly, taking less well-paid jobs may help sustain the migrants while they search for better opportunities, but presumably at the cost of a lower probability of finding the latter than if they had remained unemployed and spent all their time looking for jobs. Those who choose to do the search from the point of origin, on the other hand, will not move until they have secured a job.

The decision to migrate may not be just in the hands of the migrants themselves. In many rural areas in the Third World, the relevant decision unit is that of the family, since the prospective migrants also constitute a source of labor and income for their respective families.[25] However, the total income of a peasant family is often derived from a number of different activities, some of which may not be related to agriculture at all.[26] In a setting where incomes are close to the subsistence level, capital is a scarce resource, nature is harsh, and prices are subject to fluctuations, strategies that opt for a diversification of activities may be preferred to putting all the eggs in the same basket. Especially, if the risks connected with migration are not positively correlated with those of agriculture at the point of origin, sending one or more family members away may reduce the variance of family income and hence contribute to minimizing the probability that the latter will fall short of the subsistence level – an important consideration for poor, risk-averse families. Conversely, migration could be supported by other types of income that, for example, will allow for a longer search for jobs. The family may finance both migration and job search in return for future remittances.[27]

Family and friends may play another role as well. Both the pecuniary and mental costs of migration may be reduced considerably if migrants have contacts when they arrive. Those who have already migrated are integrated in various types of networks at the place of destination and therefore have more reliable information about job availability and working conditions than new migrants. They also frequently provide those who come after with food and shelter for some time and help shorten their search for suitable employment.[28] Thus, the risk element that is always present in the migration process may be reduced, which in turn means that those whose friends and relatives have migrated are more likely to migrate than those who lack contacts.

There is also a third way in which people other than the migrants themselves may enter as a determinant of the migration decision. The community from which the migrant comes may act as a reference group for the migrant:[29]

> A person who is poor relative to his home village reference group may elect to migrate... in order to improve his ranking relative to the home group. On the other hand, a person who is even poorer, yet relatively well off compared to others from his particular village, may not move for the same level of gain, if his utility is strongly influenced by his ranking relative to his reference group. This framework offers an interesting dynamic feature; removal of the relatively deprived from a community lowers the relative position of those remaining, which may consequently engender further migration. Over time, also, the reference group of migrants is likely to shift to their... [new] setting, but this may not worsen the migrant's sense of well-being if the reference group is formed from other... migrants from a similar setting, for which the continued inflow of migrants earlier migrants are usually those who are better off. Nonetheless the change in reference group could leave the migrant more deprived relative to this new group...[30]

All migration is not permanent. Much of it is temporary. The migrants stay at the place of destination for a limited period and then either return to where they came from or move on to some other place. What is it that induces this type of behavior? One of the main explanations advanced in the literature runs in terms of the target worker hypothesis. Those who migrate temporarily do so in order to earn enough to make a given investment possible or to buy a certain commodity. (Migration acts as a substitute for borrowing in situations where the credit market is imperfect.) Hence, they never intend to stay but from the very outset plan to leave at some future point in time.[31] Their savings are often higher than the savings of those who plan to stay on or those who were born in the area.[32]

Another explanation is that something may have gone wrong. Most models of migration stress risks and uncertainties with respect to employment and/or wages. The migrant may not get what he or she expects, and if the outcome diverges too much from the expectations returning or moving on will become attractive. That things turn out to be harder than expected may also be true for target workers, and this may then induce them to stay longer than intended, in the extreme case for the rest of their lives.[33] These workers as well, may accumulate more savings than the natives of the host country.

Temporary intra-rural migration may also be a function of the characteristics of agriculture. The cropping pattern may vary between different localities in such a way that the peak periods in terms of demand for labor do not coincide. Often, however, seasonality is not sufficient. If the income generated on the plots of the prospective migrants is deemed sufficient for the needs of the family (given the costs of migration), migration may be rare.[34]

Characteristics of Haitian migrants

The main conclusion to be drawn from our brief survey of migration theories is that there is no single theory that explains all the population movements that take place in the Third World. People may migrate for many different reasons. It is thus necessary to know more in detail who the Haitian migrants to the Dominican Republic are, if we want to explain why they migrate, above all which their economic characteristics are.

The terminology employed to describe the Haitian migrants to the Dominican Republic who work in the sugar fields or elsewhere in the agricultural sector is slightly confusing. Sometimes all of them are referred to as *braceros* [day laborers], but the term is also used to denote only seasonal migrants or seasonal migrants that have been recruited legally, on a labor contract. Illegal immigrants are known as *anba fil*, that is, they have entered the Dominican Republic clandestinely, 'below the wire'. Immigrants who reside permanently (legally or illegally) in the country are known as *viejos*. Finally, the somewhat derogatory term *congoses* (*kongo* in Haitian *kreyòl*) is often used for the seasonal immigrants, possibly only those who have a labor contract. (Sometimes it refers to all migrants, including the *viejos*.) In the following, we will look at the main conclusions from four field surveys carried out between 1981 and 2001. We will then try to avoid this terminological mess and clearly indicate which category we are dealing with.

1981

In 1981, Martin Murphy interviewed a sample of 75 legal immigrants and 45 *anba fil*.[35] The vast majority of the former (90 percent) could be classified as peasants back in Haiti. Of these, 88 percent claimed to 'own' land in Haiti, but only 26 percent held land of 'their own'. About half of them were single, their average age was below 30 years, 68 percent of them had no formal schooling, and the average number of years of education was 1.3. The average legal immigrant was working his third *zafra* in the Dominican Republic and over 70 percent had worked there before. Around 25 percent claimed to speak French, which probably was an exaggeration.

The *anba fil* shared these characteristics. Close to 90 percent were peasants, 82 percent claimed that they 'owned' land, but only 14 percent had land of 'their own'. On average, they were about 10 years older than the *braceros* and slightly more than half of them were 'married'. Like the legal immigrants they had no formal education, and the vast majority spoke no French. On average, they had spent almost 14 years in the Dominican Republic and Murphy concluded that they seldom returned.

Financially, states Murphy, it is 'irrefutable' that 'these immigrants (both *braceros* [legal immigrants] and *anba fil*) are poor, using whatever scale to determine poverty...'[36] In particular, they came from an environment characterized by a general shortage of cash. Many of the legal immigrants appeared to be target workers, resorting to migration as a way of diverifying their income sources. They were spending 25 percent of their earnings in the Dominican Republic, bringing the rest back home

> ...to pay off previously incurred debts, to make structural improvements of...housing, or to make capital investments in the purchase of agricultural parcels, and most commonly of all, to purchase young

> livestock-animals which... [they hope] to raise to slaughter age, turn a profit, and reinvest that capital in the purchase of more livestock or land.[37]

Murphy concludes that as far as the legal migrants are concerned, the possibility of extra earnings (the income gap postulated in most economic theories of migration) is what drives the flow of people into the Dominican Republic:

> *Braceros* [legal immigrants] work the five to seven month sugar harvest to accumulate needed capital. Even considering that the wages they are paid are extremely low, that they are cheated out of their wages at so many points, and that the living and working conditions in the cane fields are sub human; work in the Dominican sugar industry is viewed as a somewhat viable economic option.[38]

The situation of the *anba fil* was slightly different, although the same basic factors seemed to be at work. Some were peasants who owned land and who were in the Dominican Republic basically for the same reason as the legal immigrants. However, many were 'surplus' family members not needed on the farms or unemployed non-peasants. The economic position of these groups appeared to be more desperate than that of the legal immigrants, since they had nothing to return to in Haiti. Possibly an element of relative deprivation also entered the picture: 'The *anba fil* cannot return to the community without large sums of money, for he left Haiti under the illusion and with the promise that he would return a rich man.'[39]

1983

Two years later, in 1983, Franc Báez Evertsz conducted another survey among Haitian sugar workers.[40] More than half were between 26 and 45 years of age, 35 years on average, but the temporary migrants were markedly younger (28 years on average and more than four-fifths between 15 and 35) than the permanent emigrants (40 years). The typical temporary pattern is that the first round of migration takes place between 15 and 25 years of age (66 percent) and the last around 45.[41] Comparing the age at the time of migration, it was found that permanent migrants as a rule had been younger when they left (23 years) than the temporary ones (slightly over 25), which probably means that more of those who are young when they leave for the first time tend to stay permanently in the Dominican Republic.[42] About 60 percent of the first-time migrants were single, and it was not until after five or more trips that this figure fell notably, to 27 percent. (The intermediary figure was 55 percent.)[43] Almost 80 percent of the permanent emigrants had stayed in the Dominican Republic already after the first trip.[44]

Báez Evertsz' data indicate that the typical Haitian emigrant (70 percent) did not possess any land, but that 90 percent of the landless had fathers who did so. Of those who owned land 78 percent had less than 0.5 *carreaux* (0.65 hectares).[45] Close to one-third of the migrants had been unpaid workers on their fathers' land before leaving Haiti, one-fifth had been agricultural wage laborers (about two-thirds of these owned some land), more than 10 percent had been openly unemployed, and 6.5 percent had worked in the (non-agricultural) informal sector.[46]

1985

In 1985, Wilfredo Lozano and Franc Báez Evertsz interviewed Haitian workers on Dominican coffee plantations.[47] As it seems, sugar and coffee to some extent complement each other from the point of view of labor demand. Two years earlier Báez Evertsz had found that once the *zafra* had finished, the demand for labor was reduced with almost 60 percent, and while the vast majority of the surplus Haitian workers then returned home, about 8 percent of the total moved on to work in the coffee harvest.[48] In 1985, three-fourths of the labor force used there came from the sugar plantations, more or less the same percentage planned to return to the sugar fields after the end of the coffee harvest, and almost 90 percent of the temporary migrants employed in coffee production had been sugar workers before moving to the coffee plantations.[49]

Given this, it hardly comes as a surprise that the characteristics of the Haitian coffee workers resemble those of the workers interviewed by Murphy and Báez Evertsz. More than 60 percent were young (below 30). The average education amounted to 1.5 years, and a minimum of 65 percent were illiterate.[50] Three-fourths owned no land in Haiti (84 percent in the case of the temporary migrants), but close to two-thirds reported that their fathers were landowners. Lozano and Báez Evertsz conclude that the Haitian migrants to the Dominican Republic are basically 'peasant sons'.[51] Over a third of them reported to have been wage laborers at home, and one-fourth stated that they were occupied in agriculture. The rest were either unemployed or working in the informal sector.[52] Close to 70 percent had no access to land.[53]

Almost 40 percent stated that they had come to the Dominican Republic to seek work, and another 27 percent were looking for 'more money'.[54] The vast majority were well informed about wages and working conditions, either through their own previous experience (16 percent) or through friends (60 percent).[55] Thus, again the conclusion to be drawn is that the migration is triggered by economic factors.

1985–87

Next, there is the evidence gathered by Samuel Martínez during 1985–87 on both sides of the border, from interviews with 70 men on the Ingenio Santa Ana, in the southeastern Dominican Republic and 31 returned migrants in the Cayes-Jacmel area in Haiti.[56] His data are not quite comparable with those of the other surveys, mainly because the political situation in Haiti immediately after the fall of Jean-Claude Duvalier in 1986 'hindered the collection of quantitative data, particularly concerning the sensitive issue of land tenure...'[57] However, the evidence provided by Martínez by and large confirms the earlier findings.

Among the men who were 35 years or older (including the absentees), two-thirds had made at least one trip to the neighboring country, the first one usually at the age of 23. Most had made more than one trip, the median number being four, and as many as ten trips in a lifetime was not unusual. Martínez estimated that between 1955 and 1986 on average 14 percent of all the men between 15 and 60 had gone to the Dominican Republic. Within a year 88 percent had returned and within 2 years 91 percent, that is, migration was mainly a temporary phenomenon.[58] The desire to return was confirmed by the interviews on the Dominican side: 'Nearly all Haitians in the Dominican *bateyes* [sugar company compunds] insisted that they would return to Haiti tomorrow if given the money to do so...'[59]

This indicates that migrants desire to use whatever money the migrants may earn in the Dominican Republic for expenditure in their home country. That this is the case is also borne out by the living conditions of the migrants on the sugar estates. Martínez quotes Báez Evertsz' findings that the Haitian cane cutter on average displayed a nutritional deficit, both in terms of calories, proteins, vitamins and minerals and that (in 1983) he had to spend about 80 percent of his budget on food:[60]

> ...the Haitian *bracero* [day laborer] knows that, no matter how hard he works, he will gain nothing in long-term income security by remaining on the sugar estates. Only by returning to Haiti can he convert his Dominican money into assets of his own, with which to meet future family health, ceremonial, and educational needs.[61]

Martínez stresses the need to meet 'obligations' back in Haiti. These 'obligations' vary across the life cycle. Young men often leave in order to get the means to establish a conjugal union. Thus, between one-third and one-half of the houses in the areas investigated by Martínez had been financed by money earned on the other side of the border. More than 60 percent of those interviewed stated that this was what motivated their first trip to the Dominican Republic.[62] Establishing oneself as an adult, however, requires other investments as well:

> Dependent young men in households of humble means cannot rely on their guardians to provide them with anything more than basic food, clothing, and shelter. They have to fend for themselves, for instance, to acquire the one pair of dress shoes and good change of clothing deemed appropriate for important trips to town and other serious occasions, or to buy a piece of jewelry, a wristwatch, or some other prestige item to hold as a symbol of adulthood and urbanity.[63]

Martínez found that the first trip was an event that resulted 'not from the orders or advice of his guardians but from the migrant's own initiative',[64] that is, the relevant decision unit was not the household but the individual. Not even the cost of transportation involved the family:

> ...the cost of going to the Dominican Republic is nowhere near as great an obstacle to departure as the cost of relocating to an urban area or of traveling to North America. Therefore, a man who contemplates crossing the border as a cane worker generally finds little use in mobilizing the financial support of relatives at home.[65]

When returning, the migrants contributed to some extent to the household economy, but far less than during the 1960s or 1970s, because the size of their savings did not allow them to, and they were certainly not expected to become 'economic leaders' (like those who migrate to North America). On the contrary:

> People in rural southeastern Haiti understand that a man rarely brings home much money from the Dominican Republic. Relatives and neighbors sooner view *Sèndomèg* migrants [migrants to the Dominican Republic] as people in need of assistance than as individuals who are in a position to disburse aid to others.[66]

This, of course, raises the question of the emigrants' economic situation. As we have already mentioned, Martínez was unable to gather any data with respect to landowner status or any other indicators of wealth. However, having obtained the migration history of virtually all those who had returned to Haiti and settled there, he concluded that not all who went to the Dominican Republic to cut sugar cane came from the poorer strata of rural Haiti. On the contrary, 'in spite of unequal access to land, men from the middle and lower peasant families seem equally prone to make at least one voyage to the Dominican Republic in their youth.'[67]

However, the poorer of these were likely to make more trips: 'Few men who enjoy relatively abundant access to family land in young adulthood make many voyages to the Dominican Republic, but men who lack enough land on which to subsist commonly make four or more trips.'[68] Thus, we should still expect the poor to be overrepresented among the emigrants. Martínez is, however, careful to point out that the negative correlation between landed wealth and number of trips is 'far from perfect'.[69] A poor man cannot afford to fail too many times, and one who is better off 'might be in line to inherit several parcels of land but only be granted access to one or two, which leaves him for the moment almost as badly off as a son of a land-poor family'.[70]

Even those who are relatively better off may have to make multiple journeys. Building a house was something that could not be accomplished through a single trip to the Dominican Republic. Typically, the money earned must be invested in something else, notably livestock, that produceed earnings in Haiti, and between one and four additional trips must be made, before the necessary capital was accumulated. Less than two-thirds of the trips produced a surplus which was large enough to be invested in Haiti, but having nothing at all to show after a number of trips was not common. Less than 30 percent of the returnees interviewed by Martínez were in that position, while more than half (at least 55 percent, and probably more) were certain that their efforts had yielded an economic benefit in the form of land, a house, or livestock.[71]

Once the transition into adulthood had been made, defined as the building of a house and the establisment of a conjugal union, 70 percent emigrated again, 'to earn money to buy seed, livestock, and, ultimately, land or to buy household necessities, make house repairs, and pay for their children's education'.[72] Once a sufficient level of income security was attained in Haiti, the trips ceased, however. Less than fifteen percent had made ten or more journeys to the Dominican Republic.[73]

2001

Finally, we have the somewhat limited data obtained in a survey of living conditions in Haiti carried out jointly by the Norwegian research institute FAFO and the Institut Haïtien de Statistique et d'Informatique between March and May 2001.[74] These indicate that the emigrants going to the Dominican Republic come mainly from the *départements* which are geographically closest to the neighboring country. Thus, almost 75 percent of all reported emigrants from the Département du Sud-Est were found across the border, and the figures for the Centre and Nord-Est regions were 71 and 42 percent, respectively, to be compared with 0.9 percent for distant Grande-Anse and 2.6 and 2.9 percent for the Ouest and Sud departments. Over 75 percent of all households in the Sud-Est, over 63 percent in the Centre and 42.5 percent in the Nord-Est had one or more relatives in the Dominican Republic, to be compared with 1.7 percent in Grande-Anse, 4.3 percent in the Ouest and 6 percent in the Sud. Generally speaking, emigration to the Dominican Republic is more important for rural households than for urban ones. More than 25 percent of the emigrants from the former were found there against 18 percent in urban areas other than the capital and a mere 2.6 percent in the latter.

The 2001 survey also indicates that among poorer houeholds, a larger share of the emigrants are men (over 65 percent in the two lowest income quintiles, against 57 in the highest). The reason for emigrating, not just to the Dominican Republic, but to other countries as well, was either work (ranging from 65 percent in the lowest income quintile to over 76 in the highest) or finding work (over 26 percent among the poorest decreasing monotonically to 12 percent among the richest). This pattern was valid for all age groups (56–78 percent with the peak between 30 and 60) except the very youngest one, below 15 (26 percent).

Conclusions: The empirical evidence

In *Haiti in Caribbean Context,* David Nicholls offers the following summary of the characteristics of Haitian emigrants:

> It is sometimes assumed that the Haitian migrants must have come from the poorest sections of the community. [...] On the subject of the ... recent migration to the Dominican Republic ... [Mats Lundahl] refers to 'the poorer sections' of the rural population of Haiti as those whom 'we would expect to emigrate'.[75] Economists, unlike other social scientists, are in the fortunate position of being able

> to deduce human behaviour from certain motives which they confidently assume to be paramount, without having to waste time on the tedious business of empirical investigation... the conclusions of those who have actually investigated the situation is that the migrants do not in fact come from the poorest class of the landless and that the majority are landowners. The sea voyage to Cuba, the Bahamas and the USA, of course, demands more expenditure than the overland journey to the Dominican Republic, but even in the latter case a high proportion of migrant cane cutters are proprietors of land in Haiti. The migrants, then, need money for the journey and for the bribes which may be necessary to ensure employment. The poorest would not be able to raise enough; the small landowner is able to secure a loan or to sell part of his property and so have sufficient money to migrate.[76]

In the light of the foregoing examination of the available systematically collected evidence it does not appear as if Nicholls' position can be sustained. This evidence points very clearly to the fact that the vast majority of those who migrate to the Dominican Republic must be classified as 'landless' or 'poor', either because the family owns no or little land, or because they are too young to get access to much of it. By the same token, they hardly sell or mortgage land to finance their trips. Such claims seem to lack empirical foundation.[77]

Poverty also tends to be the central term when Haitians discuss the reason for migration. Martínez concludes that 'inquiries about the reasons why someone has left Haiti could not be sustained for long without talk of *mizè* [poverty] coming to the fore.'[78] That the migrants may not be the *very* poorest is another, completely different, matter.[79] It is well known from other parts of the Third World that the very poorest may be more tied to their place of origin than those a bit better off, for example, because they are unable to defray the expenses (transportation, etc.) that are necessary to make the trip, or because they are 'bound to the village, by law or custom, to work off old family debts they cannot repay'.[80] The general evidence, however, has to be interpreted with caution, since most of it deals with rural–*urban* migration, where education, skills of various kinds and contacts are of paramount importance for jobs in the modern sector, which obviously excludes the very poorest. 'Instead they are increasingly pushed into the informal or traditional urban sector, or into rural-rural migration...'[81]

Thus, it is very difficult to avoid the conclusion that the majority of the Haitian migrants to the Dominican Republic are young peasant sons who are uneducated and poor, either permanently or during the particular phase of their life cycle when they undertake the migration trips. They make an individual decision to seek work and get a cash income which they want to spend back in Haiti. In order to do so, they are prepared to subject themselves to the terrible working and living conditions that they will find in the *bateyes*, conditions that they have information about before they leave their home country. Many, but by no means all, are target workers with a particular type of investment in mind.

Rural poverty in Haiti

What does the profile of poverty look like in Haiti? Generally speaking, the countryside is poorer than the cities in Haiti, and the vast majority is *very* poor. The most recent figures come from a USAID-sponsored investigation of over 4000 rural households carried out between 1994 and 1996 and from the joint Norwegian–Haitian survey from 2001.[82] If we define the indigency line as the local cost of reaching the FAO minimum nutritional standard of 2240 calories per day and person with a diet that matches the composition of food expenditure of the average household, this, in 1996, in terms of annual income amounted to US$160. Adding non-food expenditure to this cost, so as to make the percentage of food expenditure in the total match the average for poor rural households (71.8 percent), gives us the definition of the poverty line, equal to an annual figure of US$220 in 1996. With these definitions, about two thirds of the rural households fall below the indigency line and over 80 percent below the poverty line, that is, the only rural inhabitants that are not poor are those in the top quintile.

The survey also revealed that the peasants are highly dependent on purchased food. A mere 28 percent of the food consumption expenditure was satisfied by on-farm production. This, in combination with the general poverty, made food consumption account for two-thirds of the total expenditure, on average, with little variation between the quintiles. Agriculture was the dominant source of income, accounting for 59 percent in the poorest quintile and 78 in the top one, the average being 72 percent. Most of the land (almost two-thirds) was owned by the peasants themselves. The main alternative to ownership was sharecropping, a practice that was more prevalent among the poorest households (18 percent of the total farm area) than among the richest (7 percent). (We will come back to the interpretation of this below.) The poorest households usually had their plots twice as far away from the *kay* [houses] as the richest households. 'This is not a trivial phenomenon: a walking distance of an hour or more to a plot entails a severe tradeoff between cultivation and other, concurrent (especially non-farm) labor activities, and this can be a disincentive to choosing crops requiring intensive cultivation techniques', using more cash inputs, hired labor and/or soil conservation.[83] Protection against soil erosion was found to increase the productivity of the land with 22 percent.

The marginal product of labor was found to be close to zero (76 gourdes per added man-year), while increases in the use of purchased inputs yielded a 90 percent return, Haitian farms being starved of capital. As could be expected, the low labor productivity created a pressure to leave the farms, especially among the poorest families, who, we recall, derived 41 percent of their incomes from off-farm activities. Also, 29 percent of all households had members who had migrated, but only 8 percent (of all households) reported receiving any remittances from the migrants.

The findings of the 2001 survey are less detailed than those from the mid-1990s. They do, however, by and large confirm the latter. Poverty in Haiti is more common in rural than in urban areas. Living in the countryside, as opposed to the capital, reduced the expected income by 58 percent. The extent of poverty also varies considerably between regions. Contrary to the conventional wisdom, it turned out that the Département du Nord-Est (and not Nord-Ouest) was the poorest one. No less than 84 precent of the population there lived on less than $1 per day. Overall, the non-poor households received more wage income and transfers than the poor and extremely poor where self-employment and self-consumption were the rule. The formal labor market was central when it came to escaping poverty. Schooling mattered as well. Around 50 percent of the children from poor and extremely poor households were enrolled in primary education, against two-thirds of the non-poor. Also contrary to the conventional wisdom, landlessness did not seem to have much to do with poverty. Eighty percent of the rural households had access to land. The plots were small and relatively equally distributed. The existing differences did not have much impact on income.

The root causes of poverty

Since poverty appears to play a central role for the decision to migrate, it becomes important to find out what causes poverty. Haiti is by far the country in the Western Hemisphere with the lowest per capita income, presently (2008) around US$600.[84] This figure, however, hides an unequal distribution of income, with lower figures not least in rural areas.[85] The Haitian peasant attempts to make ends meet on a total land area which on average is less than 1 *carreau* (1.29 hectares).[86] This area furthermore has a strong tendency to shrink over time, as the population grows, and this goes hand in hand with a decreasing rural average income.[87]

The decreasing availability of land in the Haitian countryside is not just a case of more people gathering on a given area. Unfortunately, the process contains features of cumulative causation which make it accelerate over time and hence make the situation of the peasants progressively worse.[88] The culprit of the process – its trigger – is the growth of the population. The growth rate, 2 percent per annum or less, gross of migration, is not particularly high by Third World standards.[89] In the Haitian topographical context it is, however, fatal. Little by little, cultivation has been extended from better, more accessible lands in the plains to the mountainsides. Today, peasant plots are found on *mòn* [mountainsides] that are virtually vertical in some instances.

Coffee trees are being uprooted on the mountainsides to leave room for the cultivation of food crops. This process has been going on for several decades, and it does not appear to have been counteracted by any increase in the relative price of export crops during this period that would make the peasants plant coffee again. On the contrary, the trend appears to have been in the opposite direction, with the relative price of food crops going up instead, reinforcing the effect of the growth of the population.

Unfortunately for the people who are caught in the logic of the interplay between factor growth and changes in the output mix, this sequence will also have secondary effects of a most severe kind. The reason for this is that the shift from land-intensive to labor-intensive crops increases the risk of soil erosion. The most important export crop, coffee, is a tree or a bush with a canopy and a root system, both of which help to protect and bind the soil on the steep mountainsides. When the coffee is gone, the exposure of the soil increases drastically, especially during the sowing and planting season which is also when the rains set in and wash the soil down the slopes and into plains and rivers.

Once the soil destruction is set in motion, it feeds itself. Adding more people on a given area or reducing the area for a given population amount to the same thing: they both increase the man/land ratio, and it is precisely the change in the overall factor proportions that drives the process. Thus, soil erosion will lead to an increased production of food crops and a reduction of export output, which in turn will increase the extent of soil destruction, and so on. Meanwhile, the population continues to grow. Thus both the numerator and the denominator of the man/land ratio are altered. The process tends to become cumulative, production more and more labor-intensive and the fields more and more eroded. As a result, peasant incomes decline over time, that is, the peasants become poorer and poorer.

The increased poverty is, however, not shouldered alike by all. Adolescents and young adults tend to be hit harder than the older generation. Poverty in Haiti to some extent is a life-cycle phenomenon. The field surveys quoted in the present work indicate that the Haitian migrants to the Dominican Republic to a large extent are young and poor, but also that not all of them will remain at the same level of poverty their entire life. They may not become rich when they grow older (even by Haitian standards), but they may at least be earning more than when they were young.

The relation between increased life-cycle related to poverty and migration receives some support from the evidence collected by Gerald Murray in Haiti.[90] The traditional way for a Haitian male youth to obtain his first plot of land is through a pre-inheritance grant from his parents, usually one-fourth of a *carreau* (slightly more than 0.3 hectares), in his late teens or early twenties. The income produced with the aid of this plot accrued to the youngster. To receive the plot, he had to provide work on his parents' land. Over time, however, the Haitian population has grown, and the scarcity of land has increased. Since in principle all children have the same right to inherit, farms have tended to become smaller. This, in turn means that, on the one hand, the need for filial labor has decreased to the corresponding extent and, on the other hand, that the age at which the pre-inheritance grant is received has been delayed and/or that the size of the grant has diminished. In their late teens and early twenties, most peasant boys will still be working on an independent plot, but the manner in which they got access to the plots has changed. Instead of receiving a grant, the young men these days get their plots by entering into sharecropping agreements, frequently with their own parents.

What the latter pattern (if it is systematic) is due to is not entirely clear.[91] This, however, is less of a concern in the present context. The important fact is that population growth has increased the scarcity of land in Haiti and this, in turn, has put young men in an increasingly difficult situation. Thus, teenagers and boys in their early twenties are forced to look for alternative income sources. Otherwise, they will make very little money until the time when they receive the traditional grant. Thus, migration to the Dominican Republic, in spite of all its ugliness, should stand out as an increasingly attractive alternative.

All Haitian poverty is not concentrated to certain phases of the life cycle, however. For most people, it is a steady companion from the cradle to the grave, and it should go without saying that the erosion process has a negative influence on the productivity and incomes of in principle all peasants. Thus, the reasons why men migrate also when they are, say, in their thirties or forties are no different from the causes as far as young boys are concerned. It is mainly the degree of poverty that differs.

The economics of the migration decision

Which role, then, does poverty play in the decisions connected with migration? Let us proceed to examine how some of the principles suggested in the section on migration theories can be applied to the empirical findings. The interesting thing is not whether it is the poorest or the not-quite-so poor that emigrate but whether those who do in fact migrate do so because they think they will in some sense be better off if they go. In fact, the empirical investigations presented above point very strongly in that direction. The Haitians go to the Dominican Republic because they think they can improve their lot by doing so.

This is precisely what most orthodox migration theory centers upon. The most well-known formulation in the development context is the standard Harris–Todaro model.[92] In this, migration is a function of the difference in expected wages between the place of destination (DE) and the place of origin (HE):

$$M = M(w_{DE} - w_{HE}) \tag{1}$$

The prospective migrant knows relatively well how much he would earn by remaining in Haiti and, as it seems, he is also well informed about how much he is likely to get across the border. Thus, even the simplest Harris–Todaro formulation sheds considerable light on the migration decision.

It is sometimes argued that the Harris–Todaro model (and related approaches) cannot explain the phenomenon of return migration. If conditions are better on the other side of the border, the emigrants should not come back. Yet, in the Haitian case, they obviously do. This feature is not difficult to accomodate, however. In the first place, the model is cast in terms of *expected* wages. Thus, there is always the probability that the migrant has been misinformed, that he will get cheated, shortchanged, or will get less out of his trip than he thought when making the decision. This clearly happens, but the majority of the temporary migrants make more than one trip, and you cannot fool all of the people all of the time.

More interesting is that it is possible to incorporate the decision to return home in the model. Sugar growing is a highly seasonal affair. The *zafra* lasts from December to July, at most. When it is over, the majority of the Haitian workers find that their expected wage in the Dominican Republic falls to zero. Hence, they go back to Haiti. Their expected wage there may also be zero, but they are still likely to return. Why this is so can also be explained with the aid of the Harris–Todaro formulation, suitably reinterpreted. Assuming that the migrant has obtained a certain sum from his efforts and that no more is to be had either by remaining or by going back home what will guide his decision is where he thinks he will do best in terms of the utility he derives from spending (on consumption or investment):

$$M = M(U_{\mathrm{CHE}} - U_{\mathrm{CDE}}) \qquad (2)$$

in the simplest case, where the entire income is consumed. Back in his own familiar environment, where he is better acquainted with the supply of goods, the available investment opportunities and the price structure, and where it is easier for him to move around, is obviously where the migrant prefers to spend his money.

In this way, for at least some (mainly early) part of the life cycle, the migrant will maximize his expected income by periodically migrating to the Dominican Republic, but maximizing the utility he derives from it by spending as much as possible in Haiti. As he gets older, his income earning capacity in Haiti will presumably increase. He will get some land, either as inheritance or by buying or leasing it, possibly financing the transaction with money earned in the Dominican Republic. This, *ceteris paribus*, should mean that the relative power of attraction of Haiti increases. As he gets older, he will normally also grow physically weaker, which may reduce his expected wage across the border. Possibly, risk aversion, combined with social factors, also has something to do with it. Life in the *bateyes* is never easy and the migrants are

> ...depending on meager and uncertain wages for... [their] livelihood, far away from... [their] kin. It is easy to see why returning to

> Haiti, pursuing a diversified subsistence strategy, and resuming one's place in kin-based and neighborhood networks of reciprocity at home might seem as a less risky option.[93]

Thus, over the life cycle of the individual, we would expect to find a stronger attachment to Haiti. This is presumably even more true for those who are target workers and who go to the Dominican Republic to earn money for a particular purpose. The maximization of utility over the lifetime of the individual thus requires an early period with residence periodically abroad and consumption or investment mainly at home, to be followed later in life by a more sedentary pattern of income earning and spending.

Conclusions

Our knowledge of the facts and causes of migration from Haiti to the Dominican Republic is far better today than a decade or two ago. Yet, a lot remains to be done. In this chapter, I have drawn a sketch which rests on a combination of empirical facts and theoretical principles of the most probable causal mechanisms. This sketch should, however, be made subject to more rigorous testing in the future. Comparatively, little of the research of Haitian–Dominican migration has so far built on an explicit use of economic theories of migration when it comes to asking questions of empirical relevance. I think that it precisely here that future efforts should put the emphasis. In addition, the 'Haitian side' has been under-researched so far. With the notable exception of Samuel Martínez' study, no systematic surveys have been made in the areas from which the migrants come. This is the second major lacuna to be filled out, possibly by following groups of emigrants from their point of origin in Haiti to their destination in the Dominican Republic and back again. That would provide us with a much fuller story than the ones told hitherto.

Acknowledgments

I am grateful to the participants at the seminar *Transnacionalidad, cultura y políticas migratorias*, Santo Domingo, October 29–30, 1998, where the basic ideas of the essay were first presented, to Jaime Behar, Magnus Lembke, and James Wardally for constructive criticism, and to Tom Wiens for clarifying some technical aspects of World Bank indigency and poverty line calculations to me.

Notes

Published in *Iberoamericana*, Vol. 39, 2009, published by the Institute of Latin American Studies, Stockholm University. Reprinted by permission.

1. Amnesty International (2007), p. 1. See also, for example, Corten and Duarte (1995) and Martínez (1995), pp. 6–7.
2. The earlier history is dealt with, for example, in Lundahl (1983), Chapter 8.
3. Anti-Slavery Society (1979).
4. World Council of Churches (1980).
5. Lemoine (1981).
6. ILO (1983).
7. Veras (1983).
8. Veras (1985).
9. Moya Pons et al. (1986).
10. Plant (1987).
11. Americas Watch, National Coalition for Haitian Refugees and Caribbean Rights (1989).
12. See Cuello (1997), for the detailed contents of the agreements.
13. See, for example, García (1983), Cuello (1985), and Vega (1995), for details.
14. Cf., for example, Martínez (1995), pp. 46–49.
15. For more exhaustive surveys, see, for example, Yap (1977), Williamson (1988), and Massey et al. (1993), Borjas (1994), Lucas (1997), and Gallup (1997).
16. For this, see Silié et al. (2002).
17. Lucas (1997), p. 728.
18. Ibid., p. 729.
19. The consequences in terms of wage levels are examined in Lundahl (1983), Chapter 8.
20. See, for example, Carrothers (1956), for an overview.
21. Lucas (1997), p. 730.
22. Sjaastad (1962).
23. Todaro (1969), Harris and Todaro (1970).
24. Fields (1975).
25. Mincer (1978), Stark and Levhari (1982).
26. Cf., for example, Bigsten (1985), Bangura (1996).
27. Stark and Lucas (1988).
28. Nelson (1959), Yap (1977), and Taylor (1986).
29. Stark (1984), Stark and Yitzhaki (1988).
30. Lucas (1997), p. 754.
31. Nelson (1976), Fan and Stretton (1985).
32. Galor and Stark (1990).
33. Beringhaus and Seifer-Vogt (1988).
34. Connell et al. (1976), p. 79.
35. Murphy (1986), Chapter 9. The same data appear in Moya Pons et al. (1986), Chapter 4.
36. Murphy (1986), pp. 265–66.
37. Ibid., pp. 266–67.
38. Ibid., p. 271.
39. Ibid.

40. Báez Evertsz (1986).
41. Ibid., pp. 75–77.
42. Ibid., p. 78. Báez Evertsz hypothesizes that it is the *older* children that tend to become permanent emigrants, but strictly speaking this does not follow from his data.
43. Ibid., p. 82.
44. Ibid., p. 105.
45. Ibid., pp. 87–89.
46. Ibid., p. 94.
47. Lozano and Báez Evertsz (1992).
48. Báez Evertsz (1986), pp. 316–17.
49. Lozano and Báez Evertsz (1992), pp. 88, 106.
50. Ibid., p. 58.
51. Ibid., p. 63.
52. Ibid., p. 64.
53. Ibid., p. 69.
54. Ibid., p. 71.
55. Ibid., p. 143.
56. Martínez (1995).
57. Ibid., p. xi.
58. Ibid., pp. 80–81.
59. Ibid., p. 85.
60. Ibid., p. 86.
61. Ibid., p. 88.
62. Ibid., p. 93.
63. Ibid., p. 94.
64. Ibid., p. 95.
65. Ibid., p. 96.
66. Ibid., p. 97.
67. Ibid., pp. 104–05.
68. Ibid., p. 105.
69. Ibid.
70. Ibid., p. 110.
71. Ibid., p. 98.
72. Ibid.
73. Ibid., p. 99.
74. The data from this are available in République d'Haïti (2003).
75. The quotation is from Lundahl (1983), p. 138.
76. Nicholls (1985), p. 198. Cf. also ibid., p. 191: 'It is perhaps surprising to learn that most of the migrant workers [to the Dominican Republic] do not come from the class of landless rural proletariat but they are small landowners, particularly from the areas around Léogane and Jacmel.'
77. Priests are usually stronger believers in phenomena that have not been empirically verified than economists. Nicholls' verdict (cf. the preceding footnote) is based on data collected by André Corten (1974) (Spanish version quoted by Nicholls published in 1974, French original reprinted in Corten (1986), Chapter 4). In the article quoted by Nicholls, Corten simply mentions that 'the majority of the cane cutters interviewed in the Dominican Republic declared to be landowners, instead of belonging, as would seem

normal in the case of "poverty-migration" [migration-misère], to the most impoverished category of the population: the "landless"' (Corten (1986), p. 96), without providing any details at all. In a later work (Corten and Tahon (1985), pp. 56, 70–76; cf. also Corten (1986), Chapter 8), Corten and Tahon make reference to two sets of interviews, one carried out in 1970 (presumably the one on which the quotation is based) among 85 Haitians and another in 1981, when 51 people were questioned. During the former around half of the interviewees declared to have a piece of land of their own or a piece of family land. Eleven years later, the figure had increased to more than two-thirds. At the same time, however, almost 80 percent in 1970 and over 70 percent in 1981 were classified by Corten and Tahon as rural or agricultural 'proletarians', a 'proletarian' being defined as 'someone who was alienated ... from his means of subsistence ...' (Corten and Tahon (1985), p. 22). These two statements are completely contradictory. Thus, it is difficult to know what to make of Corten's data. Possibly, the classification as 'proletarian' is dependent on lack of access to land *in the Dominican Republic* (Corten and Tahon (1985), pp. 76–77, (1986), p. 257), but that hardly makes any sense for people who have land, that is, 'means of subsistence', in Haiti.

78. Martínez (1995), p. 174.
79. Obviously 'poorer' does not mean 'very poorest'.
80. Lipton (1977), pp. 218–19. The quotation is from p. 218. Cf. also Connell et al. (1976), p. 197.
81. Connell et al. (1976), p. 206.
82. The results of the former study are summarized in Wiens and Sobrado (1997). The statistics of the latter investigation are in République d'Haïti (2003), and the main findings are reported in Sletten and Egset (2006).
83. Wiens and Sobrado (1997), p. 9.
84. World Bank (2010), p. 378.
85. Statistics on the distribution of income and wealth in Haiti are notoriously uncertain (cf. Lundahl [1996]), but few would dispute this statement.
86. A 1994–96 USAID sponsored survey of more than 4000 households revealed an average cultivated area of 1.23 hectares (Wiens and Sobrado (1997), p. 8).
87. Cf. the data summmarized in Lundahl (1997), p. 4.
88. Lundahl (1979), Chapter 5.
89. Lundahl (1997), p. 4.
90. Murray (1977), Chapters 7–10.
91. Murray views it as a device used by the parents to mobilize filial labor, but as I have pointed out elsewhere (Lundahl (1983), Chapter 6), this interpretation hardly stands up to scrutiny in a situation where the price of land is increasing in terms of labor.
92. Harris and Todaro (1970).
93. Martínez (1995), p. 101.

References

Americas Watch, National Coalition for Haitian Refugees and Caribbean Rights (1989), *Haitian Sugar Cane Cutters in the Dominican Republic*. New York: Americas Watch and National Coalition for Haitian Refugees.

Amnesty International (2007), *Dominican Republic: A Life in Transit – The Plight of Haitian Migrants and Dominicans of Haitian Descent*. AMR 27/001/2007, March 21. http://74.125.77.132/search?q=cache:onH1pt8oSo8J:www.amnesty.org/en/news-and-updates/report/haitian-migrants-denied-basic-rights-dominican-republic-20070321. Downloaded February 19, 2010.

Anti-Slavery Society for the Protection of Human Rights (1979), *Migrant Workers in the Dominican Republic*. Report for 1979 to the United Nations Working Group of Experts on Slavery. Mimeo, No place.

Báez Evertsz, Franc (1986), *Braceros haitianos en la República Dominicana*. Second edition. Santo Domingo: Instituto Dominicano de Investigaciones Sociales.

Bangura, Yusuf (1996), 'Economic Restructuring, Coping Strategies and Social Change: Implications for Institutional Development in Africa', in: Mats Lundahl and Benno J. Ndulu (eds), *New Directions in Development Economics: Growth, Environmental Concerns and Government in the 1990s*. London and New York: Routledge.

Beringhaus, Siegfried and Seifer-Vogt, Hans-Günther (1988), 'Temporary vs Permanent Migration: A Decision Theoretical Approach', *Journal of Population Economics*, Vol. 1, 195–211.

Bigsten, Arne (1985), 'What Do Smallholders Do for a Living?', in: Mats Lundahl (ed.), *The Primary Sector in Economic Development*. London and Sydney: Croom Helm.

Borjas, George J. (1994), 'The Economics of Immigration', *Journal of Economic Literature*, Vol. 32. 1667–717.

Carrothers, Gerald A.P. (1956), 'An Historical Review of the Gravity and Potential Concepts of Human Interaction', *Journal of the American Institute of Planners*, Vol. 22, 94–103.

Connell, John, Dasgupta, Biplab, Laishley, Roy and Lipton, Michael (1976), *Migration from Rural Areas: The Evidence from Village Studies*. Oxford and London: Oxford University Press.

Corten, André (1974), 'Migraciones e intereses de clases', in: Gérard Pierre-Charles (ed.), *Política y sociología en Haití y la República Dominicana*. México, DF: Instituto de Investigaciones Sociales, Universidad Autónoma de México.

Corten, André (1986), *Port au Sucre. Prolétariat et prolétarisations. Haïti et République Dominicaine*. Montréal: Les Éditions du CIDIHCA.

Corten, André and Duarte, Isis (1995), 'Five Hundred Thousand Haitians in the Dominican Republic', *Latin American Perspectives*, Vol. 22, 94–110.

Corten, André and Tahon, Marie-Blanche (1985), *Proletariado y procesos de proletarización en República Dominicana*. Santo Domingo: Editora Alfa & Omega.

Cuello, H. José Israel (1985), *Documentos del conflicto dominico-haitiano de 1937*. Santo Domingo: Editora Taller.

Cuello, H. José Israel (1997), *Contratación de mano de obra haitiana destinada a la industria azucarera dominicana (1952–1986)*. Santo Domingo: Editora Taller.

Fan, Yiu-Kwan and Stretton, Alan (1985), 'Circular Migration in South-East Asia: Some Theoretical Explanations', in: Guy Standing (ed.), *Labour Circulation and the Labour Process*. London: Croom-Helm.

Fields, Gary S. (1975), 'Rural-urban Migration, Urban Unemployment and Underemployment, and Job-search Activity in LDCs', *Journal of Development Economics*, Vol. 2, 165–87.

Gallup, John L. (1997), 'Theories of Migration'. Development Discussion Paper No. 569. Cambridge, MA: Harvard Institute for International Development.

Galor, Oded and Stark, Oded (1990), 'Migrants' Savings, the Probability of Return Migration, and Migrants' Performance', *International Economic Review*, Vol. 31, 463–67.

García, Juan Manuel (1983), *La matanza de los haitianos: Genocidio de Trujillo, 1937*. Santo Domingo: Editora Alfa & Omega.

Harris, John R. and Todaro, Michael P. (1970), 'Migration, Unemployment and Development: A Two-sector Analysis', *American Economic Review*, March, Vol. 60, 126–42.

ILO (International Labour Organisation) (1983), 'Report of the Commission of Inquiry Appointed under Article 26 of the Constitution of the International Labour Organisation to Examine the Observance of Certain International Labour Conventions by the Dominican Republic and Haiti with Respect to the Employment of Haitian Workers on the Sugar Plantations of the Dominican Republic', *International Labour Office*, Official Bulletin, Special Supplement 66 (Series B).

Lemoine, Maurice (1981), *Sucre amer: Esclaves aujourd'hui dans les Caraïbes*. Paris: Nouvelle Société des Éditions Encre.

Lipton, Michael (1977), *Why Poor People Stay Poor: A Study of Urban Bias in World Development*. London: Temple Smith.

Lozano, Wilfredo and Baez Evertsz, Franc (1992), *Migración internacional y economía cafetalera: Estudio sobre la migración estacional de trabajadores haitianos a la cosecha cafetalera en la República Dominicana*. Santo Domingo: Centro de Planificación y Acción Ecuménica.

Lucas, Robert E.B. (1997), 'Internal Migration in Developing Countries,' in: Mark R. Rosenzweig and Oded Stark (eds), *Handbook of Population and Family Economics*, Volume 1 B. Amsterdam: Elsevier Science.

Lundahl, Mats (1979), *Peasants and Poverty: A Study of Haiti*. London: Croom Helm.

Lundahl, Mats (1983), *The Haitian Economy: Man, Land and Markets*. London and Canberra: Croom Helm.

Lundahl, Mats (1996), 'Income and Land Distribution in Haiti: Some Remarks on Available Statistics', *Journal of Interamerican Studies and World Affairs*, Vol. 38, 109–26.

Lundahl, Mats (1997), *Towards the Abyss? The Political Economy of Emergency in Haiti*. Research for Action 40. Helsinki: UNU World Institute for Development Economics Research (WIDER).

Martínez, Samuel (1995), *Peripheral Migrants: Haitians and Dominican Republic Sugar Plantations*. Knoxville, TN: University of Tennessee Press.

Massey, Douglas S., Arango, Joaquín, Hugo, Graeme, Kouaouci, Ali, Pellegrino, Adela and Taylor, J. Edward (1993), 'Theories of International Migration: A Review and Appraisal', *Population and Development Review*, Vol. 19, 431–66.

Mincer, Jacob (1978), 'Family Migration Decisions', *Journal of Political Economy*, Vol. 86, 749–73.

Moya Pons, Frank et al. (1986), *El batey: Estudio socioeconómico de los bateyes del Consejo Estatal del Azúcar*. Santo Domingo: Fondo Para el Avance de las Ciencias Sociales.

Murphy, Martin Francis (1986), *Historical and Contemporary Labor Utilization Practices in the Sugar Industries of the Dominican Republic*. PhD thesis. New York: Columbia University.

Murray, Gerald Francis (1977), *The Evolution of Haitian Peasant Land Tenure: A Case Study in Agrarian Adaptation to Population Growth*. PhD thesis. Columbia University, New York.

Nelson, Joan M. (1976), 'Sojourners vs New Urbanites: Causes and Consequences of Temporary Versus Permanent Cityward Migration in Developing Countries', *Economic Development and Cultural Change*, Vol. 24, 721–57.

Nelson, Phillip (1959), 'Migration, Real Income, and Information', *Journal of Regional Science*, Vol. 1, 43–74.

Nicholls, David (1985), *Haiti in Caribbean Context: Ethnicity, Economy and Revolt*. Houndmills, Basingstoke: Macmillan.

Plant, Roger (1987), *Sugar and Modern Slavery: A Tale of Two Countries*. London and New Jersey: Zed Books.

République d'Haïti, Ministère de l'Économie et des Finances, Institut Haïtien de Statistique et d'Informatique (2003), *Enquête sur les conditions de vie en Haïti (ECVH-2001)*. Port-au-Prince: Programme des Nations Unies pour le Développement (PNUD).

Silié, Rubén; Segura, Carlos and Dore Cabral, Carlos (2002), *La nueva inmigración haitiana*. Santo Domingo: FLACSO.

Sjaastad, Larry A. (1962), 'The Costs and Returns of Human Migration', *Journal of Political Economy*, Vol. 70, 80–93.

Sletten, Pål and Egset, Willy (2006), 'Poverty in Haiti', *Iberoamericana*, Vol. 36, 41–59.

Stark, Oded (1984), 'Rural-to-urban Migration in LDCs: A Relative Deprivation Approach', *Economic Development and Cultural Change*, Vol. 32, 475–86.

Stark, Oded and Levhari, David (1982), 'On Migration and Risk in LDCs', *Economic Development and Cultural Change*, Vol. 31, 191–96.

Stark, Oded and Lucas, Robert E.B. (1988), 'Migration, Remittances, and the Family', *Economic Development and Cultural Change*, Vol. 36, 465–81.

Stark, Oded and Yitzhaki, Shlomo (1988), 'Labor Migration as a Response to Relative Deprivation', *Journal of Population Economics*, Vol. 1, 57–70.

Taylor, J. Edward (1986), 'Differential Migration, Networks, Information and Risk', in: Oded Stark (ed.), *Migration, Human Capital and Development*. Greenwich, CT: JAI Press.

Todaro, Michael P. (1969), 'A Model of Labor Migration and Urban Unemployment in Less Developed Countries', *American Economic Review*, Vol. 59, 138–48.

Vega, Bernardo (1995), *Trujillo y Haití. Volumen II (1937–1938)*. Santo Domingo: Fundación Cultural Dominicana.

Veras, Ramón Antonio (1983), *Inmigración–haitianos–esclavitud*. Santo Domingo: Ediciones de Taller.

Veras, Ramón Antonio (1985), *Migración caribeña y un capítulo haitiano*. Santo Domingo: Editora Taller.

Wiens, Thomas and Sobrado, Carlos E. (1997), 'Rural Poverty in Haiti', in: The World Bank (ed.), *Haiti Poverty Assessment, Volume II: Technical Papers*. Washington, DC.

Williamson, Jeffrey G. (1988), 'Migration and Urbanization', in: Hollis Chenery and T.N. Srinivasan (eds), *Handbook of Development Economics, Volume 1*. Amsterdam: North Holland.

World Bank (2010), *World Development Report 2010*. Washington, DC.

World Council of Churches (1980), *'Sold Like Cattle': Haitian Workers in the Dominican Republic*. Geneva: World Council of Churches.

Yap, Lorene Y.L. (1977), 'The Attraction of Cities: A Review of the Migration Literature', *Journal of Development Economics*, Vol. 4, 239–64.

Part III
The Failed Transition

Chapter 8, 'Another Failed American Occupation?' was published in 1994. The chapter deals with the American invasion of Haiti in 1994 when Jean-Bertrand Aristide was reinstated as president after the military coup in 1991. It describes the conflict between Aristide and the military, notably over the control of the police force, in the context of the predatory state. The chapter also analyzes the most serious mistake of the first occupation 1915–34, the creation of a 'political' army, and argues that the Haitian army had to be dissolved, since it did not serve any positive purpose, and that a regular police force be created instead.

Chapter 9, 'From Kleptocracy to Democracy?' was published in 1996. It begins by noting the fading international interest in Haiti as of 1996. Thereafter, the struggle for democracy is analyzed. A short portrait of Aristide is offered, and an account of the 9 months between his assumption of power and the military coup is given. This is followed by an analysis of the military government 1991–94 and the economic consequences of it. Next, the economic policy of the period after Aristide's return is sketched. The last sections of the chapter deal with Haiti's most pressing problems: the reform of the judiciary, the continuing deterioration of the agricultural sector, the resurrection of light manufacturing after the blow dealt to it by the international embargo during the military government and the desirability of upgrading it technologically, and, finally, the difficulty of consolidating democracy after the 1991–94 setback.

Chapter 10, 'Problems of Policy Reform in the Haitian Economy', was published in 1996. The chapter offers an analysis of the problem of economic policy-making in an essentially predatory state. It begins by the presentation of a formal modal of this type of state, where a ruler maximizes a utility function with private income and the probability of remaining in power as the only elements by choosing the optimal size of his polity and the optimum degree of obfuscation. This model is applied to Haiti. Thereafter some of the peasant autoregulatory defense mechanisms against outside exploiters though the creation of a 'parallel' society are discussed, and so is the gradual merger between this and the 'official' society. The next section discusses how the economic policy of the Baby Doc years was influenced by the fact that the state was predatory. This is followed by an account of the three policy reform attempts that took place from the fall of Baby Doc in 1986 until the end of the first Aristide presidency in 1996, and the negative influence of politics on the outcomes.

Chapter 11, 'Sustained Growth in Haiti: Pipe-Dream or Realistic Possibility?' was published in 1999. The chapter examines the possibility of sustained growth in the Haitian economy. It begins by a picture of the main mechanisms behind the declining standard of living in the countryside and an account of the main safety valve: migration to urban areas and out of the country. This is followed by a sketch of an agrarian reform effort undertaken by the first Préval government and of the introduction of some non-traditional crops that may help to ameliorate the situation in rural areas.

Thereafter the attention is turned to the industrial sector. Branches enjoying tariff protection are contrasted with the export-oriented assembly sector. The blow dealt to the latter between 1991 and 1994 is analyzed, and the problems of recovery and competitiveness are highlighted. The possibility of growth in the handicraft and tourist sectors is analyzed. The fact that most of the Haitian economy is informal is brought out, and the consequences of this are discussed. Finally, two key inputs in the growth process which both have been highly deficient are brought out: education and infrastructure. The concluding section argues that the short- and medium-term prospects for growth were gloomy. The political situation was paralyzed, and this would have a negative impact on economic growth.

8
Another Failed American Occupation?

There will be no American invasion of Haiti. The mediation of ex-president Jimmy Carter has succeeded in the sense that the three leading Haitian militaries, the commander-in-chief, Raoul Cédras, the chief of staff, Philippe Biamby, and the chief of police Michel François, have agreed to resign from their posts. When the Americans disembark, it will not be as an invasion force but as a guardian of public order. The only question is whether this will contribute to the solution of Haiti's problems.

This is not the first time that American troops will be on Haitian soil. Seventy-nine years ago another American president, Woodrow Wilson, sent the Marine Corps to Haiti. The landing of the Marines constituted the beginning of an occupation that would last for almost 20 years: until 1934. The reasons were to some extent the same as today. Politics had degenerated. Haiti had had 22 presidents since 1843. A single one had managed to sit through his entire period. Most had been ousted more or less violently. When the Marines went in, the incumbent president, Vilbrun Guillaume Sam, had just been murdered by a furious mob.

The occupation was a complete failure. The American administration did not manage to introduce democracy in Haiti. When the Marine Corps had left, politics degenerated. Dictators came and went until a climax was reached 1957–86 under the two Duvaliers: François (Papa Doc) and Jean-Claude (Baby Doc). Thereafter, chaos has prevailed in the country.

After interrupted elections in November 1987 and a farcical second round in January 1988, a provisional government council dominated by the military was succeeded by a president – Leslie Manigat – who could not keep his office for even half a year. After another round of military rule and a provisional president, the charismatic Catholic priest Jean-Bertrand Aristide was elected president by a majority of two-thirds in December 1990. In September the following year, the military had managed to throw him out. Now President Clinton intends to reinstate him.

What exactly is at the core of the conflict between Aristide and the military? Why did Cédras, Biamby and François refuse for so long to resign under the pressure of international sanctions that had been in force since Aristide was thrown out and which were gradually escalated thereafter?

The conflict between Aristide and the military is about the control of the police. In Haiti, there is no police force which is independent of the military, but the police is simply a branch of the latter – and the most numerous one at that. Aristide tried to change this. With the aid of foreign experts, he attempted to set up a police corps under civilian command, separated from the armed forces. The military, however, cannot tolerate such a state of things – for several reasons.

In the first place, a civilian police force would imply massive dismissal of military personnel, in a situation where very few other jobs exist. Secondly, a civilian police force would constitute a countervailing power vis-à-vis the military and reduce the influence of the military in politics. Above all, it would be a great deal more difficult for the military juntas to install and dispose of presidents. Most important of all, however, is that control over the police creates illegal incomes for the military, on the one hand directly, through various forms of extortion of the citizens, and on the other hand by creating plenty of scope for smuggling (not least of narcotics) and other corrupt activities.

Here is the very core of politics, as it is traditionally carried out in Haiti. In 1809, Haiti had the first land reform in Latin America. The old plantation system which had served as the foundation for the French colony of Saint-Domingue until 1791 hereby received the death blow. Through the reform during the nineteenth century, a class of free peasant smallholders which still exists was created. The reform, however, had completely perverse political consequences. The Haitian upper class could not monopolize the land and hence could not get an income from agriculture without working the soil themselves. Instead, politics became their foremost source of income. The fight for the presidency became a fight over the government treasury, which was filled by export taxes, import tariffs, and foreign loans. Haiti became a predatory state. The difference between the private income of the rulers and government income was blurred. Kleptocracy became the prevailing mode of government.

The degeneration of politics during the nineteenth century explains why the presidents did not last. Cliques came and went, and all of them had the same goal: to put the tax revenue into their own pockets. Only the presidents that took care to build up a large apparatus of repression managed to stay in power for longer periods. Unfortunately, degeneration had come to stay. Twenty years of American occupation could do nothing to change this fact. No Haitian predatory presidents have been as successful as the two Duvaliers. When Baby Doc was forced into exile in 1986, the Duvalier family was said to be in possession of $1.6 billion.

The selection of politicians in Haiti is a negative one, and today's militaries are no exception to that rule. Their fight against Aristide is the fight of the thoroughly perverted clique politics against the democratic mode of government. Their main assumption is that the people are there for the good of the government – not vice versa.

The Haitian Supreme Commander, Raoul Cédras, and his friends have been fighting not only for their own existence but also for the survival of the rotten Haitian political system. This is important to keep in mind when you start wondering what will happen when the American and international forces have landed. The fate of democracy in Haiti will be determined by what the Unites States (and other nations contributing to the peace-keeping forces) chooses to do.

The occupation 1915–34 failed among other things because the Americans chose to do the wrong thing: not least did they create what with time became the present army, an army to keep the citizens at bay – not an army to defend the country against external foes. By the same token, they failed to lay the foundations of a future democracy.

The occupation forces mistrusted the Haitians and therefore, through the Marine Corps, manipulated the different elections and plebiscites that were held. The presidents during the occupation were mere puppets. The result could be but one: continued dictatorship and continued kleptocracy.

This is the historic mistake that a second intervention, almost 50 years after the first, must correct. Above all the army (and the paramilitary groups close to it, mainly the old, officially non-existent, *tonton macoutes* from Duvalier's time) must be dissolved and effectively unarmed. There is no other measure that will have the same returns in both political and economic terms.

The examples are to be found elsewhere. After the civil war in 1948 Costa Rica abolished its army. The country has never had any reason to regret this decision. On the contrary, it is hard not to view this as one of the most important reasons for why the Costa Rica has developed into a model democracy with by far the highest per capita income in Central America.

Haiti does not need an army any more than Costa Rica does. The country is not subject to any external threats. Fidel Castro is no longer in the position where he can embark on foreign ventures, and Haiti's relations with the neighboring Dominican Republic are reasonably good. The external security is guaranteed in a different way – by the presence in the Caribbean region of the most powerful nation in the world. What Haiti needs is simply a normal police force that enjoys the support and confidence of the citizens.

Finally, the peace-keeping forces that will remain in Haiti until after the regular presidential elections next year must provide maximum support to the process of democratization. It is of utmost importance that Aristide – the president of the country, who has been elected by the people – will be put in the position where he can act effectively and form a government, with the widest possible majority: preferably a government of national unity with representatives of all the important democratic parties. It is not enough to maintain law and order in a superficial way during a transition period. Then the process may easily grind to a halt, and Haiti will experience more kleptocratic dictatorships in the future.

The risk is, however, high that the United States and its allies will choose to let the Haitians solve their problems by themselves without caring about whether the army is dissolved or not. In that case, the probability is high that the entire occupation will become a failure. The root of the evil remains as a dark threat and may preclude the democracy that is being established from becoming anything else but a nominal democracy.

Haiti is facing enormously difficult provision problems. Before the economic sanctions began, the income per capita was more or less at par with that of Tanzania. In reality, the standard of living was considerably lower. Exactly where the country finds itself today is impossible to know, but there is no doubt about the fact that a severe decline has taken place. There are hardly any alternatives to the low-yielding agriculture carried out in plots of half a hectare or one hectare.

The boat people problem is as much of an economic phenomenon as a political one. In the past, these problems have been aggravated by pure gangster politics. Democracy is no sufficient condition when it comes to creating a decent material standard for the poorest people of the Western Hemisphere, but it is definitely a necessary one.

When the American Secretary of State, William Jennings Bryan, was informed about conditions in Haiti a couple of years before the invasion in 1915, his only comment was: 'Dear me, think of it! Niggers speaking French.' Let's hope that President Clinton has better advisors at his disposal.

Note

Published in *Finans Tidningen* (Swedish version), September 21 and 22, 1994.

9
From Kleptocracy to Democracy?

For a short period in 1994, the international community directed its attention toward Haiti. This was during the period which preceded the decision of the United States to intervene and topple the sitting military regime and reinstate the legal president of the country, Jean-Bertrand Aristide. Thereafter, the interest has gradually diminished, not least in the United States. President Clinton hardly wants another Somalia on his back, and the year 1996 in addition was election year. Fidel Castro is hardly in the situation where he will risk any foreign policy adventures. Hence, American assistance to Haiti is being reduced. The country is no longer interesting for the big neighbor in the north.

This lack of interest is, however, unwarranted. Even though Haiti is simply a 'small' country of the size of Belgium or Maryland, it has a great deal to offer for those who want to analyze the problems that poor underdeveloped countries face when they want to introduce democracy. The modern struggle for democracy in Haiti began when the dictatorship of Jean-Claude Duvalier fell from power, in February 1986. Then power was assumed by a provisional government dominated by the military. The presidential elections that were to be held in November 1987 were interrupted by the army and by the former *tonton macoutes*. When the elections which made Leslie Manigat president were held, in January 1988, the voter turnout was abysmally low. It did not take too long before Manigat was ousted.

Jean-Bertrand Aristide: Priest and president

Jean-Bertrand Aristide was elected president in December 1990. He was born in 1953 and comes from a peasant family. Aristide attended a Catholic (Salesian) school in Port-au-Prince, and he graduated from a priest seminary when he was 21. After a year in the Dominican Republic, he returned to Haiti to study psychology at the university in Port-au-Prince. Aristide quickly became politically uncomfortable for the Catholic Church in Haiti, since he insisted that the poor should come first.

In order to get rid of him, the Church sent him to Israel for bible study. When he came back to Haiti in 1982, he was ordained, and after a mere 3 months of duty, he was sent to Montreal where he finished a Master's degree in theology and in addition took PhD courses in psychology. In 1985, he returned to Haiti.

Aristide was stationed in the poor parish of Saint-Jean Bosco in Port-au-Prince, and at the same time, he taught in the largest seminary of the city. During the period up to the fall of Baby Doc in February 1986, Saint-Jean Bosco became a center and Aristide somewhat of a symbol for the increasing resistance against the Duvalier regime. 'The little church' – *ti legliz* – was based on the fundamental principle of the Latin American liberation theology – the poor are to be delivered from their subordinate position in society – and it was organized as a counterweight to the formal catholic hierarchy, which lacked understanding of the plight of the poor and whose representatives often sided with the sitting regime.

Aristide survived a number of attempts against his life organized by the Duvalierists. Also after the fall of Baby Doc he, however, stood out as politically uncomfortable in the eyes of the church, and in May 1986, he was ordered to refrain from further political activity. The military-dominated junta that ruled Haiti demanded that he should be removed, and in August 1987, the message arrived from Rome that he was to go to a small community outside Port-au-Prince. This was, however, not accepted by Aristide's parishioners and the masses of Port-au-Prince, who prevented his transfer. Two weeks before Christmas in 1988, Aristide was finally expelled from the Salesian brotherhood.

Arsitide has been portrayed as a Communist demagogue by his adversaries. Within the CIA it has been contended that he suffers from grave psychological problems, that he is a manic depressive and a megalomaniac. He was allegedly treated for these problems in two Montreal hospitals in 1990. The bluff was called when a reporter from the *Miami Herald* obtained a permission from Aristide to get access to his journals from the two hospitals (plus two more Montreal hospitals), and it turned out that none of them had any files on him.

What upset the CIA was probably the Aristide rhetoric. This in the first place had a number of characteristics that could be interpreted as

Communist, even though Aristide himself has stressed that Marxism is not one of his sources of inspiration. He called capitalism a 'deadly sin' and a 'deadly economic infection'. He thought that the United States had exploited Haiti and that the Americans cooperated with the Haitian military and the *tonton macoutes*. He called the United States a 'military dictatorship', considered the political values of Che Guevara to be close to his own and predicted that the poor would one day rise and take from the rich what rightly belonged to them. The fight for justice should, however, be non-violent.

In the economic and social field, Aristide stressed justice and equality. The Catholic Church should work for the poor and stop being hypocritical. Large landowners should share their land with the landless and the poor. This partly self-contradictory message of course left the field open to a number of interpretations.

Aristide's opponents accused him of falling back on the parliament of the streets and of using political violence systematically to reach his goals. This is, however, a gross exaggeration. During his time in the presidency, human rights associations could record a mere 7 political lynchings – usually of Duvalierists, soldiers or ex *tonton macoutes* – against 50 during the 11 months that preceded his presidential period – and there are no indications that Aristide either ordered them or agreed to them.

During the 8 short months that Aristide was allowed to remain in power he could of course not do very much. His macroeconomic program (reduced budget deficit, restrictive monetary policy, improved tax collection, and loans from the International Monetary Fund and via the Paris Club) contributed to the stabilization of the economy during the short period when it was allowed to work. The budget deficit was reduced to 0.1 percent of GDP, the public enterprises began to run a surplus, the black market exchange rate was reduced, and the rate of inflation came down from 20 percent in December 1990 to 12 percent in September the following year. The size of the currency reserves increased. The size of the corrupt administration was shrunk, and the magnitude of smuggling, notably of drugs, was reduced.

The military dictatorship 1991–94

By and large, the results obtained by Aristide were wiped out by the military junta that overthrew him in September 1991. His fight against corruption and drug smuggling threatened the very existence of the military. The constabulary that had been created by the military in the

1910s and 1920s, as well as the army that succeeded it, mixed two fundamentally different functions in an unfortunate way: that of the military and that of the police. In practice, the police was under military, not civilian, control, and the same type of personnel served in both. After the fall of Baby Doc in 1986, the military in practice took over the government until 1991, and after the 8 short months of Aristide in power, they were back for another 3-year period. During the 6–7 years when Haiti was *de facto* run by the army, from the fall of the Duvalier regime to the return of Aristide, the military systematically used its position as police, in direct contact with the population, to generate illegal incomes, from smuggling, extortion, 'private' taxation, and so on. The commander-in-chief, General Raoul Cédras, for example, who had a monthly salary of the equivalent of US$900, was deemed to have a fortune of more than $100 million when he left Haiti.

The consequences of the unhampered plunder were devastating. Between 1991 and 1994, GDP per capita fell with around one-third in real terms, from a level which was already very low. Today, the level seems to be around $250–260 per annum – a catastrophically low figure – definitely the lowest in the modern era. Three circumstances are of particular interest.

First, the political chaos and the everyday violence which Haiti was thrown into all but killed the only dynamic sector of the economy: the assembly industry. Between 1966 and 1984, it had increased the share of manufactures in total exports from 4 to 66 percent, and in 1990 it employed around 46,000 people. At the end of 1994, this sector had almost been wiped out.

Second, Haiti has one of the most difficult erosion problems in the world. When the population grows more and more, people have to make a living on a given land area. The consequence of this is that the peasants tend to switch from products which require few working hours per hectare to products which require many. In practice, this means that the perennial coffee plants have been uprooted and food crops have been planted instead – on incredibly seep lands. The tropical downpours quickly erode these cultivations. At the same time, the demand for firewood increases. In Haiti, it is difficult to find any economically viable substitutes to charcoal. Hence, the rate of erosion is increased also by the increasing demand for charcoal, and this has probably never been higher than during the international boycotts 1991–94 when Haiti suffered an acute shortage of oil and gasoline. Through the erosion, the yields in agriculture fall, and in the longer run, the capacity of the peasants to make a living is reduced.

Third, to all this must be added that much of what the common man managed to assemble one way or another ended up in the pockets of the governing clique. Average income figures hence yield a picture which is too bright for the vast majority of Haitians.

Military rule also led to macroeconomic instability. GDP fell with one-third, and the rate of inflation increased more than fivefold between 1991 and 1994. The budget deficit increased from 1 percent of GDP to almost 5 percent. Tax revenues fell from 8 percent of GDP to 3 percent as both the level of activity and imports fell, and the tax administration was weakened. Simultaneously, expenditures increased from 8 to 9 percent. The deficit was financed through credits from the central bank and canceled foreign debt payments. In September 1994, the Haitian arrears on the foreign debt amounted to $126 million and those on the domestic debt to 11 million. At the same time, foreign trade had shrunk drastically. The value of exports decreased from $202 million in 1991 to 57 million in 1994, and imports were reduced from 449 million to 141 million. The deficit was financed mainly by humanitarian aid. At the end of 1994, Haiti's foreign debt amounted to 47 percent of GDP, and the debt service, that is, interest and amortization payments in relation to exports (of 1991) to 13 percent. The currency reserves had more or less been depleted already in 1992.

The return of Aristide

The Aristide who came back to Haiti in 1994, in the wake of international sanctions and in the end a regular invasion led by the United States, was not quite the man who had left the country in 1991. His rhetoric had been tuned down. Aristide now stressed peace, reconciliation, and security. His passion for equality and income redistribution remained, but his views of the means to be employed were partially different.

During the 3 years that Aristide had spent in the United States, he had had an opportunity to study the American tax structure and the public assistance programs. He realized that tax reforms, increased employment, humanitarian aid, and social welfare could contribute to the reduction of the gap between rich and poor.

He had also become convinced that the best way of achieving increased employment and reduced poverty went through the private sector, and he hence stressed free enterprise and good relations with the business community much more than in 1991. These relations would undergo a marked improvement.

Also Aristide's second period as a president began with a change of economic policy. The package which was presented to the donor community in Paris already before his return, in August 1994, stressed basic needs. Resources were primarily to be allocated to education, health care, food, agriculture, and to a reform of the judiciary and the army. The social expenditures were to be increased by 70 percent while military spending was to be cut back immediately, by 50 percent. Measures to create employment would receive priority. The extent of state participation in direct production was to be reduced. The public enterprises which had drained the government treasury during a number of years were to be reformed and privatized. The public administration was to be slimmed and future government efforts should primarily be directed toward the infrastructure.

The package also contained a traditional stabilization and structural reform program. Above all, government tax revenues were to increase to 8 percent of GDP (the 1991 level) though a combination of new taxes, an increase of the area of application of some already existing taxes and more efficient collection. The government subsidies on oil were to be abolished. Foreign trade was to be liberalized so as to stimulate export-led growth. As a first step, the tariff level was to be reduced by 50 percent on average, to 4 levels, ranging between 0 and 15 percent, with the final goal of abolishing all tariffs. The interest rate level, which had been negative in real terms during the military regime, would be left to the market and the expansion of the money supply (M2), which had amounted to some 30 percent per annum 1991–94, would be contained. For this program, Haiti obtained foreign loans of $900 million over a period of 5 years.

For the 1996–98 period, the targets of the reform program were an annual real GDP growth of 6 percent, a reduction of the rate of inflation to the international level, and the strengthening of the balance of payments to such an extent that Haiti could make do without special balance of payments support. During 1995, however, it was necessary to increase the budget deficit and the private consumption from the abnormally low level where it had been during 1991–94, as a consequence of the international embargo. Nevertheless, the Haitian economy began to display certain signs of increased stability already during 1995. Most of the operationally defined targets set up as part of Haiti's agreement with the IMF had been reached. The rate of inflation had come down to 29 percent in September, the abnormal commodity scarcity which had prevailed during the embargo had been removed, and the value of the Haitian currency in terms of dollars was stable. At the same time, exports were increasing. Some 80 assembly factories had reopened their doors around mid-1995 and had employed 9000 people.

When Haiti once more elected a president in December 1995, René Préval obtained an astounding majority of the votes – 88 percent – but the voter turnout was much lower than when Aristide was elected: a mere 28 percent. Twenty-five of the twenty-seven opposition parties had boycotted the elections. The election campaign had been short, and Préval was generally seen as the chosen candidate of Aristide.

Judicial reform

When Préval took office in February 1996, the political situation in Haiti was a great deal better than it had been for a long time. This, however, in no way means that the problems of the country have been solved.

One of the most urgent reform areas is the judiciary. As most other institutions, it decayed during the Duvalier period and the subsequent military rule. When Aristide returned in October 1994, it had more or less ceased to function. Human rights were mercilessly trampled down.

In 1993, the OAS and the UN surveyed the Haitian judiciary. The conclusions were awesome. The military and their allies terrorized judges, prosecutors, and lawyers. In October 1993, the Minister of Justice, Guy Malary, was murdered in broad daylight, and in February the following year, the chief prosecutor in Port-au-Prince was abducted in his home and was never more heard from. Most judges and lawyers were badly educated and lacked motivation. The courts lacked the most elementary equipment. Often even law books were lacking. Most Haitians avoided to have anything to do with the judicial system. Powerful circles in society could in practice behave any way they liked. The country lacked a professional police corps. The judicial procedures prescribed by the law were systematically neglected. Police stations and prisons did not keep any records whatsoever. Prison conditions were inhuman.

When Aristide returned, a series of reforms were inaugurated. The most important of these was the separation of the police from the army. The size of the army was decreased, first from around 7000 to 1500 and then, at the end of 1995, to zero. A separate police force under civilian control was set up. A new police academy was created and in August 1995 around 1200 police cadets had finished their education there. In February 1996, the figure had increased to 4000. The paramilitary groups which 1991–94 had terrorized the population were dissolved or at least forced underground. The office of *chef de section* was abolished. The education of judges and prosecutors was initiated; the salaries were increased for the judges at the lowest levels; and law texts were distributed to the courts. A renovation and humanization of the prisons was begun.

A tremendous lot, however, remains to be done. Many local courts still do not function, and the result is that people often take the law into their own hands. Arrest orders are often issued on loose grounds – not least rumors and popular discontent – and frequently by officers who do not have any right to arrest people. Those arrested have to wait longer that what is prescribed by the law (more than 48 hours) to be heard. May judges are still afraid of arresting former members of terror groups. The bases of the sentences are often dubious, and corruption continues to be present within the judiciary.

In addition, the new police corps is still weak. The education period has been short, and equipment like helmets and shields is lacking, which often leads to use of arms in riot situations.

Without a functioning court system, the police cannot work and then it is impossible to come to grips with street violence and political violence. This is important both in terms of human rights and for the future development of the Haitian economy.

The judiciary in addition must be able to guarantee that property rights are respected, that contracts are honored and that they are not interpreted in court so as to favor the part that pays best or in other illicit ways interfere with the work of the judges. Otherwise transaction costs will be so high in the economy that they will strangle the economic development which – in the best place – will take place in the future.

The economy

The economy is another key issue for Préval – a problem intimately related to the problem of preserving democracy. If Haiti continues that retrogression of the past 50 years, and above all if the drastic decline which took place 1991–94 is not reversed, social chaos may ensue, and it will be difficult to consolidate the democratic gains which were after all made in 1995 and 1996.

With a GDP per capita of $250–260, Haiti is among the 15 or 20 poorest countries in the world. President Aristide hoped that his country would 'move from misery to poverty with dignity'. The very near future, however, looks very gloomy. During 1995, foreign assistance amounted to the equivalent of 25–30 percent of GDP, and the economy grew at around 4 percent per annum. During 1996, however, a reduction of the assistance has taken place, not least from the United States, which reduced its contribution with 40 percent. This quite probably will imply that the rate of economic growth will once more become negative.

Also in the longer run, the future looks dark. The interaction between population growth and erosion inexorably depresses per capita income in the countryside. There is no simple way of stopping the process which in addition has all but killed traditional export production: coffee, sugar, cotton, and cocoa. This cumulative decline will in all probability continue. Military rule, in turn, almost killed the export industry, the most important source of foreign exchange. As President Préval expressed it in an interview in *Le Monde*: 'We are a country which no longer produces anything and which imports virtually everything.'

Haiti also faces enormous difficulties when it comes to creating an agricultural sector which is sustainable and which in addition can feed the population. The pressure on the land is already too heavy, and the population has nowhere to go. The emigration which has taken place from Haiti during the past decades has been unregulated, and the Haitians have as a rule not been able to gain legal entry to other countries. This means that if Haiti has any economic future, it is likely to be found in the industrial sector. Industry, however, has its own problems. Between the military coup in 1991 and the return of Aristide in 1994, many enterprises left Haiti, and whether they will ever return is doubtful. A good example is furnished by the baseball makers. In the mid-1980s, Haiti was the world's largest producer of baseballs. More than 6000 people were employed in the sector. In June 1995, maybe 300 were left. Most firms had closed down and/or moved – some to China – presumably for good.

The problems of the manufacturing sector are, however, not only 'political' but also – and perhaps in the first place – structural. The relative success of the assembly industries in the 1970s and 1980s built only on low wages. The raw materials for the baseballs came from the United States, and the market was found there as well. The only thing that was done in Haiti was the sowing of the balls. Even though the assembly industries may be revived, this does not necessarily lead to economic growth, since the links with the rest of the economy are few. The raw materials in their majority come from abroad, and it is actually in the labor market that you can trace the effects.

A more long-run problem is that the small industry will face difficulties in increasing the income level in a more durable fashion. Haiti lacks educated labor which makes it difficult to go into high-growth sectors, since these usually require a more advanced technology. The reasons behind the low educational level are to be found both on the supply and on the demand side. The Haitian predatory state never thought it essential that the citizens receive a good education and hence has not spent any resources on upgrading the school system. Education is an activity with marked economies of scale: the higher the educational level in a country, the easier it is to increase the volume of knowledge even more. And vice versa: the worse the educational situation, the more difficult it becomes to generate additional knowledge. This, in turn, leads to a low private rate of return on education in countries like Haiti. These countries are 'locked' into a 'low-level education trap', which they cannot escape from through a gradual increase of the level of education, since this does not pay.

Even though Haiti cannot find any way to improve the educational situation, it will be difficult to get investments in branches which require more specialized technology. In the international economy, countries specialize according to their comparative advantages, on such goods and services as they can produce relatively inexpensively. Industries with advanced technology requiring research and development hence tend to end up in the already rich regions of the globe. It is often a question of developing very specialized intermediate goods which can be used in the manufacturing of the final products. This is easiest in countries where a strong demand for diversified goods and services already exists and which in addition have previous experience of this type of production.

In Haiti, the situation is radically different. The country imports all the complicated products that it consumes, and the only industrial sector that exists is the simple assembly industry. During the foreseeable future, Haiti's comparative advantage will be found in the low wages. The international pattern of trade hence contributes to locking Haiti into a low-productivity trap where the only existing sectors are traditional agriculture, assembly production, and the mix of activities that generally characterizes the informal urban sector in the Third World.

Democratization

A third major problem is the continued democratization of Haitian society. Democracy is in no way a clear-cut notion – at least not in Haiti. The political tradition of the country is that the masses will rather take to the streets to make themselves heard than to let themselves be represented by elected representatives in parliament and in local bodies. The two elections held after the return of Aristide to Haiti did not imply any progress in that respect but left a lot to desire in terms of honesty.

For the democratization process to be successful continued international support and supervision will be necessary. The risk is, however, high that the support will be reduced quickly once you can see that the process has 'got going'. In the United States, President Clinton has had to avoid another Somalia at any cost, and he has hence seen to it that the American presence in Haiti has been quickly reduced. The United Nations, in turn, had planned that the supervision force should leave the country precisely at the critical moment when the change of president was to take place, a completely bizarre decision. The Security Council, however, decided that a force of 1200 soldiers and 300 police should remain, together with Canadian personnel outside the UN mandate.

A prolongation is necessary since in principle there is nothing to guarantee that the new police will not behave like the old army, the circumstances permitting. What it is all about, in the end, is to break with the bad tradition, and this requires supervision and education during a long period of time.

The democratization problem is, however, not only – and not primarily – an international problem. Haiti is a country which to a far too large extent lacks what Robert Putnam has termed social capital, that is, 'norms of reciprocity and networks of civic engagement'. Such norms and networks create confidence among the citizens and make it easier for them to engage in all kinds of transactions – economic, social, and political – with other people. They increase the costs of breaking agreements, and they facilitate the diffusion of information. Social capital probably displays increasing returns: the more social capital that exists already, the easier it becomes to increase this capital.

Savings associations, cooperative labor teams, and so on function on the local level in Haiti, but it has never been possible to achieve this type of cooperation on the national level. There, instead the unfortunate political tradition that developed during the nineteenth century has dominated the picture, and as soon as the grass roots have attempted to organize politically, this has led to confrontation with the traditional structures, centered on hierarchical domination and plunder, which have immediately mobilized violence to put them down.

By and large, in Haiti there are three different political interest groups: the former Duvalierists and the groups that cooperate with them, the neo-conservative, reformist block – the 'bourgeois' parties of Haiti – and the Lavalas of Aristide, which contains various social democrat and more radical groups. The cohabitation between these groups has often been anything but happy. The first group is not interested at all in democracy. The other two are, but the road to democratic government rather goes through a 'pact', like in South Africa, than through confrontation, election fraud, and election boycotts.

This is not simple. The 'bourgeois' groups see their position threatened by the Lavalas mass movement and demand a market economy which rests on safe property rights. Among some of them, there is considerable sympathy for the military junta that ousted Aristide. Nevertheless, for the sake of future democracy, it is important that Lavalas seeks a compromise with these groups.

Politics in Haiti has to a far too large extent been equal to personal politics and private interests, and this has been the main reason for the confrontations. The winners in the political game have always cleaned the table, a party has been a leader and his followers, and the leaders have seldom accepted democratic principles within their own parties. The parties have been mobilized only in times of elections and have then been thrown on the garbage heap.

Now the time has come to create a system which precludes the institutionalization of personal politics inside what the outside world innocently conceives of as democratic rule. Politics must build on broad consensus solutions which in turn contribute to making negotiations the accepted political work form. The system must facilitate a broad and orderly popular participation which makes it impossible to reintroduce the predatory state through the back door.

Note

Published in *Internationella Studier* (Swedish version), Vol. 28, 1996.

10
Problems of Policy Reform in the Haitian Economy

The traditional 'interventionist' view of economic policy builds on two implicit assumptions: that the government is willing to act for the benefit of the population and that policy implementation is costless.[1] Both of these assumptions, however, may be violated in practice. All real economies, not least those of the Third World, know full well that policy intervention is not costless. First of all, information is costly, which means that, however well-intentioned, policy measures may be mistaken simply because the factual and analytical base on which they rest is erroneous. Second, all implementation requires a bureaucracy. The level of competence of this bureaucracy may not necessarily match the complexity of the tasks it faces, and the bureaucracy may itself have implicit goals which differ radically from the official goals and, therefore, bias the outcome of the policy. Third, economic policy is largely a question of coordination, and coordination entails costs. Fourth, all policy measures alter the existing distribution of income and thereby set in motion countervailing forces fomented by the losers to neutralize the effects of redistribution.[2]

The list does not end here, but for the purpose of this study, it should suffice. Haiti is not exempt from any of the problems enumerated above, but from a historical perspective, they appear only as minor nuisances, as defects that in principle can be corrected. The main defect of Haitian economic policy has rather been of the first kind. With few exceptions, Haiti has been plagued by governments that have had no interest whatsoever in promoting economic efficiency, growth, and redistribution in favor of the poor. To put it simply, the Haitian state has been a predatory one, and this has created a logic which differs dramatically from that of the benevolent social guardian of the economics textbooks.

In this chapter, we attempt to follow the logic of the predatory state as it has operated in Haiti for more than a century and a half. Thereafter, we point to some of its main consequences, notably the separation of the majority of the population from the decision-making bodies and the macroeconomic morass bequeathed by the government of Jean-Claude Duvalier in 1986. Finally, we provide a brief account of what has taken place since that date, underscoring various reform efforts and setbacks, and discuss the prospects for future economic reform.

A model of the predatory state

The Haitian rulers of the past focused most of their efforts on obtaining private incomes through control of the government machinery. Essentially, they may be pictured as possessing a utility function with two arguments: one is income and the other is the probability of remaining in power.[3] In order to achieve these two objectives, they had to make two types of decisions: how many accomplices to cut in on a given deal and how to go about securing their prey, either overtly or covertly.

Formally, the ruler then maximizes a utility function

$$U = U(Y, P), \tag{1}$$

where Y is ruler income and P the probability of the ruler remaining in power. Utility is increasing in both arguments, but at a decreasing rate.

Income, in turn, is given by the difference between revenues (R), 'taxes collected', and the costs (C) for obtaining these revenues (e.g., collection costs):

$$Y = R - C. \tag{2}$$

Revenues and costs are both functions of the size of the ruling clique (M) and the degree of obfuscation (O), that is, the degree to which the true purpose (income extraction) of a policy is hidden from the population:

$$R = R(M, O), \tag{3}$$

$$C = C(M, O). \tag{4}$$

'Obfuscation' in the present context simply means that different methods may be employed to extract a given income, some of which are more visible or transparent, while others are more opaque. (For example, direct confiscation of assets is highly visible, while taxes and tariffs that serve only to enrich the ruler may be defended, for example, as being 'for the good of the national economy'.) It is assumed that both increasing clique size and increasing the degree of obfuscation are subject to decreasing returns and that costs increase at an increasing rate in both arguments. Enlarging the ruling clique makes it possible to extract more from the citizens, but each new member adds less than this immediate predecessor to the extraction capacity, and members can only be recruited at an increasing cost. Increasing the degree of obfuscation makes it easier to fool the citizens, but at a decreasing rate, and the costs of finding new means of deceiving the public are increasing.

This, then maximizes ruler income when marginal revenue (with respect to clique size and obfuscation, respectively) equals marginal cost. In other words, we have (*ceteris paribus*) revenue and cost functions of the traditional type shown in Figure 1, where clique size or degree of obfuscation is measure along the horizontal axis.

Subtracting costs from revenues yields a ruler income curve which has the shape of an inverted *U*, that is, income increases with clique size and obfuscation, but only up to a certain point. Thereafter, it decreases again.

A similar argument may be constructed when it comes to the probability of the ruler remaining in power. Small polity size (or a low degree of obfuscation) makes for a high probability of being removed by outside forces, but as the values of these independent variables increase, so does security, at a decreasing rate. As clique size and obfuscation increase, however, so does the probability of the ruler being ousted by his own people, through a palace coup. Large cliques split more easily, and factions are formed which may want to depose the ruler, and presumably this risk increases at an increasing rate. Also, as the degree of obfuscation increases, the insiders may interpret this as a sign that the ruler is extracting more and will hence feel it increasingly tempting to dispose of him and take over themselves. Again, we obtain an

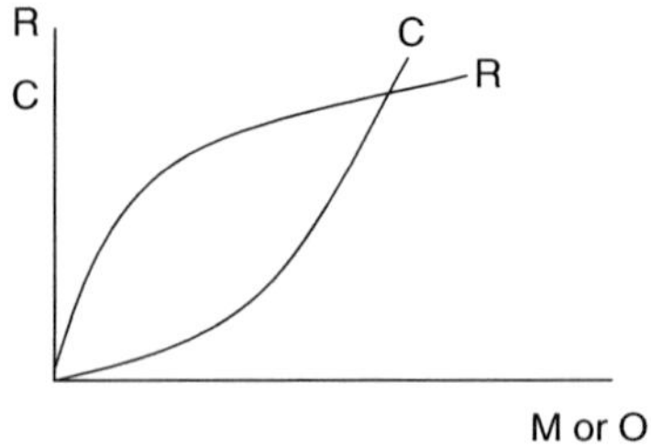

Figure 1 Ruler revenue and cost functions

inverted *U* for the probability of remaining in office as a function of either clique size or obfuscation, with a maximum where the marginal risks of outside revolution and inside coups are equal.

If the ruler had had only one argument in his utility function, finding the optimal levels of income or security would have been easy. Where there are two arguments, the income curve and the security curve will generally not peak at the same clique size or obfuscation degree. There will normally be a trade-off at the margin, where the ruler can obtain more income only at the expense of less security or vice versa. It is easy to show that the optimum for the ruler is obtained where

$$\frac{P_M}{P_O} = \frac{(R_M - C_M)}{(R_O - C_O)}. \tag{5}$$

The ratio of 'marginal securities' must equal the ratio of marginal incomes.

It is impossible to state generally whether the income curve peaks at a lower clique size or obfuscation degree than the security curve. However, in the case of Haiti, it is fairly certain that where clique size was concerned, the income curve peaked first, that is, rulers going primarily after income ran a high risk of being removed from office by outside forces. This was the common pattern during the nineteenth century, as I have analyzed elsewhere.[4]

What is important is the logic itself: Haitian rulers have been concerned with milking the population and with remaining in office. In doing so, they have had to choose the number of persons with whom they were prepared to share the spoils and how openly to pursue their plunder. This logic also has a corollary: Politics in Haiti has led to a negative selection of politicians (and other groups taking part in the political game – notably the military) for a very long time. As we know it, Haitian politics and government have been a far cry from the notion of the benevolent social guardian. This, of course, has had serious implications for all levels of Haitian society, some of which are explored below.

The separation of the governors from the governed

Where there is a predator, there must also be a prey, and the prey in the Haitian case has been the majority of the population, notably the peasants, for whom *leta* has always been synonymous with extraction, either in the form of labor or in the form of taxation. This dates back to the beginning of Haitian independence when the early rulers put the ex-slaves back to work on the plantations under conditions reminiscent of slavery and under military supervision, among other things to ensure a work-free income for the emerging elite.[5] This system broke down after 1809, when Alexandre Pétion began to redistribute the land. A peasantry came into being during the course of the nineteenth century and, simultaneously, direct exploitation of labor was replaced by a system of exploitation of the many by the few which built on taxation. Essentially, this is the system which persists to the present day.

The Haitian masses responded to exploitation by minimizing contacts with the exploiters, by creating what was essentially a 'parallel' society to the centralized one which the rulers attempted to construct, by pursuing an exit option, if we are to use the terminology coined by Albert Hirschman.[6] Peasant society centered on the individual, it was basically egalitarian, and it built on the principle of reciprocity. According to Gérard Barthélemy, it rested on autoregulative devices which essentially served to preserve the parallel society, on the one hand by harmonizing the behavior of the individuals constituting it and on the other by blocking the rise of differences between the individuals so as to prevent hierarchical structures from arising.[7]

The most important autoregulative institution has always been the family and the socialization of the individual through family education. Cooperative work structures – *koumbit* – are employed instead of work for a cash wage, since the latter is not compatible with reciprocity in that it places the worker in a 'lower' category. The Catholic religion contributes to the identification of the individual with the collective, while the voodoo rites performed in private allow for individualism through the worship of a multiplicity of *lwa*. Sorcery is employed as a defense against aggression by a society which otherwise lacks defense mechanisms. An exceedingly complicated land tenure system, characterized by the absence of written titles, in which the individual is at once owner, sharecropper, and tenant, simultaneously leasing land to someone else, serves to make purchases by outsiders difficult.

Through these autoregulative mechanisms, an equilibrium is created in peasant society, one which rests on shared poverty and a common definition of needs which serve as a bulwark against the attempts of the outside society to create increased demand and hence open for the production of a surplus which may be appropriated by the rulers of this society. Accumulation of riches is permitted over a lifetime, but the riches – normally land – are thereafter redistributed in connection with funeral expenses. Contacts with the outside society cannot be avoided, since this society constantly makes demands on the peasants, but penetration is made difficult. Multiple names may be used to create confusion, and the real center of authority is hidden. When the outside structures crumble, the peasants quickly step in and take over, as is the case when a regime falls and land that has been concentrated in the hands of the decaying clique is simply taken over and redistributed by the peasants, or when the latter squat on the land of absentee landowners. Ultimately, when dissuasion and persuasion fail to fend off the outsiders, violence may be resorted to.

On the other hand, the peasants also need the outside society. It is next to impossible for young peasants to accumulate the money they need to have access to land without migrating abroad, at least temporarily, for example, to the Dominican Republic, to cut cane.[8] Migration is also necessary as a safety valve, to get rid of those who, for some reason, do not conform to the rules established by peasant society.

Peasant society has always come under attack from outside forces, and, inevitably, these attacks have been more aggressive during the past few decades than before, especially after the rise of François Duvalier to the presidency and his construction of a new power structure, resting, among other things, on the rural *chefs de section* and the voodoo priests and priestesses.[9] Also, the behavior of peasant society has tended to converge with that of outside society over the course of the last half-century. Peasant society has gradually opened itself towards the exterior, to a large extent being forced to do so, because of growing poverty. The desire for education, as a means of escaping the circle of poverty, has increased, and the peasants look unfavourably upon physical isolation as a result of bad communications. Migration inside and outside Haiti is also responsible for bringing change.

At the same time, the outside has moved closer to peasant society with the advancement of *noirs* beginning with the presidency of Dumarsais Estimé (1946–50) and thereafter with the two Duvaliers (1957–86), notably François. Voodoo, whose followers were persecuted, only a few decades ago, has moved out into the open. *Kreyòl* has gained ground in relation to French, not least as a written language and a means of instruction. Thus, the two Haitian societies are gradually merging, under the pressure of poverty, migration, and social change. Today, around one-fourth of the total population lives in the capital. Still, the gap between governed and governors persists, as the plunder continues. We will later return to what this means for the design of development policy.

The influence on economic policy

This is not the place to go into the history of the predatory state in Haiti. That story is available both in other chapters of this book and elsewhere.[10] Instead, we will examine the final phase of the 'heyday' of kleptocracy: the Baby Doc years, so as to gather an idea of how economic policy was affected by predation.[11]

Baby Doc inherited a complete machinery for siphoning off funds from the treasury: unbudgeted accounts – not least via the Régie du Tabac et des Allumettes, the state tobacco monopoly which collected taxes not only on tobacco and matches but also on a large number of other consumer goods.[12] These funds never showed up in the budget, but their employment (the *tonton macoutes* and the presidential family) was subject to a high degree of obfuscation, until the president finally had to give in to IMF demands in 1982, when Haiti was in deep balance of payments trouble, and centralize tax collection and close most of the unbudgeted special accounts. Jean-Claude also continued the organized racket of collecting funds from the Haitian sugar cane workers in the Dominican Republic. Thirdly, aid money was diverted, at an increasing risk, however, as the attitude of the international community against Haiti hardened.

Clearly, regressive redistributional maneuvers such as these resulted in an inefficient allocation of resources in society, with funds being spent on the consumption of the ruling clique – some conspicuous, like $3–5 million on the wedding of the president, others more discrete – rather than on investment in physical or human capital that could have served to enhance the production capacity of the economy. In addition, the redistribution itself used up resources, in the form of payments to an otherwise useless bureaucracy and repression apparatus, which could have been used on the production of goods and services demanded by the citizens. By the same token, economic growth was held back, with per capita income falling steadily over time.

Jean-Claude Duvalier and his clique were never content with simply resorting to the devices that François Duvalier had relied upon, but the predatory state toward the end of the 1970s entered a 'fine tuning' or 'modernization' phase during which, as it seems, the degree of obfuscation increased.[13] Private business was conducted by the presidential family, with the aid of the state machinery, mainly through Baby Doc's father-in-law, Ernest Bennett, and his various companies. Bennett rapidly made it to the top in the notoriously difficult, oligopolistic, coffee export market – from a very modest initial market share. He was also involved in large-scale smuggling of a number of commodities, such as sugar, flour, rice, and cotton textiles, but, even more importantly, drugs from Colombia to the United States.

Another common method was to operate via the network of government-owned enterprises which held monopoly positions in the domestic market. Five such enterprises were either established or purchased, beginning in 1979: soybean oil, wheat flour, sugar (two mills), and cement. These were all hopelessly inefficient from an economic standpoint, their only *raison d'être* being to generate income for the *Duvaliéristes*. Overall, the Duvaliers had almost unlimited access to government funds via checks drawn on ministries, government agencies, and state enterprises for any amount desired.

This, in turn, generated huge deficits in the government budget – no less than 13 percent of GDP in 1980–81 – and these deficits had to be financed either by credits from the banking system to the public sector, with concomitant crowding out of private investment, or by an expansion of the money supply via the government printing press. As a consequence, domestic demand was boosted, imports increased, and foreign currency flowed out of the country. Imports had to be cut, capital flight ensued, the gourde (which by law was pegged to the dollar) became overvalued, and a black exchange market was established where the dollar sold at a premium. Finally, the IMF had to be called in, some token reforms were undertaken and 'fiscal discipline' was imposed through the slashing of development expenditures. When Baby Doc was finally thrown out of office in 1986, the Haitian economy was in severe macroeconomic disarray – simply as a result of unhampered plunder.[14]

The long-run trend had also been negative. If we use 1980 as the endpoint, it becomes evident that the Haitian economy had been undergoing what amounted to at least 50 years of stagnation and decline. During this entire period, GDP per capita remained stagnant at best and declined at worst. For the next 5 years, GDP decreased steadily, by 0.9 percent yearly, and GNP took an even deeper plunge: 2.7 percent each year. The agricultural sector was losing the race against population growth. In 1986, food production per capita was 13 percent below its 1979 value and total agricultural output per capita was 14 percent lower.[15] This was not only a result of increased population pressure on the land but also of a price and tax policy which punished export production and encouraged food crop production, that is, which served to speed up the process through which the balance between the former and the latter was altered in favor of the ecologically detrimental production of food crops.[16]

In the import-competing part of the manufacturing sector, a protectionist policy had been pursued without any trace of success from 1949 to 1986, one which simply fostered monopoly, high costs, inefficiency, and high prices which the consumers had to pay, in a market which was far too small to allow for any economies of scale. The government monopolies were pure rackets which had nothing whatsoever to do with sound economic principles.[17]

The second component of manufacturing – the light assembly export industry – on the other hand, had witnessed spectacular growth from the mid-1960s to the mid-1980s, increasing its share of the total value of exports from 4 percent in 1966 to almost two-thirds in 1984 and employing some 30,000 people at the latter date – in spite of the anti-export bias which resulted from the protection of the import-competing segment.[18]

Tourism, in turn, had been experiencing problems already during the 1970s as a result of the impact of the recession on the US economy. The early 1980s were even worse. The human rights situation, coupled with the AIDS issue, the political unrest, and the world recession, made receipts from tourism and other travel drop to such a degree that in 1984 they were no higher than they had been in 1972. Two years later, when the Minister of Public Health officially declared that 10 percent of all Haitians might be infected with the AIDS virus, tourists were scared away once again.[19]

The three reform attempts

The Conseil National de Gouvernement (CNG), which took over the helm after the fall of Baby Doc in 1986, was thus faced with a double dilemma. In the first place, it had to stabilize the economy in the short run. Second, it had to face the even trickier issue of how to set a notoriously stagnant economy on a growth path. To make matters even more difficult for the new government, the two issues were interrelated. To set the economy on a growth path without simultaneously stabilizing the economy was simply not possible, but stabilization of the balance of payments required improved export performance – that is, growth. Under the leadership of the Minister of Finance, Leslie Delatour, a combined stabilization and structural adjustment program was launched. Foreign trade was liberalized. Export taxes on agricultural goods were removed and imports were liberalized, substituting tariffs for quantitative restrictions at more uniform rates than before, so as to remove the anti-export bias and increase efficiency in the import-competing sector.[20]

At the same time, the government budget deficit problem was tackled. Some of the worst black holes in the economy – the inefficient public enterprises – were either closed down or lost their monopoly privileges. Government payrolls were purged of non-existent zombie workers and the notorious *tonton macoutes* were dissolved. Expenditures were redirected toward 'development-oriented' sectors: agriculture, public works, education, and health.

The tax system was reformed as well. Income taxes were simplified, and the top bracket rate was reduced, in the hope of decreasing tax evasion. Specific taxes with high collection costs were abolished. An effort to increase the efficiency of collection increased. Altogether, these measures reduced the fiscal deficit from 7 to 5 percent of GDP from 1984–85 to 1985–86 and subsequently to less than 1 percent of GDP. This in turn made it possible to decrease the rate of increase of the money supply and to curb the rate of inflation. Even the price level began to fall.[21]

The international donor community responded favorably. An inflow of funds was generated, which, in spite of low coffee prices and depressed earnings from tourism, producing a current account deficit, led to an improved reserve position in 1985–86 and 1986–87. Thus, the reform package appears to have worked relatively well from a stabilization viewpoint, in an economy which had been whacked completely out of joint by the unhampered plunder that took place in the early 1980s.

The policy reforms were not allowed to run their course without disturbances, however. Presidential elections had been scheduled for 1987, and already by mid-year, political unrest began to spread. The labor market was plagued by strikes and work stoppages, the investment climate deteriorated, and the mock 1988 elections and the subsequent military coups that brought first Namphy and then Avril into power did little to restore confidence.

After the interruption of the elections that should have been held at the end of November 1987, the confidence of the international donor community was shaken as well. The IMF, the World Bank, the United States, and other leading contributors suspended most of their aid to the government. The result was an immediate budgetary crisis which was further compounded by problems of collecting revenue as the political situation grew increasingly unstable. Smuggling increased, companies declared lower profits, and the electricity company had problems both collecting bills and preventing illegal tapping of lines.

The situation called for emergency measures: cutting back government expenditures, introducing new taxes, and making an effort to make collection more efficient. Domestic borrowing had to be resorted to, which in turn stimulated monetary expansion and caused balance of payments problems. The build-up of international reserves was halted early in 1989 when foreign exchange holdings were down to a single week's imports. The arrears on the foreign debt accumulated, and the black market premium on the dollar increased to 40 percent. The rate of inflation jumped to 12 percent in 1988–89, from a negative figure 2 years before.[22]

In the meantime, GDP per capita continued to fall, with an estimated 2 percent every year on average during the 1980s.[23] In 1989, an estimated 61 percent of the population earned less than $100 annually.[24] This situation would have been impossible were it not for the fact that between 700,000 and 1,500,000 Haitians living outside the country in 1990[25] contributed by sending money back home.

In December 1990, Jean-Bertrand Aristide was elected president with a landslide majority of two-thirds in elections that, surprisingly, could be held without interference. The Aristide government assumed its functions in February 1991. Again a stabilization program was launched. Negotiations for a stand-by loan were initiated with the IMF, and in July 1991, the Paris Club agreed to a $50 million loan to finance public sector investment during the coming 18 months. An orthodox policy package was presented which included balancing the government budget, controlling the volume of domestic credit, increasing the efficiency of tax collection and a restrictive monetary policy.[26]

Aristide also continued the 1986 policy of trimming the corrupt public administration:

> ... in his first few months in office, over 2,000 federal jobs were eliminated. He eliminated the Bureau of Tourism and made deep cuts into such dubious endeavors as the 'Ministry of Information', which was trimmed by almost 50 percent. In another celebrated instance when state bookkeepers could not account for over one million dollars in ostensibly *collected* taxes, Aristide himself showed up unannounced in the office and politely but firmly asked to see the books. Throughout the country, various ministries and offices were 'closed for restructuring'.[27]

What is more, the *chefs de section* – the rural 'sheriffs' who in a totally arbitrary way had represented the 'law' in rural Haiti – were abolished. The anti-corruption drive also included an effort to reduce smuggling, not least of drugs, which had been the most important unofficial source of income for the army. The effort was at least partly successful and the

US Drug Enforcement Agency could report that the amount of cocaine going through Haiti on its way from Colombia to the United States had decreased in 1991.[28]

Once again stabilization indices showed progress. The Direction Générale des Impôts could report receipts that were one-third above the 1990 level, and customs receipts showed an even better performance: 50 percent.[29] The government budget deficit was reduced to its lowest level in 5 years: 0.1 percent of GDP.[30] The state enterprises (mainly the flour mill, the cement factory, and the national Port Authority), all of which had been sources of financial abuse and corruption, were generating surpluses instead of deficits since May 1991. The black market premium on the dollar began to shrink, and the rate of inflation was brought down from 20 percent in December 1990 to 12 percent in September 1991.[31] The international reserve position was improved in spite of a deficit on the external trade and service accounts. The external debt was reduced, as a result of forgiveness from France and United States, to a level corresponding to 35 percent of GDP.[32]

Again, there was some modest hope for stabilization and, perhaps, in the longer term, for measures that would allow Haiti to break out of this long-run stagnation and retrogression. This hope, however, was dashed once more by political events. On October 1, 1991, President Aristide was forced by the military to leave the country. Joseph Nérette, Supreme Court judge, was sworn in as provisional president – a mere façade for General Raoul Cédras.

At the root of the coup was the fear of the military that Aristide would succeed in separating the police from the military, since that would also have meant loss of a number of opportunities for private enrichment for the armed forces.[33] Most important, the military would lose control over smuggling activities – the most lucrative source of income for the armed forces.

Aristide had to be forced out. The predatory state was back in power. Plunder was once again the order of the day. An embargo was imposed on Haiti by the OAS, but this embargo remained largely ineffective for a long time. The Dominican border was never effectively sealed, so smuggling to a large extent compensated for legal trade. The embargo was 'at best, sieve-like', reported the *Financial Times* at the end of 1992.[34] In particular, it did not seem to affect the incomes of the military. Cocaine traffic once again got into full swing. Those hurt were the general population. The price of gasoline skyrocketed, making the transportation of both people and goods difficult. The peasants had problems getting their produce into the cities and obtaining their regular supply of urban consumer goods. The rate of erosion accelerated through increased tree-felling. Charcoal had never been a more economical substitute for oil in the history of Haiti. The legal business community suffered as well.[35] In 1992, Haiti's GDP per capita fell by close to 15 percent.[36]

The sanctions against Haiti were tightened in June 1993, this time by the United Nations. Oil and arms were to stay out of the country, and the American assets of the coup makers would be frozen.[37] Immediately thereafter, the Governors Island Accord between Aristide and the Haitian military provided a first step toward the return of the legal president. In August, a transitional government, nominated by Aristide, was in place, and at the beginning of September, the sanctions were lifted.

After the subsequent political turmoil, with increasing violence as the main ingredient, the transitional prime minister stepped down in December. Sanctions were again tightened in May 1994. This time, they included all trade except purely humanitarian imports. The economy took a further downturn. Finally, in September, President Clinton had had enough of the Haitian military. The United States stepped in with troops for the second time in the history of Haiti. Aristide could finally come back, with a year and a few months to go before he had to step down in February 1996.

For the third time, the reform process in Haiti is back to square one, with the economy at a lower level than ever. GDP per capita is estimated to have fallen by 5.7 percent yearly in real terms between 1991 and 1994 to a probable level of US$260 or less the latter year.[38] A structural adjustment program has been launched which includes privatization of a number of government enterprises, abolition of tariffs, and a drastic reduction of the public payroll.

The structural adjustment program has already been subject to strong criticism from left-wing sources. Aristide is seen a 'selling out' to big business. These attacks, however, reveal a total lack of understanding of Haiti's past and a purely mechanical analysis of the present. Haiti's problem has always been that the country has had *too much of the wrong kind of state*, not too little of the right kind. Hopefully, the present government can begin to change this, but change takes time.

Also, as the Haitian case clearly demonstrates, changes are easily reversed. Democracy is far from safe in Haiti. The predatory state could easily make yet another comeback. Reducing the domain of the state, however, makes predation more difficult and hence reduces the attraction of political power for those who are after a quick profit: therein lies the real importance of the reduction of the size of the state in Haiti.

Conclusions

I began this chapter by pointing to two assumptions which tend to be implicit in economic policy making. One of these was of special relevance in the case of Haiti: the willingness of the government to intervene in order to improve the lot of the population. As the subsequent discussion revealed, this assumption has hardly ever been fulfilled in practice. The state in Haiti has been a predatory one, and this has distorted economic policy completely.

The best example of how the logic of the predatory state has carried the day is furnished by the last few years of the rule of Jean-Claude Duvalier. Unhampered plunder brought the economy into complete disarray and called for both macroeconomic stabilization and structural adjustment when Duvalier fell in February 1986.

After the fall of Baby Doc, three efforts were made to reform economic policy. The first was carried out in 1986–87, by the CNG government. That effort was interrupted by the political turmoil in connection with the farcical presidential elections at the end of 1987 and the beginning of 1988. The second attempt, carried out by Aristide's government in 1991, was interrupted by the military coup which forced Aristide to leave the country in October that same year. The third effort has just begun.

Clearly, the main problem of economic policy reform in Haiti has not been the contents of the reforms, even if these have been harshly criticized in some circles. Both the CNG package and the 1991 Aristide measures brought about positive changes. Politics, or rather, politicking, however, has played havoc with these reforms. A reform is introduced, it runs for a year or two at most, and then it is interrupted. The new Aristide government was working against the clock. Aristide had to step down in February 1996. Before that Haiti had to go through presidential elections. It is very difficult to know what this event will mean for the economic reform process. A completely perverted political process has strangled reform for almost 200 years in Haiti. Will that process come to an end now? I wish I had the answer.

Notes

Published in *Forum Empresarial*, Vol. 1, 1996, published by Centro de Investigaciones e Iniciativas Académicas, Facultad de Administración de Empresas, Universidad de Puerto Rico. Reprinted by permission.

1. Krueger (1993), p. 53.
2. Blomqvist and Lundahl (1992), pp. 237–38.

3. Lundahl (1985b), Danielson and Lundahl (1994).
4. See Lundahl (1985b), Lundahl and Vedovato (1989).
5. See Lundahl (1979), Chapter 6; Lundahl (1985a); and Lundahl (1984a).
6. Hirschman (1970).
7. Barthélemy (1989).
8. See Lundahl and Vargas (1983).
9. See Lundahl (1984b).
10. Lundahl (1985b).
11. Lundahl (1992), Danielson and Lundahl (1994).
12. Lundahl (1984b).
13. Maingot (1986–87), p. 83.
14. Lundahl (1992).
15. Ibid.
16. See Lundahl (1979), Chapter 5 and Bourdet and Lundahl (1991).
17. Lundahl (1992).
18. Ibid., p. 16.
19. Ibid., pp. 18–19.
20. Ibid., pp. 22–24.
21. Ibid., p. 23.
22. Ibid., p. 24.
23. Inter-American Development Bank (1995), p. 3.
24. PNUD, Unité de Coordination et de Suivi de l'Environnement (ECMU) (n.d.), p. 2.
25. Farmer (1994), p. 119.
26. Clermont (1993), p. 11.
27. Farmer (1994), p. 168.
28. Ibid., p. 169.
29. République d'Haïti (1994), p. 9.
30. Ibid., pp. 35, 10.
31. Ibid., p. 11.
32. Ibid., p. 47.
33. Laguerre (1993), Chapter 7.
34. Quoted by Chomsky (1994), p. 36.
35. Farmer (1994), pp. 193–94, 201–02.
36. International Monetary Fund (1995), p. 19.
37. Farmer (1994), p. 210.
38. International Monetary Fund (1995), p. 2; Inter-American Development Bank (1995), p. 3.

References

Barthélemy, Gérard (1989), *Le pays en dehors*. Port-au-Prince: Éditions Henri Deschamps.

Blomqvist, Hans C. and Lundahl, Mats (1992), *Ekonomisk utveckling: En introduktion till u-ländernas ekonomiska problem*. Stockholm: SNS Förlag.

Bourdet, Yves and Lundahl, Mats (1991), 'Patterns and Prospects of Haitian Primary Exports', *Latin American Issues*, No. 9, A Monograph Series on Contemporary Latin American and Caribbean Affairs, Allegheny College, Meadville, PA and University of Akron, OH.

Chomsky, Noam (1994), 'Introduction, to Paul Farmer', *The Uses of Haiti*. Monroe, ME: Common Courage Press.

Clermont, Charles (1993), 'Haití: Situación económica en la víspera de una estabilización política', *Cuadernos de la Coyuntura Caribeña*, No. 1, 7–19.

Danielson, Anders and Lundahl, Mats (1994), 'Endogenous Policy Formation and the Principle of Optimal Obfuscation: Theory and Some Evidence from Haiti and Jamaica', *Comparative Economic Studies*, Vol. 36, 51–78.

Farmer, Paul (1994), *The Uses of Haiti*. Monroe, ME: Common Courage Press.

Hirschman, Albert O. (1970), *Exit, Voice, and Loyalty: Responses to Decline in Firms, Organizations, and States*. Cambridge, MA and London: Harvard University Press.

Inter-American Development Bank (1995), *Emergency Economic Recovery Program, Haiti*. Report of the Joint Mission (November 7–20, 1994). January 3. Washington, DC.

International Monetary Fund (1995), *Haiti – Recent Economic Developments*. SM/95/43. March 1. Washington, DC.

Krueger, Anne O. (1993), *Political Economy of Policy Reform in Developing Countries*. Cambridge, MA and London: MIT Press.

Laguerre, Michel S. (1983), *The Military and Society in Haiti*. Houndmills, Basingstoke and London: Macmillan.

Lundahl, Mats (1979), *Peasants and Poverty: A Study of Haiti*. London: Croom Helm.

Lundahl, Mats (1984a), 'Defense and Distribution: Agricultural Policy in Haiti during the Reign of Jean-Jacques Dessalines, 1804–1806', *Scandinavian Economic History Review*, Vol. 37, 77–103.

Lundahl, Mats (1984b), 'Papa Doc: Innovator in the Predatory State', *Scandia*, Vol. 50, 39–78.

Lundahl, Mats (1985a), 'Toussaint L'Ouverture and the War Economy of Saint-Domingue, 1796–1802', *Slavery and Abolition*, Vol. 6, 122–38.

Lundahl, Mats (1985b), 'Government and Inefficiency in the Haitian Economy: The Nineteenth Century Legacy', in: Michael B. Connolly and John McDermott (eds), *The Economics of the Caribbean Basin*. New York: Praeger.

Lundahl, Mats (1992), 'The Haitian Economy Facing the 1990s', *Canadian Journal of Latin American and Caribbean Studies*, Vol. 17, 5–32.

Lundahl, Mats and Vargas, Rosemary (1983), 'Inmigración haitiana hacia la República Dominicana', *Eme Eme, Estudios Dominicanos*, Vol. 12, 3–51.

Lundahl, Mats and Vedovato, Claudio (1989), 'The State and Economic Development in Haiti and the Dominican Republic', *Scandinavian Economic History Review*, Vol. 37, 39–59.

Maingot, Anthony P. (1986–87), 'Haiti: Problems of a Transition to Democracy in an Authoritarian Soft State', *Journal of Interamerican Studies and World Affairs*, Vol. 28, 75–102.

PNUD, Unité de Coordination et de Suivi de l'Environnement (LECMU) (n.d.), *Haïti 1994. Indicateurs environnementaux de base, Étude préliminaire*. Port-au Prince: PNUD.

République d'Haïti, Cabinet Particulier du Président de la République (1994), *Témoignages sur les performances économiques du gouvernement Aristide/Préval*. June. Port-au-Prince.

11
Sustained Growth in Haiti: Pipe-Dream or Realistic Possibility?

For several decades, the Haitian economy has been one of the most fragile in the Caribbean region. Essentially, this is due to the insufficient natural resource base of the country, with the slowly but steadily increasing population pressing on a shrinking agricultural land area. Employment opportunities have been few outside of agriculture, and the inevitable result has been that per capita income has declined over time for at least half a century, probably more.

We will begin by sketching the fundamental mechanism behind the declining standard of living in rural areas. The second section explores the main present safety value: migration – out of the country and into urban areas. We then consider some agrarian reform efforts and non-traditional crops that could contribute to ameliorating the situation in the countryside.

The chapter thereafter discusses the reasons behind the failure of import substitution in manufacturing, in contrast to the success of the export-oriented assembly industries until the devastating blow dealt by the international sanctions against Haiti in 1991–94, in the wake of the coup against President Jean-Bertrand Aristide. This is followed by an analysis of the industrial recovery that began after the end of the sanctions, the competitiveness in the short- and medium-run of the most important branches, and some ingredients in a possible industrial strategy. Following the discussion of manufacturing, we will turn to a sector that is usually neglected in analyses of the Haitian economy – handicrafts – and examine its main present shortcomings and needs. Handicrafts are closely related to tourism – a sector that needs to be developed more than at present.

Most of the Haitian economy is informal, that is, the economic actors are operating without much contact with the authorities. The special problems that this leads to are discussed next. Finally, two key inputs in the development process that have hitherto been lacking and which play an important role in most sectors, education and infrastructure, are considered. The concluding section provides an overall evaluation of the possibility of increased growth in Haiti in the short- and medium-term.

Population growth, erosion, and poverty

Between 65 and 70 percent of the Haitian population of some 7.2 million people live in rural areas.[1] All of these people, one way or another, are dependent on agriculture for their living, although, as a result of the increasing weakness of this sector, non-agricultural pursuits over time have come to match, and possibly even overshadow, agricultural production as a generator of income in rural households.[2]

The rate of population growth in Haiti, gross of emigration, is estimated to be around 2.5 percent per annum.[3] Unless the new entrants in the labor force emigrate or are accommodated in other sectors, the responsibility for employing them will fall on agriculture. Room must be made for them on the land, but, given the topography of Haiti, this is no trivial problem.[4] Between 20 and 30 percent of the cultivated land is completely unsuited to agriculture, and no less than 60 percent has a slope exceeding 20 percent.[5] The interaction of population growth and soil erosion under these circumstances sparks a cumulative process that increases rural poverty every year.[6]

In Haiti, two types of crops are cultivated: land-intensive and labor-intensive. Traditionally, the most important among the former has been the main cash crop, coffee, while the latter category consists of food crops of different types, peas and beans, root crops, and maize. From the point of view of environmental conservation, coffee has the great advantage of being a perennial plant, with roots that bind the soil on the mountainsides and with a canopy that protects the ground from the direct impact of the heavy tropical rains. The cultivation of food crops, in turn, has a completely different impact. Once the population grows in a given area, and given relative commodity prices (between the two types of crops), the crop mix will change. The man–land ratio in agriculture increases, and since the land area does not grow as well, it becomes impossible to maintain the original composition of output.[7] The Haitian peasants shift out of coffee production and plant more food crops instead. The uprooting of the coffee trees and the substitution of food crops increases the exposure of the soil to rain and wind and hence increases the possibility of erosion.

Erosion is fueled in a second way as well. The vast majority of the Haitians are completely dependent on charcoal and wood for energy, and this means that trees must be cut down in a country where extremely little forest remains.[8] Charcoal and firewood have been without competitors in terms of price not only since the oil shocks in the 1970s but long before that. For practical purposes, the price of the trees employed to make charcoal consists of the value the peasants put on the time it takes to cut and process them, as the trees mainly come from lands with unclear title and not from the peasants' own farms.

During the international sanctions that were applied to Haiti at various times between 1991 and 1994, in the aftermath of the military coup against President Jean-Bertrand Aristide, the demand for charcoal increased drastically. Oil, kerosene, and gasoline prices increased manifold. (Thus, in August 1994, oil was selling in the unofficial market for 12–18 times the official price.)[9] This made charcoal production increase fivefold in some areas, and the rate of deforestation increase by as much as 30 percent in the humid and semi-humid mountain areas.[10] The supply of charcoal increased as well. In certain places, there were few other ways of making a living during the sanctions. Given the demand, however, it was easy to enter the charcoal market, as a producer and vendor – an effect that may remain, and even be reinforced, in the long run, unless agriculture picks up again.

Few forest resources are left in Haiti, and if tree-felling continues, then these resources will be lost within a few decades. The 1991–94 sanctions also contributed to the acceleration of the erosion process via changes in the crop mix. Agricultural exports (not least of mangoes) declined both because markets were cut off and because some imported inputs were made unavailable.[11]

The erosion process described above operates at given commodity prices. If the relative price of export products increases, then the possibility arises that the process could be counteracted, the peasants again planting coffee. Also, if the price of substitutes for charcoal could be made to decline in relative terms, other, less environmentally damaging, fuels would be used. Unfortunately, however, this scenario does not constitute a valid description of the Haitian reality. On the contrary, the tendency has been in the opposite direction during the past few decades, with the price of export goods declining in terms of foodstuffs and charcoal becoming ever more attractive in comparison to other combustibles.[12] Thus, the erosion process has received an added impetus from relative price movements.

'Hard' empirical data are scarce in Haitian agriculture. Nevertheless, the cumulative process is clearly visible in the countryside. The peasants are uprooting their coffee trees and are planting food crops instead and have been doing so for many years. For whatever they are worth, agricultural production statistics indicate a secular decline in the output value per capita for at least four decades. In the mid-1980s, the average had fallen by 20 percent in comparison with the mid-1950s figure, and thereafter the downward trend continued, with as much as a 7 percent decrease on average during the 1991–94 sanctions episode.[13] Altogether, there is little doubt that the Haitian peasant is getting poorer and poorer.

Traditional agriculture does not have a bright future in Haiti. The existing trends are alarming. In 1950, the area available for cultivation amounted to 0.38 hectares per capita of the population. At present, the figure is likely to be 0.16 hectares, with a population of 7.5 million.[14] As of today, Haiti cannot feed its population adequately using what is being produced domestically. On average, over 40 percent of what the average Haitian eats comes from abroad, 34 percent as commercial food imports, and the rest (7 percent) as food aid.[15] This mining of the soil cannot continue much longer if a catastrophe is to be avoided.

Migration

The secular decline of rural per capita income has created a push out of the countryside, into the cities or to other countries. Emigration (legally or illegally) has brought net population growth down to around 2 percent per annum,[16] but, unless the present trends in fertility – five children per woman – are changed, this safety valve will be hard pressed to handle larger numbers of people even in the short run. Population projections are not encouraging: an estimated 20 million Haitians in 2040 – almost three times as many as today.[17]

Migrants to urban areas within Haiti are facing a difficult situation. During the last two or three decades, Port-au-Prince, the main recipient, has experienced increasing problems when it comes to handling the task. The city had less than half a million inhabitants at the beginning of the 1970s.[18] The figure has since increased to 1.4 million, and out of Haiti's 7.2 million inhabitants, altogether 2.3 million live in urban districts. In 2025, if present fertility and migration trends continue, the population of the capital will be some 4 million, with another 2 million living in other urban areas.[19] The consequences in terms of housing, sanitation, congestion, safety, and crime are easy to imagine, with a socially very unstable Port-au-Prince as a little Calcutta in the Caribbean.

Emigration has brought Haitians to the United States, Canada, France, the Dominican Republic, and a number of Caribbean islands, notably the Bahamas, and the Turks and Caicos. The United States, Canada, and France house over a million and the Dominican Republic about half as many.[20] Even tough the flow of boat people to Florida has dropped drastically, after the end of the sanctions, from almost 25,000 in 1994 to a mere 700 2 years later,[21] this exodus will continue in the years to come. Possibly, emigration to the United States will pick up again, as indicated in a recent report from a humanitarian foundation:

> The slow pace of recovery of the Haitian economy and political uncertainty has contributed to a continued sense of hopelessness within the population. Such desperation fuels a desire to leave, and a trickle of Haitians continues to leave Haiti in small boats, often to be intercepted and returned by U.S. Coasts Guard vessels. The potential for a migration or refugee emergency thus remains high and could be unleashed quickly by a political or economic crisis.[22]

The conclusion is obvious. Unless a viable alternative can be found inside Haiti to traditional, unsustainable agriculture, emigration will continue, probably at an accelerated pace. What then are the alternatives? Let us begin with agriculture itself. What possibilities for change exist in the sector where the majority of the Haitians are concentrated?

Agricultural reform?

The Haitian government is well aware of the need to do something that improves living conditions in the countryside. To this end, an agricultural policy has been devised that is based on four different priorities: development of large irrigation systems in the plains and rehabilitation of water retention and distribution systems in the mountains to improve infrastructure, increased security of land tenure for the peasants, improved access to land, extension and financial services in combination with marketing of Haitian agricultural goods abroad and investment in agro-industries, and, finally, agricultural research.[23] What good this will do is, however, highly uncertain. Most fundamental is that the erosion and population problem is not put at the center of attention. A related problem is that the budget resources of the Haitian government are very limited. The risk is high that resources will be spread across too many areas.

The government may or may not have realized this. Hitherto, actual policy has been strongly concentrated on changes in the system of land tenure. This began as a response to agrarian unrest in the Artibonite Valley. Tenure had been made insecure by an invasion of landless sharecroppers, and violent conflicts had erupted over land. In addition, there were disputes between local communities.[24] Faced with this, the government decided to simply take over the disputed land and if necessary redistribute it. An Institut National pour la Réforme Agraire (INRA) was created in April 1995,[25] and on the Fête de l'Agriculture, May 1, the following year, usufruct rights to 5000 hectares of state land and disputed areas were allocated,[26] followed by another 6000 hectares a year later. Subsidized credit and reparation of deficient irrigation systems completed the picture: '*Tè ak dlo ak kredi ak ankadreman teknik fè refòm agrè*.'[27]

These measures have been well received in Haiti. All peasants are for agrarian reform, and the government knows that. The process is scheduled to continue in the future, presumably with the Plantation Dauphin in the north, once the world's largest sisal plantation, and a new land law is virtually ready.[28] There is, however, another side to the land reform efforts. The concentration on redistribution seems to have blocked all other policy measures in the agricultural sector, and land reform as such does nothing to stop erosion from spreading because it fails to tackle both the crop mix problem and the rehabilitation issue. Instead, the concentration is on a short-run matter: increasing agricultural production, with the obvious risk of over-exploitation. The peasants receive only usufruct rights, not title, which means that the basic uncertainty with respect to ownership is not removed. In this situation, the danger that they will attempt to squeeze as much as possible out of the soil in as short a period as possible is high. Tenure may even have become *more* precarious than before on lands not involved in the redistribution, because title disputes can easily provoke government intervention and decisions that lead to uncertain results.

A recent major study of Haiti's agriculture, carried out by the FAO, stresses the need for an integrated strategy for agriculture. Such a strategy would have to be broad in scope and pay attention both to the prevention of erosion by increasing the permanent cover of the soil, by rehabilitating irrigation systems, and by providing inputs.[29] This is in principle a correct approach, but where do you begin? The problem of the agricultural sector in Haiti is that it is in a state of cumulative decline as a result of the interaction of population growth and soil destruction. Virtually, all the inputs that could be conducive to change are lacking – credit, education, technological change, and so on – and it is difficult to know where to begin and how to design a strategy that maximizes the impact. Not least, the crop mix aspect must be dealt with, since it is at the very heart of the decline. What the sector needs is crops that are at the same time labor-intensive and environmentally sustainable.

The search for such crops has barely begun in Haiti, and this is hardly the place to come up with detailed suggestions on the individual crop level. A few examples will suffice. The Inter-American Institute for Agricultural Cooperation (IICA) has initiated a coffee production scheme with the double aim of creating a better image of Haitian coffee in the international market, based on higher quality, and bypassing the *spekilatè* and the exporters (the traditional intermediaries) in the marketing chain.[30] The scheme covers around 20,000 growers in the Jacmel and Gros Morne areas. Organically cultivated coffee is grown alongside other peasant crops instead of competing with them. This on the one hand contributes to the ecological stabilization of the hillsides, and on the other hand gives the cultivators an opportunity to avoid excessive concentration in one crop that does not provide any cash income during the dormant season.

The organic coffee is bought at whatever market price is prevailing at harvest time. It is thereafter prepared according to the labor-intensive 'wet' method to obtain a quality that is higher than that of traditional coffee, produced with the aid of the 'dry' method. The resulting product is exported directly to the United States, where it is sold in the gourmet segment of the coffee market, on a 5-year contract that gives the growers a price that is higher than the average obtained in Haiti. The difference between this price and the one paid at harvest time is distributed to the participants in the scheme.

Non-traditional coffee is an example of a crop that faces an increasing demand. The market for high-quality gourmet coffee is expanding rapidly in the United States, and this appears to be reflected in the incomes of those participating in it. (The traditional intermediaries have been forced to increase the prices they offer to the producers to be able to compete.) Still, what will happen to the scheme is highly uncertain. Finance is not secured for more than 1 year, and this may prevent the planned expansion into the northern part of Haiti. In addition, a price war may be lurking around the corner, should the scheme be so successful that it threatens the interests of the traditional intermediaries; what the outcome of such a war may be is difficult to know.

What the coffee example demonstrates is that it is possible to find crops whose value per unit of weight or volume is high, which can be marketed successfully abroad in market segments where the income elasticity of demand is high and which increase employment and incomes in the peasant economy. Finding other crops with similar characteristics will require a number of specialized studies of market conditions, labor requirements, natural growing conditions environmental effects, and compatibility with traditional peasant farming.

Candidates may not be lacking, however. Haiti has in the recent past been one of the largest exporters of mangoes in the world, before the sanctions began to reduce the mango stands. These exports can presumably be revived in the somewhat longer run, since mangoes have the additional advantage of constituting an essential part of the Haitian diet. They could also be processed by agro-business. Horticultural products are another case in point, being successful already in some humid mountain areas. Flowers are another possibility, and most tropical spices should grow well in Haiti. The neighboring Dominican Republic provides an encouraging example. In the Cordillera Central an experimental pepper-growing project is on stream and seems to work well, not least from the employment point of view. It is very labor-intensive, and it provides opportunities both for men and women, without demanding drastic changes in traditional work roles.[31]

Non-traditional crops hence seem indispensable if Haitian agriculture is to survive in the long run, but the crops selected must provide proper incentives to the peasants. Other changes may be required as well. Eventually, the role of peasant agriculture in general may have to diminish. At least since the American occupation of Haiti (1915–34), and the introduction of foreign-owned plantations, the theme of large-scale agriculture has been virtually taboo in the country. Still, larger units may have a role to play. At present, the average size of peasant holdings (less than a hectare) has shrunk to the point where these no longer can feed a normal-size family. They are geographically divided into many plots, and, because all children have inheritance rights to equal-sized plots of equal quality, this, pulverization will continue in the future. It will become increasingly difficult to wring an adequate income out of this structure. In Haiti, the largest landowner is the state, and on land where state ownership is established without doubt, the possibility exists to invite modern foreign, export-oriented companies that employ superior techniques and require labor on a reasonable scale to produce such crops as pineapple, which is successfully produced in the Dominican Republic.[32]

Manufacturing: Import substitution

What do the Haitian cities have to offer those who have to leave the countryside? Unfortunately, not very much. The industrial sector has never been very big in Haiti; during the 1991–94 sanctions, the most viable part suffered heavy setbacks, and the effects on employment are still strongly felt.

Manufacturing consists of two separate segments, without much contact between them. The first to be established was the import-competing one. This was able to work only thanks to high tariff protection in combination with different types of monopoly privileges from the end of the 1940s until the fall of Jean-Claude Duvalier in 1986.[33] It is difficult to qualify this whole venture as anything but disastrous. Normal principles of competition were set completely aside. Instead, the game consisted in the establishment of contacts in high places by 'entrepreneurs' cornering the markets for imports and production of goods with a strong domestic demand. Naturally, the ones paying for this were the consumers. At the end of the 1970s and the beginning of the 1980s the situation became even worse as a series of government-owned companies were established in sugar, soybean oil, cement, and wheat flour. None of these was ever economically viable. Their only *raison d'être* was that they served as a mechanism of pumping money into the pockets of the Duvalier family.

The transitional government that took over after the fall of Duvalier in February 1986 proceeded to reduce the level of protection. One of the two sugar factories was closed down, and the monopoly privileges of the cement and wheat flour companies were abolished. This forced a drastic adjustment on the import-competing sector, and in the 1990s, the combination of political unrest and international sanctions forced most of the firms remaining in the sector to close down.[34] What remains of the state-owned ventures is today on the list of privatization objects.

The import-substitution episode is a sad story, and the main lesson to be learnt is that high protection levels simply create rents, and these rents will inevitably be sought by politically well connected individuals who will not run companies efficiently. The goods that are eventually produced tend to come from sectors where Haiti has a comparative *dis*advantage. Whatever employment is generated in this highly artificial fashion is created only at a very high real cost to the economy. No linkage effects arise, since the absence of competitive pressure limits output and growth, and with that also the demand for inputs from other sectors. Import substitution thus turned out to be a complete dead-end in virtually all respects: its net contribution to the economy was negative.

Manufacturing: The assembly industries

The second manufacturing sub-sector is the export assembly industries. These had to compete in international markets and hence displayed a much higher degree of vitality and dynamism in the 1970s and 1980s than did the import-competing firms. Their share of exports increased quickly, from less than 5 percent in the mid-1960s, to over two-thirds before the mid-1980s. Employment followed suit and expanded to the point where in 1990 more than 250 firms in the sector hired some 46,000 people.[35] Each of these employees, in turn, was supporting three or four dependants on average.[36] Thus, between 185,000 and 230,000 Haitians – or close to 20 percent of the population living in Port-au-Prince – relied on the assembly industries for their existence.

The export sector had to overcome a number of obstacles in order to grow. In the first place, protecting the import-competing firms made for an anti-export bias by increasing the domestic price of their output in terms of export goods. Second, they had to struggle with the price, quality, and delivery of infrastructural services. Third, the lack of both general education and specific training among the workers posed problems. Finally, some of the main inputs of the public sector consisted of red tape and arbitrary interventions. On the other hand, the assembly plants benefited from the low minimum wage level (which was not always respected), the lack of trade unions, the exemption of import duties on inputs and export duties on finished products and of income and license taxes, and finally, the favorable tariff treatment in the main market: the United States.[37]

Unfortunately, the ascending curve of the assembly sector was abruptly broken when the coup against President Aristide took place in 1991. The resulting international sanctions to some extent exempted the export industries, but not enough to cushion them from being severely hit. Of the 252 firms operating in 1990, only 44 were left in early 1995, and employment was reduced from 46,000 to less then 5000 as the companies closed down.[38] The sanctions led to market disruption, steeply rising energy costs, unavailability of spare parts, scarcity of inputs in general, and loosening of work discipline during the political turmoil that ensued. As is well known, assembly industries are inherently footloose. Most firms hence closed or left the country. The dynamism created in the economy was gone.

Industrial recovery

What will happen to the industrial sector in the near future is unclear.[39] The effects of the sanctions can still be felt. Employment has picked up little by little as companies have reopened: 13,000 in mid-1995, 18,500, in 101 firms, a year later, and, as of May 1997, somewhere between 20,000 and 25,000.[40] The average per firm has been brought to the same level as in 1990: 183 employees; but the total has reached only half that year's figure. Both domestic and foreign investors view Haiti as a risky venture, and this puts a brake on the speed of the recovery process. The foreign customers, in turn, were forced to shift to other supply sources during the sanctions. (Those who remain are essentially the same as before the sanctions.) The recovery so far has been confined almost exclusively to domestic producers, and only companies that were active before the coup have reopened their doors.

Little else has changed. The comparative advantage – low wages – remains the same in Haitian manufacturing. In the assembly sector, unionization is virtually non-existent, and the fact that the minimum wage increased from 15 gourdes per day to 36 in May 1995 seems to have had little impact. (Before that the figure had not changed since decade ago and the wages paid in the assembly sector are usually above this minimum.)[41]

At the end of 1995, a study appeared which compared production conditions in Haiti with conditions in Mexico, Jamaica, the Dominican Republic, El Salvador, Cuba, and China.[42] This study looked into, among other sectors, assembly work (sporting goods, toys, clothing, and electronics), processing (agro-industries and industrial artisanry) and constructed weighted indices of comparative advantage based on 26 variables connected with the legal and administrative situation, economic policy, manpower, including wages, services, and industrial zones. The results were discouraging. Low wages, a liberal policy *vis-à-vis* foreign investors and a geographic location close to the United States could not compensate for shortcomings in most other respects. It was only with respect to Cuba that Haiti possessed a comparative advantage in the short run. In clothing, toys, and sporting goods, the indices for Haiti were approximately at the same level as those for the Dominican Republic. The other countries outdid Haiti in all sectors.

Macroeconomic developments since the return of Aristide, not least the results of the Programme d'Urgence et de Reconstruction Économique, are in the main conceived of as favorable in business circles, but another impression prevailing there is that the state so far has failed to guarantee law and order, not least physical security. It is difficult to find industrial buildings in safe areas. Second on the list of business complaints is what somewhat euphemistically is called the 'difficult and unpredictable social environment', that is, the expression in the streets of the frustration of broad population segments when pondering what the future may bear, as a result of, among other things, lack of communication from the government about the rationale behind economic reforms. This factor carried a higher weight than such economic factors as the lack of industrial infrastructure, lack of support from the government bureaucracy (expressed e.g., through recurrent delays in formality matters) and high nominal interest rates on industrial loans (on average 24 percent per annum).[43]

Thus, the immediate situation looks bad. Confidence is low in business circles and so is industrial productivity. What may happen in the somewhat longer run is difficult to know. The 1995 study gives no reasons for optimism on this point. The competitiveness of the assembly factories may improve marginally in relation to the competitors in the Caribbean and Central America, but only provided that the social and economic situation of Haiti stabilizes and the reform ambitions are not shelved. However, their handicap in relation to Mexico and China will still persist in virtually all branches, and neither agro-industries nor industrial artisanry will be competitive. This picture could in most cases be changed if the pace of administrative reform is accelerated, finance is improved, Haiti is integrated into the North American Free Trade Association (NAFTA), and the gaps to the competitors with respect to human resources, services, and infrastructure are closed, but these are options that are hardly available in the short run.[44]

The long run presents other difficult problems. Today, operations in assembly manufacturing build only on low wages. An interesting question is whether it will in the future be possible to 'trade up' and produce goods with somewhat higher technological contents conducive to higher, and preferably increasing, wage incomes and linkages to other sectors in the Haitian economy. This, unfortunately, does not appear to be the case. At least three factors tend to make it difficult to move away from the low-wage end unless we are talking about the very long run.[45]

In the first place, the inputs required by technologically more sophisticated industries tend to be very specialized. They are often non-traded intermediates that must be produced more or less on the spot by local firms in close collaboration with their customers precisely because the designs involved need to be tailor-made. This, in turn, tends to create a 'trap' that it is very difficult to break out of. Causality runs in both directions. On the one hand, there must be enough demand for the manufacturers of intermediates to be willing to make the effort, since the specialized skills required translate into high fixed costs. On the other hand, if these skills do not exist, no specialized intermediates will be produced, and the final goods producers dependent on them will never open their doors.

The crucial factor when it comes to breaking this vicious circle is education. The general education record of Haiti is, however, the worst in the Western Hemisphere,[46] and as far as specialized technicians and other skilled employees are concerned, the situation is even worse. This can be remedied only in the long run by a gradual, concerted effort of expanding vocational and technical training at the secondary and tertiary levels.

Skill creation may not be enough. There is also a structural characteristic that is difficult to overcome. In the present international division of labor, Haiti is a net importer of non-traditional manufactures. This means that any effort to develop differentiated industrial goods will have to face the competition of low-priced imports when developing the R&D activities needed for trading up. Hence, the latter may never become profitable, and Haiti will in that case be locked into the lower end of the industrial ladder, producing just low-wage goods with the aid of simple techniques.

Having said all this, despite the devastating effects of the sanctions, the assembly industries continue to be the most dynamic segment of the Haitian economy. The sector has recovered relatively well, given the difficult external circumstances. This, in turn, must be compared with the fact that traditional agriculture is not a viable option and that, barring large-scale migration, changing the agricultural sector will have to be accompanied by measures that create employment outside agriculture and hence ease the pressure on the ecologically vulnerable hillsides. In the light of history, escape from poverty has taken the road of industrialization in all the nations that count as developed today. Haiti must do the same.

In this context, one strategy that has not been employed so far in Haiti is that of creating industrial free zones or export processing zones,[47] whereas in the neighboring Dominican Republic, no less than some 175,000 industrial workers are employed in 33 free zones, where they produce mainly garments. Other competitors in the Caribbean have also expanded employment in this way: Guatemala, 100,000 and Honduras, 45,000.

The sitting Commission Présidentielle pour la Croissance et la Modernisation Économique commissioned a study on the effects of free zones in Haiti.[48] This study elaborated a basic framework according to which the zones should be private but placed under supervision of the Direction Générale des Douanes. They should be administered by an organization with a majority representation of private business associations. In practice, most of the conditions outlined in the study are already fulfilled in Haiti. No export duties exist, tax and import duty exemption is the rule for export-oriented industries, and capital moves freely out of Haiti. Rather, the main benefits from locating in a free zone stem from access to buildings, physical security, and general infrastructure. It is much easier to control a geographically delimited free zone than a number of factories spread out over a wide territory. The zones could also be given priority when it comes to such items as power, water, telephone lines, and so on, and one should expect that the geographical concentration of companies should facilitate transportation considerably.

The infrastructure problem requires further discussion, and we will hence come back to it below. Before that, however, we should take a look at the handicraft and tourist sectors, for the simple reason that the development of these activities to a large extent faces the same difficulties as the manufacturing sector.

Handicrafts

A sector that is usually left out of the analysis of the Haitian economy is handicrafts, rural as well as urban.[49] Haiti has a long handicraft tradition that goes back at least to the 1920s, and the starting point of the sector's modern history could be traced to the early 1970s. Tourism began to recover after the dark Papa Doc years, and craft exports were facing a growing international market after years of stagnation. Increasing quantities of metal and wood products, baskets, tapestries, macramé, crochet, and other weaving products were sent abroad. However, these exports soon ran into problems. In the early 1980s, the market began to be saturated with Haitian goods during a period when price competition from producers in other countries started to be intense. Since Haitian producers by and large failed to adapt to changing tastes as far as patterns, design, and quality were concerned, Haitian goods were falling behind in the Caribbean tourist market.

The demise of Jean-Claude Duvalier and the return of Haitians from exile abroad produced new incentives for handicraft production: inspiration from abroad in combination with a renewed interest in popular Haitian culture and national themes. The demand for Haitian handicrafts increased both abroad (among the Haitians in the diaspora) and at home. The sector was seeing a bit of a 'renaissance', further reinforced by the triumph of the democratic forces at the end of 1990.

The renaissance did not last long, however. Handicrafts were rammed as hard by the sanctions as any other sector in the Haitian economy. Between 1985 and 1990, Haitian artisans, located mainly in rural areas, had contributed some 10–15 million US dollars of exports each year. After the 1991 coup, they were forced to cease their production and many, needing the cash, even sold their tools. Handicraft exports dropped from about $9 million in 1990 to a mere 1.4 million in 1994, and the share of handicrafts in total exports dropped from 12.6 to 6.1 percent. The cost of raw materials in many instances skyrocketed, with increases ranging from 100 to 400 percent. At the same time, the money inflow from relatives abroad, which had been used to finance activities, was cut off. The handicraft sector was decapitalized, and as early as 1992 many craftsmen shifted to commerce and similar activities instead.[50]

To what extent the handicraft sector may have recovered after the end of the sanctions is impossible to say, notably for rural areas, where definition and classification of activities is notoriously difficult. Those active are concentrated in basketry and fiber craft, wood sculpture and other woodwork, as well as embroidery and needlework. Of these, needlework and woodwork have faced problems as a result of increased international competition. Overall, traditional crafts are having problems since they have to compete with industrial products both for markets and for qualified designers. Still, only a minority of the artisan population of Haiti works for industrial firms.[51]

The tourist market, in Haiti and in the rest of the Caribbean, not least the Dominican Republic, is the main market for the handicraft sector. However, industrial craft products with a pronounced 'Haitian' touch have found a niche in the United States, and the more individualized, high-quality items have no problems selling in the international market, although quantities are small.[52]

If these markets are to be developed, the handicraft sector must overcome a number of obstacles. In 1996, a survey of handicraft production in Haiti identified the following major constraints: education and training, design, production, funding marketing, organization of the sector, government policy, and legislation. The rapidly changing international markets require training for adaptation and diversification. The buildings and tools employed are often not designed with the goods they help to produce in mind. It is difficult to find raw materials, the finish often leaves things to be desired, and the producers are unfamiliar with pricing practices. Designs are frequently out of touch with tastes overseas, and changing them requires considerable time. It is difficult to find new marketing outlets, not least since producers often have only dim ideas about what the market looks like.

In this context, it should be noted that the Haitian state does not provide much support, while the governments of the competitor countries tend to be extremely active. The general lack of adequate transportation in Haiti in turn increases the price that the final consumer has to pay. Unless they are prepared to pay high interest rates, small producers have problems finding adequate finance. Cooperation and common representation of interests is lacking. Finally, the government has failed to promote handicrafts through legislation, implementation of already existing laws, and development of special incentive schemes.

Thus handicrafts in Haiti have to cope with a formidable array of problems. In addition, the sector stands out as extremely heterogeneous, with one end in almost industrial production and the other in primitive products made by single producers. This must be kept in mind when support and solutions are to be devised. The main difference here, between industrial production and traditional crafts, is based on organization and division of labor. The single artisan has to perform all the operations alone. The industrial enterprise, on the other hand, makes systematic use of the division of labor and thereby achieves a productivity level which is impossible for the individual to reach by himself.

This observation bears directly on the problems of handicrafts. On the one hand, it is desirable that the sector strengthens its relations with manufacturing, so that as many artisans as possible can be transferred into higher-productivity pursuits within the latter sector. It is, however, not enough, since the handicraft sector also contains a group of artisans that are difficult to incorporate into industrial production. For these, support in the form of credit and marketing and, not least, technical assistance in developing designs and avoiding repetitive patterns that rapidly saturate the market is desirable.

Tourism

One of the most important markets for handicrafts is provided by tourism. In addition, tourism is a labor-intensive sector that under favorable circumstances can make a contribution to employment. Haiti has a reliable climate, with the mean temperature varying by a mere 5°C between the coolest and hottest months of the year. The rainy seasons do not coincide with the tourist peak seasons at the end of the year and during the summer. In addition, the colorful culture and history of the country give Haiti a comparative advantage *vis-à-vis* its competitors in the Caribbean region.

Still, the fate of tourism in Haiti has varied considerably over the years. The history began with the Bicentennial Exposition in Port-au-Prince in 1949, and the number of visitors to the country increased steadily from 5000 in 1945 to almost 60,000 in 1960.[53] The following years, however, were the darkest ones of the Papa Doc regime (and in the modern history of the country, for that matter), and numbers dropped to 19,000 in 1964, with visitors staying no more than 3 days on average. The death of Duvalier in 1971 and the improved image abroad during the first years of Jean-Claude's presidency made tourists return. The total number of visitors reached a peak of 339,000 in 1979. However, all of these were not tourists. The majority was Haitian emigrants visiting their country of origin, people in the aid community, and foreign businessmen. At this time, some 2500 hotel rooms were available in the country.

At the beginning of the 1980s, tourism contracted again. The world economy entered a recession, the Baby Doc government was increasingly accused of human rights violations, and Haiti appeared on the list of 'H's' suspected to be behind the spread of AIDS in the United States.[54] This negative news was followed by political unrest in Haiti. Total receipts from tourism in 1984 amounted to no more than they did in 1972. It was hoped that the fall of Baby Doc in 1986 would change the situation, but as the political situation deteriorated, the prospective tourists preferred not to come, especially not since the Minister of Public Health stated that 10 percent of all Haitians might be infected with AIDS.

During the next few years, little happened that could change the situation. The 1987 elections were interrupted and when a president was finally elected, the following year, it was under highly dubious circumstances. The new president was rapidly ousted by the military, and when Jean-Bertrand Aristide, who was elected by a landslide majority of two-thirds in 1990, was thrown out of the country the following year, another low-water-mark was reached. The international sanctions practically killed the industry.[55] The only visitors arriving were Haitians from the diaspora visiting their relatives, and during the first quarter of 1995, it was even reported that as much as 70 percent of the hotel beds in Port-au-Prince were occupied by Haitians coming from abroad, paying in US dollars.[56] (It should then be noted that most of the visitors were staying with their families.)

Tourism has never been a success in Haiti, even when the political circumstances have been favorable. The country's share of the Antilles market never exceeded a couple of percent.[57] The notorious lack of infrastructure has put a brake on mass tourism even during periods when there has been no violence or political turbulence. Outside the capital, there are few hotel beds, and the communications between the provincial cities and Port-au-Prince have most of the time been very poor. This makes it difficult to reach such spots as, for example, Jacmel and Cayes on the south coast and Cap-Haïtien in the north. Even during the best years, at the end of the 1970s, this was true and thereafter the transportation network has deteriorated gradually. Four-wheel-drive vehicles are finding a growing market in Haiti. There are no railroads and most tourists stay clear of the overloaded and overcrowded trucks that provide the only collective transport between major cities. Hence, in practice, whoever visits Haiti for tourism is locked into the capital, where no beaches exist, unless he or she is willing to rough it.

These are issues that must receive priority if tourism is to receive a boost in the future. Whatever investment in hotels, restaurants, and so on, is needed will have to come from private, domestic, or foreign, sources, but it will not materialize unless Haiti's international image improves considerably. The feeling that the country is not a secure and stable place to go to must be made to disappear. No other sector in the economy has suffered as much as tourism from the overwhelmingly negative publicity that Haiti has received in the past. Security and stability are only necessary, and not sufficient, conditions for an expansion, however. A decent infrastructure is needed as well. Power cuts at odd hours, a chaotic traffic situation in the capital, non-availability of beaches close to Port-au-Prince, and no transportation to the areas where beaches are, in fact, available, are all things that have little appeal for the average tourist. The Cap-Haïtien area, for example, has more to offer than the capital, but ever since the American occupation, 1915–34, resources have been heavily concentrated in Port-au-Prince and its surroundings, and this pattern was strongly reinforced during the presidencies of the two Duvaliers. Thus, the tourism issue is also deeply entangled in the wider regional development question – an issue that has received very little attention in Haiti.

The Préval administration professed an interest in tourism. Haiti should be marketed as a 'different' country, with a strong and highly actively with the private sector and with other countries in the

Caribbean.[58] Inspiration should not be lacking. The Dominican Republic has seen a tremendous boom in tourism during the past decade, and parts of Haiti could presumably make use of this fact, notably the border area in the north, where Cap-Haïtien and Henry Christophe's magnificent Citadelle la Ferrière are located.

Problems with the informal economy

Most of the Haitian economy presents a special problem in that it is informal. The state has difficulties reaching actors that pay no attention to its laws and regulations. This is the case with virtually the entire peasant sector, many small manufacturers, most artisans and others active in the handicraft sector, many traders, and virtually all personal services. Some 650,000–750,000 people are estimated to be working informally in urban areas.[59]

Micro enterprises dominate the informal sector. Often, they do not consist of more than a single individual. Many are women. Owners are individuals or families. The business volume tends to be very small and no taxes are being paid.[60] Local raw materials are employed in labor-intensive, mostly technologically rudimentary operations. Those who work in the sector have little formal education, frequently none at all. Entry is completely free in the informal economy. Markets are very competitive. Incomes and living standards are low, as a result of low labor productivity, which, in turn, makes savings and capital formation difficult.

Informal entrepreneurs have to cope with special problems. They lack access to formal credit, and in cases where outside finance is required, this comes as short-term loans only, from informal sources charging high real interest rates as a result of lack of collateral and lack of supervision of how loans are used. The informal entrepreneurs have very limited access to public infrastructure facilities. Power, water, and garbage collection have to be procured in informal ways. Often, human power has to be resorted to and the capital equipment is limited to simple had tools. The buildings used (if any) may not be adequate for the type of operations performed. Industrial space is both scarce and expensive in Haiti, so location, as well, is a problem.

Very few projects have in the past dealt with the problems of the informal sector. This field has been more or less left by the Haitian state to non-governmental organizations that have worked mainly on living and working conditions and provided some credit, mainly for commerce. The market forces reign supreme, and entrepreneurs and workers have to adjust more or less instantaneously when conditions change, which may be overnight. The diversity of the sector and the large numbers of people involved call for an approach which is diversified and decentralized as well, as exemplified by the discussion of handicrafts above.

It is doubtful whether formalization would do any good. As of today, efforts are limited and concentrated to registration and formalization of the titles of the property on which the microenterprises are located.[61] Formalization would in principle make it easier for enterprises to have access to public services, notably in infrastructure. Still, it is highly doubtful whether this is a viable proposal. As we will soon come back to, the present provision of such services leaves a lot to be desired, and one important implication of formalization would be the need to pay taxes. Presumably, in the near future the informal sector will remain beyond the reach of government efforts, and whatever satisfaction of the sector's demand for education and training, credit, and infrastructure that is possible will have to continue to take place through non-governmental efforts.

Key inputs: Education

Much of the foregoing discussion has revolved around two common themes: (1) the need for education and training and (2) the need for a vastly improved physical infrastructure. These are necessary, but not sufficient, inputs if Haiti is ever to break the downward cumulative process that the country has been caught in for several decades.

Beginning with education, the history of Haiti in this respect is discouraging.[62] When the American occupation of Haiti began, in 1915, the situation, especially in rural areas, was dismal. The peasants were more or less completely illiterate. The Americans made an effort to change the educational system, away from the emphasis on literature and humanistic subjects that characterized the French tradition, toward a system putting more weight on manual and vocational practical training. The effort failed, however, and once the Americans left, the French-derived schools reigned supreme again.

Over the next few decades, few changes were experienced. When the 1950 census was taken, the illiteracy rate for the entire country was found to be almost 90 percent. Twenty-one years later, the figure still remained high – close to 80 percent (90 percent in rural districts).[63] An impossible system had been created. It used a foreign language – French – as the medium of instruction, and very few texts were available in *kreyòl*. To this was added the strong emphasis on examination at all levels of the system. The result was catastrophic. The school system did not serve as a vehicle for the accumulation of human capital, but as a filtering device – and a negative one at that. Social mobility was minimized and allowed those on the top rungs of the societal ladder to continue to control those below. The vast majority of Haitians failed to complete even the primary cycle.[64]

In the mid-1990s, some things changed, but not very many. *Kreyòl* has taken the place of French – successfully, it seems, since the official illiteracy figure has been reduced to 42 percent for the country as a whole, a figure that may, however, be an exaggeration since enrollment leaves a long to be desired. As many as 90 percent of all the children of school age enter school, but only 29 percent of the beginners in first grade go on to the secondary level, and a mere 6 percent finish that level. Only 4 percent continue on the tertiary level. Grades are frequently repeated.[65]

The quality of the education received is usually bad. Teachers are often unqualified, few, if any, textbooks are available, and the buildings used as schools are old and decrepit. Many teachers are forced to hold other jobs on the side since the salaries they receive are so low that they do not allow a decent living. Because of this, recruitment is difficult, extremely so in rural areas. Most of the schools are private and only a minority are enrolled in the state-run schools. The majority go to schools run by NGOs, churches, private persons, and so on: 66 percent in the primary cycle, 81 percent at the secondary level and 50 percent at the tertiary.[66] The quality range is very wide, from very good to catastrophic. On the national level, no massive alphabetization program exists.

There remains no doubt that the school system in Haiti needs to be both expanded quantitatively and improved qualitatively. If we are to believe official statistics, there is a considerable willingness to pay for education among families who have children of school age. Between 11 and 13 percent of the family budget is spent on schooling by those who send their children to private schools, a figure that ranks very high when compared with other countries at a similar income level.[67]

All families cannot afford to pay, however. The state, one way or another, must assume the main responsibility for education. Educational reform is now being carried out in Haiti, and joint ventures between the state and private schools have been suggested as a way of increasing the cost effectiveness of investment in education. The state would then not run the schools directly but rather subsidize operations and control curricula and quality. The budget of the Haitian government is extremely limited. In this situation, the importance of efficiency looms large, and the public school tradition in Haiti is not a successful one. With this in mind, there are good reasons to believe that the most efficient way of increasing quality and quantity in the educational sector goes via a mixed system.

One of the most crucial areas in the school system is that of technical education. This is central both for increasing productivity and for increasing employment. Manufacturing needs technicians and middle-level managers with a technical background. Otherwise bottlenecks tend to arise which preclude the productivity of other categories of employees from increasing as well. However, in the past, very little attention has been paid to technical education. Until 1995, there were only 38 technical schools, with a total enrollment of 5800. No less than 70 percent of these schools were private.[68]

Key inputs: Infrastructure

A second input bottleneck in the Haitian economy that must be removed if the rate of growth is to increase is the sadly deficient infrastructure. Power cuts occur almost daily, at completely irregular intervals. A mere 8 of every 1000 households in the country have a telephone line, in a system that does not work. (Business frequently has to resort to radio-based means of communication.)[69] The water distribution system is not dependable, and the road system is literally falling apart. Public service delivery is insufficient, untimely, and irregular in most aspects, to the detriment of virtually every single producer in the country.

An example of the existing state of affairs is given by the electricity company. At the end of the recent sanctions, the situation was desperate:

> The operations of the electricity company were particularly badly hit [during the sanctions]: no significant new equipment had been purchased since 1986; spare parts which needed to be imported were unavailable after 1991; and the progressive depletion of oil supplies resulted in continuous interruptions in electricity generation. The production of electricity from thermic plants (which represented about 65 percent of electricity production in 1991) declined from 290 millions of kWh in 1991 to 27 millions of kWh in 1994... The decline in thermic plant generation was only partly offset by additional hydroelectric generation. At the beginning of 1994 electricity production at the main hydroelectric plant (in Péligre) was stopped

> as a result of technical difficulties; by the end of the year electricity was available for only 12 hours a day in Port-au-Prince.[70]

Today, the situation has changed very little. The production of the Électricité d'Haïti is nowhere close to the existing demand. The generating capacity is too low, and about 40 percent of what is produced is either tapped illegally or disappears due to other non-technical reasons.[71] Electricity is available mainly in the capital, but only for a few hours per day during the dry seasons.[72] As a result of this, both households and firms have to supplement the public supply with electricity generated by them. Effectively, the government has shifted the responsibility for infrastructure to the private sector.

Transportation is another case in point. Haiti is a country where roads do not last long, and airports and ports leave a lot to be desired. The road network consists of some 4500 kilometers, most of which are not paved. Ten ports that can handle medium-tonnage vessels and a dozen smaller ports and wharves exist. Finally, Haiti has two international airports and four domestic airstrips.[73] Some of the formerly important ports, like the one in Jacmel, were closed down by the Duvalier administrations and left to decay. Adequate maintenance was limited to less than 20 percent of the paved roads and 4 percent of the rest. The harbor in Port-au-Prince is congested, deficiently managed, has far too many employees, and lacks the necessary equipment.[74] It comes as no surprise, then, that it is the most expensive port in the entire Caribbean.[75] Altogether, the transport system is characterized by neglect and decay.

Here, as well as in the case of electricity, adjustment is forced on the private sector. There is a trade-off between the state of the vehicles and the state of the roads. Ordinary cars are to an increasing extent replaced by four-wheel-drives, at increasing costs. Insofar as ordinary cars continue to be employed, reparation costs increase as the road network continues to deteriorate. However, the trade-off is a limited one. The deficient state of the roads severely limits the amount of merchandise that can be transported and increases the time required. To what extent improvement is possible is doubtful. Transportation stands out as one of the least cost-effective areas in the public sector.[76]

The situation with respect to infrastructure is particularly unfortunate since developments are held back by the on-going debate about privatization of public enterprises. The Électricité d'Haïti, TÉLÉCO, the Port-au-Prince harbor and airport, among others, are awaiting immediate decision, but as long as the discussion in parliament remains in a state of paralysis, very little action will be taken to increase efficiency.

Conclusions

Our survey of the Haitian economy has not revealed many features that would lead us to believe that sustained growth is imminent. The economy between 1991 and 1994 reached such a low-water-mark that heroic efforts are required just to put it back on the pre-coup level. Sustained growth appears as a very remote possibility – in the best case. In the worst case, per capita income will continue its decline, and the pressure to emigrate will increase.

In agriculture, the cumulative interaction between population growth and erosion continues, and the agrarian reform that is under way fails to address the problem of how to find crops that are both labor-intensive and ecologically sound. Thus, we should not expect any reversal of income trends in agriculture in the near and medium-term future.

The most dynamic sector in the Haitian economy during the 1970s and 1980s was the export assembly manufacturing firms. The 1991–94 sanctions almost wiped these companies out, and the recovery beginning in 1995 has not yet reached the point where figures are back at the 1991 level. Manufacturing exports face strong competition both from other Caribbean nations and from countries further away, and unless such crucial variables and political stability, physical security, education, and infrastructure undergo a drastic improvement, there are no reasons to expect Haiti's competitiveness to increase over the next few years. In the longer perspective, Haiti must break away from low-wage manufacturing if incomes are to improve, but given the dismal educational situation, this appears utopian, especially since the country would have to compete with low-priced imports of technologically more sophisticated goods.

A sector absorbing many people both in rural and in urban areas is handicrafts. This sector was badly hurt by the sanctions, and increasing output and sales may be difficult. The Caribbean market by and large appears to be saturated with Haitian crafts, and the sector needs assistance in a number of ways to be able to expand, ranging from close cooperation with manufacturing to targeting of individual artisans.

Tourism – one of the most important markets for handicrafts – is often pointed to as a potentially expansive field, but this sector has in the past been subject to more downs than ups. Today, tourism is severely constrained by the lack of infrastructure – notably electricity and transportation – and by the feeling abroad that Haiti is not yet stable and secure enough for tourists.

The fact that most economic activities in Haiti are informal poses special problems when it comes to designing strategies for growth and development. Many entrepreneurs want as little as possible to do with the authorities. By the same token, they lack the infrastructure that is necessary to increase productivity and incomes. In the past, the Haitian government has made few efforts to break this impasse, and in the near future, this situation is not likely to change.

The analysis of the different sectors of the economy points clearly to the strategic importance of the key inputs in the development process: education and infrastructure. On both these counts, Haiti displays severe deficiencies. The illiteracy rate is the highest in the Western Hemisphere; technical education, necessary for manufacturing remains rudimentary; the telephone system does not work; electricity is available only at irregular intervals; transportation is a hopeless mess; and so on. These are all factors that are difficult to improve at short notice, especially given the very limited resources at the disposal of the Haitian government. Thus, there are no indications that in the foreseeable future Haiti will be able to break out of the economic stagnation and decline that has characterized the country for several decades.

This chapter has not dealt with either macroeconomic policy problems or with politics in any detail. These themes have been touched only *en passant*, for reasons of space. (I have discussed these issues in detail elsewhere and the reader is referred to those writings.)[77] However, when these factors are added to the picture, the conclusion that sustained growth in Haiti is a pipe-dream receives further support.

During most of the period from the beginning of the 1980s to the present Haiti has experienced severe macroeconomic disturbances as a result of political factors.[78] The unhampered plunder by Jean-Claude Duvalier and the clique surrounding him during the first half of the 1980s led to large budget deficits that were monetized and which by boosting demand caused balance of payments deficits as well. The attempts to stabilize the economy, undertaken by the provisional government that took over in February 1986, were interrupted by the political chaos that ensued in mid-1987, when presidential elections were imminent. Smuggling and under-reporting of company profits undermined the government budget, and the rate of inflation increased. Thus, policy reform came to nothing.

In 1991, after the election of Jean-Bertrand Aristide to the presidency, a second stabilization effort was made. This time, the endeavor was interrupted by the *coup d'état* at the end of September that ousted Aristide. During the next 3 years, per capita income dropped catastrophically, as we have seen in the foregoing, and the economy experienced another macroeconomic disequilibrium, with a severe breakdown of the tax administration and conversion of a balance of payments surplus into a huge deficit as a result of capital flight and suspension of foreign aid. Again, policy-making was back to square one, but at a drastically lower per capita income.

A third round of policy reforms was initiated by the government of René Préval, in 1996.[79] These reforms are of the standard IMF–World Bank type. Their eventual fate is doubtful. The political process does not work to the advantage of economic growth. The government budget was voted in parliament with few months left of the fiscal year both in 1996 and 1997, and the Haitian political scene remains one of confrontation rather than one of cooperation. Following the first round of senatorial elections in April 1997, communication between the main two political groupings broke down completely. In June, the prime minister resigned. It would take one-and-a-half years before a successor could be appointed, because of stern opposition in parliamentary circles. The gap between President René Préval and his predecessor, Jean-Bertrand Aristide, who handpicked Préval to succeed him, widened day by day. Parliament was dissolved at the beginning of 1999. The following year parliamentary elections were held, elections that were denounced as fraudulent by the opposition against Aristide and his Fanmi Lavalas grouping. The opposition chose to boycott the presidential elections in November, so Aristide was elected to his second term without opposition.

Unfortunately, the two elections held in 2000 have not solved Haiti's political problems. If anything, they have contributed to worsen them. The rift between President Aristide and the political opposition is both deep and wide. The political mechanism continues to be paralyzed. How long this will continue remains to be seen, but as long as the paralysis remains, the economy will not move forward. Stagnation and decline will continue to carry the day.

Notes

Published in *Iberoamericana*, Vol. 29, 1999, published by the Institute of Latin American Studies, Stockholm University. Reprinted by permission.

1. World Bank (1997), p. 4; FAO (1996), p. 7.
2. World Bank (1997), p. 4.
3. Ibid.
4. See Lundahl (1979), Chapter 5, for a detailed discussion.

5. FAO (1996), p. 19.
6. One may ask the question whether some mechanism à la Ester Boserup (1965), when population growth stimulates technological progress, will not act as a brake on this tendency. However, this is not the case. Technological change has by and large been absent from rural Haiti. See Lundahl (1979), Chapter 12, for an extensive discussion of the reasons.
7. Cf. Rybczynski (1955).
8. Lundahl (1979), pp. 195–204; Stevenson (1989).
9. Daskal (1996), p. 7.
10. Ibid., p. 10.
11. FAO (1996).
12. Lundahl (1979), pp. 214–20; Bourdet and Lundahl (1991). These tendencies were reinforced during the 1991–94 sanctions, when export markets were cut off and oil prices skyrocketed.
13. Lundahl (1997b), p. 5.
14. Locher (1988), pp. 15–16.
15. Gagnon (1996), pp. 14–17.
16. World Bank (1997), p. 4.
17. World Bank (1996), p. 2.
18. Lundahl (1979), p. 630.
19. World Bank (1996), pp. 4–5.
20. Ibid., p. 2.
21. Open Society Institute (1997), p. 3.
22. Ibid., p. 1.
23. IMF (1996b), p. 15.
24. Evalyasyon premye faz refòm agrè nan Latibonit (n.d.), pp. 4–6.
25. IMF (1996b), p. 15.
26. Evalyasyon premye faz refòm agrè nan Latibonit (n.d.), p. 11, lists the criteria that must be met by those who are to receive land.
27. 'Land, water, credit and technical leadership make agrarian reform.' Personal communication from T. Anderson White, Port-au-Prince, May 8, 1997.
28. Ibid.
29. FAO (1996), pp. 54–56.
30. Interviews with representatives of coffee producers in Cayes-Jacmel, May 6, 1997.
31. Personal communication from Rubén Silié, Port-au-Prince, May 15, 1997.
32. Ibid.
33. Lundahl (1997a), pp. 76–80.
34. Inter-American Development Bank (1995), p. 36.
35. Lundahl (1997a), pp. 80–81; Lundahl (1997b), p. 6.
36. World Bank (1981), p. 23.
37. Lundahl (1992), pp. 409–11; Lundahl (1997a), p. 81.
38. Inter-American Development Bank (1995), p. 36.
39. On this point, I am indebted to Johnny Handal for a stimulating conversation, Port-au-Prince, May 3, 1997.
40. Interviews with Rémy Montas, Prime Minister's Office, Port-au-Prince, May 2, 1997. The 1996 figure comes from Capital Consult (1996).
41. IMF (1995), p. 5; IMF (1996a), p. 10.

42. Capital Consult (1995).
43. Information from the Prime Minister's Office, Port-au-Prince, May 2, 1997.
44. Capital Consult (1995).
45. Lundahl (1997a), pp. 83, 85–87.
46. See, for example, Lundahl (1979), Chapter 10; Tardieu (1990); and Prou (1997), for an overview.
47. Capital Consult (n.d.).
48. Ibid.
49. An excellent synthesis of the problems of handicrafts is found in Fleurant and Mangonès (1996).
50. Ibid., pp. 1, 10–11 and Annex 3.
51. Ibid., pp. 12–15.
52. Ibid., pp. 16–17.
53. The following is based on Lundahl (1992), pp. 412–13.
54. The other 'H's' were homosexuality, heroin and hepatitis.
55. IMF (1995), p. 3.
56. *Le Nouvelliste*, March 17–19, 1995.
57. Lundahl (1992), p. 412.
58. IMF (1996b), p. 16.
59. GHRAP (1995), p. 66.
60. Ibid., pp. 64–65.
61. Interview with Bernard Craan, *Centre pour la Libre Entreprise et la Démocratie* (CLED), Port-au-Prince, May 2, 1997.
62. Lundahl (1979), Chapter 10; Tardieu (1990).
63. Lundahl (1979), p. 478.
64. The details of this are found in ibid., Chapter 10.
65. Mure-Ravaud and Rodd (1997), pp. 25–26.
66. Ibid., p. 3.
67. Ibid., p. 37.
68. Silié and Hasbum (1996).
69. World Bank (1996), p. 14.
70. IMF (1995), pp. 3–4.
71. IMF (1996b), p. 18.
72. World Bank (1996), p. 14.
73. Ibid., p. 17.
74. Ibid., p. 14.
75. IMF (1996b), p. 13.
76. Ibid., p. 17.
77. See Lundahl (1979), (1983), (1997a), (1997b) and Lundahl and Silié (1998). The latter essay complements the present one.
78. Lundahl and Silié (1998).
79. Actually, the reforms were begun by Aristide, after his return to Haiti in 1994, but Aristide subsequently turned against his own reform commitments.

References

Boserup, Ester (1965), *The Conditions of Agricultural Growth: The Economics of Agrarian Change under Population Pressure*. London: George Allen & Unwin.

Bourdet, Yves and Lundahl, Mats (1991), 'Patterns and Prospects of Haitian Primary Exports', *Latin American Issues*, No. 9, A Monograph Series of Contemporary Latin American and Caribbean Affairs, Allhegeny College, Meadville, PA and Akron, OH.

Capital Consult (1995), *Compétitivité des industries d'Haïti*. Étude realisée pour le compte de la Commission Présidentielle pour la Croissance et la Modernisation Économique. December 12. Port-au-Prince: Capital Consult.

Capital Consult (1996), *Enquête industrielle, Août 1996, Résultats preliminaries*. Port-au-Prince: Capital Consult.

Capital Consult (n.d.), *Étude exploratoire pour l'implantation de zones franches en Haïti*. Préparée pour le compte de la Commission Présidentielle pour la Croissance et la modernisation Économique. Port-au-Prince: Capital Consult.

Daskal, Jennifer (1996), *Sanctions on Haiti: What Were the Costs?* Cambridge UK and Cambridge MA: King's History and Economics Centre and Harvard Center for Population and Development Studies.

Evalyasyon premye faz refòm agrè nan Latibonit (n.d.), Port-au-Prince: Biwo rejyonal INARA nan Latibonit.

FAO (1996), Haïti: Analyse du secteur agricole et identification des projets. Rapport sectoriel (final), Volume I de III: Rapport principal, 75/95 TCP-HAI 23, July 3, Port-au-Prince.

Fleurant, Gisèle and Mangonès, Kathy (1996), *Haitian Artisans: Giving Shape to One's Vision and* Ideas: *An Assessment of the Haitian Handicraft Sector*, January, Port-au-Prince.

Gagnon, Gérard (1996), *Food Security Issues in Haiti*, Final Draft, Washington, DC: World Bank.

GHRAP (Groupe Haïtien de Recherches et Action Populaire) (1995), *Dossier sur l'évolution de l'économie haïtienne 1980–1994*. Mimeo, Port-au-Prince: GHRAP.

IMF (1995), *Haiti – Recent Economic Developments*, SM/95/43, March 1, Washington, DC: International Monetary Fund.

IMF (1996a), *Haiti – Staff Report for the 1996 Article IV Consultation and Request for Arrangements under the Enhanced Structural Adjustment Facility*. EBS/96/153, September 24. Washington, DC: International Monetary Fund.

IMF (1996b), *Haiti – Enhanced Structural Adjustment Facility – Economic Policy Framework Paper for FY 1996/97-1998/*99. EDB/96/128, October 1. Washington, DC: International Monetary Fund.

Inter-American Development Bank (1995), *Haiti: Emergency Economic Recovery Program*. Report of the Joint Mission (November 7–20, 1994), Washington, DC: IDB.

Locher, Uli (1988), 'Land Distribution, Land Tenure and Land Erosion in Haiti'. Paper presented at the 12th Annual Conference of the Society for Caribbean Studies, Hoddesdon, Hertfortshire, July 12–14.

Lundahl, Mats (1979), *Peasants and Poverty: A Study of Haiti*. London: Croom Helm.

Lundahl, Mats (1983), *The Haitian Economy: Man, Land and Markets*. London and Canberra: Croom Helm.

Lundahl, Mats (1992), *Politics or Markets? Essays on Haitian Underdevelopment*. London and New York: Routledge.

Lundahl, Mats (1997a), 'The Haitian Dilemma Reexamined: Lessons from the Past in the Light of Some New Economic Theory', in: Robert I. Rotberg (ed.),

Haiti Renewed: Political and Economic Prospects. Washington, DC: Brookings Institution press.

Lundahl, Mats (1997b), *'Towards the Abyss? The Political Economy of Emergency in Haiti'*, Helsinki: WIDER (World Institute for Development Economics Research).

Lundahl, Mats and Silié, Rubén (1998), 'Economic Reform in Haiti: Past Failures and Future Success?', *Comparative Economic Studies*, Vol. 40, 43–71.

Mure-Ravaud, Georges and Rodd, Alistair (1997), *Éducation. Examen des dépenses publiques d'Haïti*. Note No. 7. March. Washington, DC: The World Bank.

Open Society Institute (1997), *Haitian Boat People: Causes and Methods of Migration*. Special Report, April, New York: Forced Migration Projects.

Prou, Marc E. (1997), 'Haitian Education under Siege: Democratization, National Development, and Social Reconstruction', in: Robert I. Rotberg (ed.), *Haiti Renewed: Political and Economic Prospects*. Washington, DC: Brookings Institution Press.

Rybczynski, T.M. (1955), 'Factor Endowment and Relative Commodity Prices', *Economica, N.S.*, Vol. 22, 336–41.

Silié, Rubén and Hasbum, Douglas (1996), *Situación de la enseñanza técnica y formatión profesional de la República de Haití*. Consultancy report for the Organización de Estados Iberoamericanos (OEI), Santo Domingo.

Stevenson, Glenn G. (1989), 'The Production, Distribution, and Consumption of Fuelwood in Haiti', *Journal of Developing Areas*, Vol. 24, 59–76.

Tardieu, Charles (1990), *L'éducation en Haïti de la période coloniale à nos jours (1980)*. Port-au-Prince: Imprimerie Henri Deschamps.

World Bank (1981), *Haiti: Economic Memorandum. Recent Economic, Industrial and Sector Development*, Report No. 3079-HA, February 17. Washington, DC: The World Bank.

World Bank (1996), *Memorandum of the President of the International Development Association to the Executive Directors on a Country Assistance Strategy of the World Bank Group for the Republic of Haiti*. Report No. 15945-HA, August 13. Washington, DC: The World Bank.

World Bank (1997), 'Haiti: The Challenges of Poverty Reduction'. March 24. Discussion paper presented at the Haiti Consultative Group Meeting, April 2–4. Port-au-Prince: The World Bank.

Part IV
A Future for Haiti?

Chapter 12, 'Hating the United States Does Not Help Haiti', was published in 2010. The first half of the chapter criticizes an article by the philosopher Peter Hallward, who argues that the United States is behind the underdevelopment of Haiti, without mentioning any domestically created problems. In Hallward's view, Haiti is simply a victim of the imperialist forces that have always blocked all serious efforts to develop the country. He points to Cuba as a positive example of how things could have been in Haiti as well. My argument is that he misses the two central features of Haitian underdevelopment: the erosion process in agriculture and the dismal domestic political tradition.

The second half of the chapter emphasizes the complicated historical relations between the United States and Haiti, from the beginning of the American geopolitical expansion in the 1860s, via the US occupation of the country 1915–34 and the Cold War, up to the present. The argument is that it does not make much sense to focus on 'whose fault it was that Haiti is underdeveloped' in the catastrophe situation. The United States has played a positive role during the catastrophe. Now the time has come for a concerted international reconstruction effort, and the United States has an important role to play in this as well.

Chapter 13, 'After the Earthquake: What Future for Haiti?' attempts to indentify the priorities and the main problems when it comes to rebuilding Haiti after the earthquake that took place on January 12, 2010 and putting the country on a path conducive to sustained social and economic development. It begins with a short account of the principles of reconstruction laid down in the government Action Plan for National Recovery and Development of Haiti.

The first problem is the reform of the Haitian state: the implementation of democracy, the provision of security to the citizens, the creation of an efficient judiciary, and the eradication of corruption. Some recent corruption statistics are presented, and some possible ways of reducing corruption are identified. The second problem is that of economic development and employment: through emigration and through the resurrection and growth of the garment industry. The problems, needs, and possibilities of the apparel sector are sketched. This is followed by a discussion of the need to reform the agricultural sector and of the difficulty of developing the tourist industry in the short run. The importance of future economic and administrative decentralization is stressed. The regions, which decayed during the entire twentieth century, must be developed, not just the capital. The Haitian diaspora may make a contribution, both by returning and by continuing to send money. The leading role of the international community is emphasized: the canceling of Haiti's debt, the administration of the reconstruction and development effort and the control of the aid pouring into the country to prevent it from ending up in the wrong pockets. Finally, the role of the United States and its interest in Haiti is discussed.

12
Hating the United States Does Not Help Haiti

Most of the time, I am rather proud of being a professor, but not always. Sometimes, I feel ashamed on behalf of certain colleagues. In an article in the *Guardian* from January 13, 2010, the philosophy professor Peter Hallward at Middlesex University presents an analysis of Haiti's problems that puts all the blame for the situation in the country on France, the United States, and the international community in general.[1] Together, they have raped the country. During the 40 years that I have dealt with Haiti, I have had to read a lot of nonsense, but Hallward's article certainly takes the prize.

Hallward has grandiose ambitions. He analyzes Haiti on a level where no Haitians exist. He has written *Hamlet* without including the Prince of Denmark. Unfortunately, the context then becomes unintelligible: 'Punitive international trade and financial arrangements ensure that... destitution and impotence will remain a structural fact of Haitian life for the foreseeable future.' Stereotypes and clichés instead of analysis, assumed relations which are simply far-fetched, and unproven claims which are presented as self-evident facts.

Hallward sees the migration from the countryside to the cities as the result of a 'relentless neoliberal assault on Haiti's agrarian economy [which] has forced tens of thousands of small farmers into overcrowded urban slums.' He quotes Brian Concannon, the director of the Institute for Justice and Democracy in Haiti. According to Concannon, the poor ended up in the cities 'because they or their parents were intentionally pushed out of the countryside by aid and trade policies specifically designed to create a large captive and therefore exploitable labour force in the cities...' The Marxist reserve army has been mobilized. Have Hallward and Concannon never been to the Haitian countryside and seen what is taking place there? The population pressure has forced cultivations up the mountainsides. The soil must be laid bare precisely when the tropical downpours set in. This inevitably leads to erosion. The destruction of the soil is the fundamental mechanism pushing people from the countryside to the cities, and it has worked, slowly but inexorably, for a hundred years, probably even longer. Does the neo-liberal violence stimulate the Haitians to make children, or is the precipitation a result of a neo-liberal rain dance of some kind? It would have been interesting to get to know the fundamental chain of causation. Exactly what does the conspiracy look like?

Peter Hallward does not say anything about the catastrophic political tradition of Haiti, a tradition which has left the masses to their fate, created by the very Haitian politicians. In Haiti, politics has always been a concern solely for small cliques who have attempted to wring private incomes out of the population, through the control of the state treasury. This tradition emerged during the nineteenth century, and it has continued up to the present. Between 1843 and 1915, the country had 22 presidents. All of them were predators. Four of them died during their presidencies. A single one managed to finish his term. The remaining 17 were deposed, more or less violently. During these 72 years, Haiti experienced no less than 102 civil wars, revolutions, coups, *attentats*... The United State must certainly have had busy days, if Hallward is to be believed.

The only Haitian who is present in Hallward's article is his idol, Jean-Bertrand Aristide, 'elected by some 75 percent of the electorate', who 'was overthrown by an internationally sponsored coup in 2004 that killed several thousand people and left much of the population smouldering in resentment.' What Hallward carefully chooses to pass by in silence is that Aristide polarized the Haitian population, that he moved politics into the streets and attempted to stay in power for longer than what the constitution allows. He never manifested any willingness to have a dialogue with the opposition, and he managed to split his own party, Lavalas. Aristide did all he could to prevent René Préval from achieving anything during the first presidency of the latter, in order to return himself as a savior, in 2000, in elections which were boycotted by the opposition – hence his landslide victory (92 percent). It is possible, and perhaps even probable, that Aristide had good intentions the first time he was elected president, in 1990, but with the wisdom of hindsight, he appears as the person who closed the 'window of opportunities' for democracy which had been opened after the fall of Baby Doc in 1986. In the end, he simply became one more link in the chain of corrupt presidents with no interest in the development of their country who have always governed Haiti.

Of this, Hallward says nothing. In his view, the consequences of the earthquake are 'the result of... [a long] history of deliberate impoverishment and disempowerment', and poverty is 'the direct legacy of perhaps the most brutal system of colonial exploitation in world history, compounded by decades of systematic postcolonial exploitation'. Ever since the beginning of the American occupation of Haiti, in 1915, 'every serious political attempt to allow Haiti's people to move (in former president Jean-Bertrand Aristide's phrase) "from absolute misery to a dignified poverty" has been violently and deliberately blocked by the US government and some of its allies'. Which are these efforts? Who made them? Hallward does not present them, either in his article or in his book.[2] Was it the Haitian presidents? Sténio Vincent? Elie Lescot? Dumarsais Estimé? Paul Magloire? François Duvalier? Jean-Claude Duvalier? Jean-Bertrand Aristide? Hardly. All these gentlemen had one thing in common with their predecessors from the nineteenth century. Whatever projects they had aimed at something very different from economic and social development. But where did the 'serious political attempt' come from, then? What is it that has been blocked?

'Decades of neoliberal "adjustment" and neo-imperial intervention have robbed... [Haiti's] government of any significant capacity to invest in its people or to regulate its economy', writes Hallward. Obviously, his ideal is the planned economy. 'Cuba has escaped the worst effects of neoliberal "reform", and its government retains a capacity to defend its people from disaster.' Indeed. An earthquake in Havana would have bounced back on Fidel Castro's firm principles, the buildings that have been erected according to socialist norms would of course have resisted and the belief of the Cubans in real socialism would have been strengthened by a 6-hour speech at the Plaza de la Revolución. The kind of economic system that would make sand stand out as a scarce commodity in the Sahara is, however, not needed in Haiti. Everything is scarce there already.

What can the Haitians learn from a system which has forced rationing books on the citizens already under 'normal' (for the Cubans) circumstances, which ruthlessly strangles the efforts of the citizens themselves to improve their living standard and which does not allow any criticism whatsoever of the regime? The probability that history will absolve Fidel Castro must be regarded as negligible. Beware the Haitians of hurricane Fidel.

Peter Hallward is professor of philosophy. His philosophy with respect to Haiti is of the cheap kind, but at this point, good advice is dear. Haiti does not need advisers like Hallward. Socrates would have rubbed his hands with delight if he had got to meet this modern sophist, and Plato would have been able to add another amusing dialogue to the rest. '... deliberate impoverishment and disempowerment...' Hallward's 'analysis' sucks.

* * *

Haiti has a long and complicated relation with the rest of the world. The country was isolated during the nineteenth century. It was surrounded by nations which all feared slave uprisings after the Haitian revolution. Paradoxically, the first country to recognize the sovereignty of Haiti was France, the former colonial power, in 1825, followed by Holland, Prussia, Sweden, and Denmark. The United States did not follow suit until 1862. Five years later, the expansionist American foreign policy took its beginning, and naturally, the Caribbean was then seen as an American interest zone.

The Americans occupied Haiti 1915–34, mainly because the United States feared that Germany would establish submarine bases in the area which would threaten the Panama canal and American shipping. The American economic interests in Haiti were negligible. The occupation was not well administered and not much of what was undertaken survived it. The racism of the times and the lack of understanding of Haitian society and culture made it take a turn for the worse.

The number one priority was the repayment of the national debt. Not very much was left for development purposes. A few American investments were made. Roads were built. The corruption within the administration was reduced. Half-hearted efforts were made in agriculture and education. Health care was improved. The Americans, however, did nothing to prepare the Haitian for democracy. An uprising was crushed brutally, and a new army was created, an army which unfortunately would have far too much political influence after the occupation.

Haiti continued to be the object of American interest also after 1934, not least during the Cold War and after Castro's assumption of power in Cuba. The desire for stability in the Caribbean dominated American policy. Democratic elections were not held until 1990. When the elected president, Jean-Bertrand Aristide, was deposed by the military the following year, he was reinstated with American assistance in 1994.

All this is history, and ought to remain history.

On January 12, 2010, the capital of Haiti was destroyed by an earthquake. The reports in the media have mainly dealt with the consequences of the quake and of what is needed to bring the country back on its feet. However, not everyone seems to have understood that you must look to the future. Some look back instead, through biased and mis-colored glasses. The Friends of Anti-Americanism have felt the fresh morning air after the catastrophe. For them, the task ahead is not to help the poor Haitians but to stigmatize the United States. A long tradition exists which puts all the blame for Haiti's problem on the outside world. France created a slave colony during the seventeenth and eighteenth centuries, and after the liberation, the United States has blocked economic and social development.

Blaming the United States, however, simply serves to obfuscate the much more important domestic causes of underdevelopment. During the nineteenth century, a predatory state was created in Haiti, and it is this state that has constituted the main obstacle to economic and social development in the small island nation, all the way up to the present day.

Most unproductive of all is to summon up a picture of a United States that has not changed since the days of President Woodrow Wilson. It was not the United States of Wilson that intervened after the earthquake on January 12. It was that of the black president Barack Obama.

It was completely self-evident that the United States had to take the lead of the immediate rescue operations. Port au Prince is a mere hour from Miami, and the United States had a unified command. The United Nations administration of Haiti was in shambles. When former Haitian prime minister Michèle Pierre-Louis got the question from *Le Figaro* if the United States intervention did not amount to tutelage, she denied it energetically. It was a question of pragmatism. Discussing history at the present time is meaningless. It's all about reconstruction.[3]

The first phase of the assistance – pure catastrophe aid – will soon come to an end. Thereafter, the nation of Haiti must be rebuilt – a new Haiti that throws its dismal history overboard. Nation-building is of course in the first place a task for the Haitians themselves, but in collaboration with the international community. It can never be a concern just for the United States.

Organizations like the United Nations and the World Bank must play a prominent role. The Haitian catastrophe is the worst in the history of the United Nations. Economic and social development is a long-run process by definition. There are no simple solutions, no panaceas. What has been destroyed must be rebuilt. The wheels of the economy must be made to turn. Haiti is not even back on square one.

Unfortunately, believing that the Haitians will manage to break with their history without help is not realistic. The domestic politicians have time after time proved that they lack both interest and ability. Here, help and support is necessary, and unfortunately also supervision. The Haitians must think in completely other directions than hitherto. It's a question of breeding new leaders and politicians who do not focus on their own vested interests but who have an understanding of what life is actually like for people living on one or half a dollar a day.

In this, no Marxist, post-modern or post-colonial phrase rhetoric is of any help. There is no reason to question the fundamental Western humanistic values. The time has come to take the humanitarian engagement of the United States seriously. In his *Newsweek* article of January 25, 2010, Obama stressed that the United States will collaborate both with the United Nations and the people and government of Haiti.[4]

There is no reason to doubt that this will happen.

Notes

First part published in *Axess* (Swedish version), No. 2, 2010 and the second part published in *Sydsvenskan* (Swedish version), February 5, 2010.

1. Hallward (2010).
2. Hallward (2007).
3. Berthemet (2010).
4. Obama (2010).

References

Berthemet, Tanguy (2010), 'Michèle Pierre-Louis: "Il faut qu'une entité commande"', *Le Figaro*, January 19.

Hallward, Peter (2007), *Damming the Flood: Haiti, Aristide, and the Politics of Containment*. London and New York: Verso.

Hallward, Peter (2010), 'Our Role in Haiti's Plight', *The Guardian*, January 13.

Obama, Barack (2010), 'Why Haiti Matters', *Newsweek*, January 25.

13 After the Earthquake: What Future for Haiti?

On January 12, 2010, the two tectonic plaques that meet below Haiti began to rub against each other. Seven minutes to five in the afternoon, an earthquake of magnitude 7.0 on the Richter scale took place, followed by 32 after-quakes of 4.0 or more during the following 9 hours.[1] The epicenter was a mere 25 kilometers from the capital, and the quake struck at a distance of just 13 kilometers from the surface of the earth.[2]

Port-au-Prince lies in ruins. The city looks like Berlin at the end of World War II. As stated in the Prologue, over 600,000 people have left for the countryside. The suburb Carrefour and the cities of Léogâne, Grand Goâve, Petit Goâve, and Jacmel are destroyed. Between 250,000 and 300,000, people are reported to be dead. Around 300,000 are injured. Three million people have been affected in some way by the disaster.[3]

The earthquake took place in an environment where the buildings were crummy, the infrastructure completely run down, and the public service was next to non-existent already before the disaster struck. The chapters in this book have dealt with the factors that have made Haiti the most underdeveloped country in the Americas. The combination of soil erosion and kleptocracy for almost a century and a half has produced a per capita income which is the lowest in the Western Hemisphere. More than three-fourths of the population lived on less than the equivalent of two US dollars per day already before the earthquake half the population on less than one (in 2000),[4] and the average income of the latter group was 0.44 dollars.[5] It was in this situation that the earthquake struck – in a country which one-and-a-half years before had been hit by four hurricanes in less than 3 weeks.

Now, the difficult task of physical reconstruction of the affected areas has begun, and thereafter the challenge of long-run economic and social development has to be faced. It will not be easy. Haiti's ecology is fragile, and the interplay between man and the environment has created a gigantic erosion problem which inexorably depresses rural incomes over time. Haiti also has a completely catastrophic political history. In the best case its governments have been mediocre, most of the time they have been dismal. And now, there is hardly any government or administration at all. Virtually, all the important command functions have been wiped out.

The International Donors' Conference Towards a New Future for Haiti at the United Nations in New York on March 31, 2010 more than met the expectations. The basic idea of the conference was to make it possible for the donors to pledge *new* long-term assistance, as distinct from the immediate humanitarian assistance, and to coordinate the development effort. The target set by the Haitian government was to raise US$3.8 billion for the first 18 months of the recovery and reconstruction effort.[6]

The donor community promised Haiti a great deal more: $5.26 billion for the first 18 months, and 9.9 billion altogether for the coming 3 years.[7] But how is the reconstruction to take place? Can Haiti be put on the path of self-sustained long-run economic development? The country must be rebuilt, and not to the level where it was on January 12, 2010, but to a level which for the first time in the history of the country may give the citizens something that looks like a decent standard of living. The task is one of building a new nation and a new economy.

What is needed then? You might as well say it at once. There are no simple solutions for Haiti after the earthquake catastrophe. Some sort of Marshall Plan is needed. But what should it contain? Everything is in shambles in the capital and its surroundings. Everything has to be repaired and reformed. It goes without saying that the reconstruction must begin at the physical end. People need dwellings and for daily life to return to something resembling normalcy, the public administration and the economy must get back on their feet.

The action plan

At a Technical Preparatory Conference for Haiti held in Santo Domingo March 15–17, 2010, the Haitian government presented the first draft of an *Action Plan for the Reconstruction and National Development of Haiti*.[8] A revised version – *Action Plan for National Recovery and Development of Haiti* – was presented in New York on March 31.[9] The foundation of the plan, which envisages a total investment of US$3864 million over

18 months, is the solidarity between all Haitians that is expected to materialize in the wake of the catastrophe:

> The situation that the country is facing is difficult but not desperate. In many ways it is an opportunity to unite Haitians of all classes and origins in a shared project to rebuild the country on new foundations. Nobody has been spared, and no one can pick themselves up again alone. We must build on this new solidarity which is expected to trigger profound changes in behaviour and attitudes.[10]

Thus, the plan calls for the participation of 'all the sectors of the Haitian society'. It contains a long-term vision with respect to the future. According to the first version:

> ***We share a dream***:
>
> We see Haiti as an emergent country by 2030; a society of simplicity, fairness and justice; united, living in harmony with its environment, culture and a controlled modernity based on the rule of law, freedom of association and expression and national planning, with a modern, strong, dynamic, competitive, open economy and a broad territorial basis, where all basic needs of the population are met and managed by a Unitary State which is strong, acts as a guarantor of the general interest and is highly devolved and decentralized.[11]

The UN Secretary General, Ban Ki-moon has called the action plan 'a visionary document'.[12] If the dream comes true, it will mean that, for the first time ever, Haiti has managed to break with its dismal political history. It will be nothing short of a revolution, a revolution as important as that of 1791. The envisaged strategy rests on the creation of wealth and jobs mainly through the private sector working within a good macroeconomic framework hand in hand with a strong state in order to make it possible to protect the environment and create social development and public service to the population in a geographically decentralized and balanced way which ensures the inclusion of all groups of Haitian society.

The government identified five main reasons for the extreme damage caused by the earthquake: excessive population density, the catastrophic state of the environment, the lack of adequate building standards, the unregulated land use and the unbalanced geographic distribution of economic activity, and the plan envisages that 'all these areas of vulnerability' will be addressed.[13]

The major part of the funding of the recovery and development effort has to come from abroad. The buildings of the central tax administration and customs were destroyed during the earthquake, and much of the commercial and financial sector which constitutes the main tax base was severely damaged as well. Since 85 percent of the government revenue came from the Port-au-Prince area before the catastrophe, this amounts to a major shortfall. Together with the immediate reconstruction needs, it puts a heavy burden on external finance for some years to come. For the remainder of the 2009–10 fiscal year, the amount of budget support needed has been estimated to US$350 million.[14]

The recovery effort has been divided into three phases: an immediate one, covering 18 months, a second one encompassing 10 years, divided into three programming cycles, 'during which the reconstruction and recovery of Haiti will become a reality, in order to put the country back on the road to development, followed by another 10 years to make it a real emerging country'.[15] The main concern of the action plan is the immediate reconstruction phase. It focuses on four different areas: territorial, economic, social, and institutional rebuilding. To administer the reconstruction and development effort, the creation of two bodies is recommended: an Interim Haiti Reconstruction Commission (IHRC) and a multi-donor trust fund, the Haiti Reconstruction Fund (HRF) to pool the donor funds and avoid overlapping of initiatives. The temporary commission will eventually become a Haiti Development Agency (HDA). It will take responsibility for Haiti's development planning, draw up and initiate projects and approve project proposals to make certain that they agree with the priorities of the action plan.

In Santo Domingo, the donor community committed itself to provide US$3.8 billion over the next 18 months to finance the priority needs, and to give the Haitian government an additional 350 million in direct budget support for 2010.[16] At the conference, it was agreed that the World Bank will administer the reconstruction fund through its International Development Association (IDA) and that the IHRC will be led by the present Haitian prime minister, Jean-Max Bellerive, and Bill Clinton for a period of 18 months. Thereafter the Haitian government under the leadership of the president will take over.[17] The commission was approved by the Haitian parliament in mid-April, and toward the end of May, an advertisement was placed in *The Economist* for an executive director.

To a large extent, the action plan looks like a wish list. It was to be expected. The plan had to be produced rapidly, under all kinds of pressures, in order to secure the necessary funds for the reconstruction and development effort. There was no way of avoiding putting the dough in first. But yeast is also vital, more than ever. Now that the funding has been secured, the time has come to identify the *real* priorities. The action plan alone does not provide enough guidance. The rest of this chapter will be devoted to that.

A new nation

Before the earthquake, Haiti was a failed, thoroughly corrupt state.[18] It is completely clear that the long march back to square one and the journey from there toward a decent material existence requires not only money but also aid, monitoring, and supervision from outside. The task is to build a new nation, no less, no more. This, however, does not require Haiti to give up its sovereignty. That is neither necessary nor desirable. The idea is not that the United States or the United Nations should occupy the country administratively. What is needed is some kind of double command on many levels, where the international community works side by side with and trains what is left of the domestic administration so that more and more tasks can be transferred. In the end, the Haitian administration must be able to function by itself, but it is illusory to believe that it does so today or will do so in a satisfactory way in the near future.

Given that a new nation must be built, a discussion of the possible future scenarios becomes inevitable. Today, Haiti is balancing on a narrow knife edge. The vital functions in society rest on external inputs. What will happen when this is no longer the case? There is no question about the fact that the catastrophe has created possibilities. In one sense, it has cleaned the table of the past. With this view, there is only one road to be traveled: the one that leads to a new future with new structures in society which lead to economic growth and a rising living standard. The task ahead is to find new formulae and new forms through organizational creativity.

This will take time, however, and the road is full of obstacles. The most pressing problem is that of arranging elections. On February 7, 2011, the presidency of René Préval comes to its constitutional end. He cannot be elected a third time.[19] If presidential elections cannot be arranged in time, the president of the Supreme Court steps in as acting president, a solution that will provoke criticism from those who want to get away from and international administration of Haiti. If the elections materialize, on the other hand, social disturbances are likely to take place, since the probability that voters can be registered in a satisfactory way is very low. A new parliament must also be elected.

Elections are called for as soon as the institutions that can guarantee the credibility of the process are in place, a point which has been stressed by President Préval as well: 'What we must absolutely avoid is that we have a temporary provisional government (beyond the date of presidential elections) that does not enjoy legitimacy.'[20] Hence, such institutions as the National Identification Office and the CEP (Conseil Électoral Provisoire, the electoral council) must be strengthened very rapidly to make voter and party candidate registration possible. (The history of the latter has been marred by such events as ambiguous vote counting and the exclusion of the party of former president Jean-Bertrand Aristide from the senate elections of 2009 on technical grounds.) As it seems, when the present is being written, the elections will take place on November 28, 2010, the date put down by the constitution,[21] and Préval has stated that he intends to stay in office for an extra 3 months, until May 14, 2011, instead of stepping down on February 7, if elections cannot be held in November.[22]

There is no guarantee whatsoever that the future development of Haitian society will be channeled into new directions. Physical reconstruction is one thing. Reconstruction of society is another. During the reconstruction phase very large sums of foreign assistance money will be circulating in Haiti, a great deal more than the country has ever received before. As we have come back to, time after time, in this book, corruption runs like a thread through the entire history of the country. Are there any indications that it will disappear in the near future? Will the worm once more bore into the apple, or will the apple grow and mature until the arrival of the harvest period? The answers to these questions are not given in any way.

The two scenarios lead directly to the question of the contents of the future Haitian politics. Up to now, a party has been more or less synonymous with its leader. The man comes first, the supporters only thereafter: *moun pou m,* my people. It has been the leaders who have created the parties, not the parties that have elected their leaders, and unfortunately the goals of the leaders have been far from synonymous with the good of the people. This kind of leaders have no place in a positive development spiral. On the contrary, they will simply act as a brake on it. Will the earthquake serve as a catalyst for a process that will create a different brand of Haitian politicians? It is impossible to know. Possibly, it can make strong, hitherto unknown, leaders step forward, but we have no way of knowing. During the immediate aftermath of the earthquake, potential leaders have had no way of making themselves heard, since the means of communications have been knocked out. The president has not been able to communicate with his people,[23] and no other leaders – old or new – either. What speaks for a new order is possibly a change of generations. Younger Haitians do not think like their elders, and they ought to have a better understanding of the need for renovation, but – again – it is in no way self-evident which the post-earthquake course of Haitian politics will be.

Reforming the state

The Haitian state never worked well, but without an honest and efficient state apparatus, long-run development will not be possible. A working democracy rests on a functioning parliament which facilitates a meaningful dialogue between the government and the opposition. The Haitian tradition deviates blatantly from this norm. Politics has revolved around confrontation and intolerance, nothing else. Political bliss is when you can govern and make decisions without interference. All the dictatorships and semi-dictatorships that Haiti has had to suffer have left a heritage which is not easy to get rid of. The political history of the country has always been the number one obstacle to change.[24]

In order to prevent politics from degenerating once more in Haiti, institutions must be built which make it possible for the citizens to hold the politicians responsible for their acts. In other words: What is needed is a functioning democracy. Despite the fact that Haiti has held elections regularly since 1990, the democratic process has not worked.[25] It has been interrupted on various occasions, and not even the very politicians who have been elected through it have respected it. The parliament has been closed occasionally, and the debate which forms part of the core of a functioning democracy has been suppressed. The old confrontation policy survived the transition from dictatorship and military rule to power changes based on elections.

One of the roles of the opposition is to scrutinize the government and the parties in power and hold them accountable for their policy decisions, asking for explanations and justifications. This has never been possible in Haiti. Democracy is difficult. In order to change things, people must know their rights, and the democratic idea must be so well anchored among the regular citizens that they begin to put pressure on the representatives that they have elected, but this, in turn requires education, an education which also includes respect for human rights, knowledge about the workings of democracy and information about the contents of politics. No such education has ever been furnished in Haiti, and unfortunately, education takes time. Changing the present state will take a generation – under favorable circumstances.

The two gaps

Meaningful popular participation in politics is also rendered difficult by the continuing existence of the two gaps that we have made reference to earlier in the book, the one between the elite and the masses[26] and the one between the state and the citizens.[27] The masses have no place in the world of the elite. They are second-class citizens,[28] and those who govern have done it for their own good, not for the good of the people.

There are no consensus-building mechanisms in Haiti: the country by and large lacks reciprocity norms and networks for cooperation between different social classes. There is very little social capital, no trust across class borders which make collaboration possible.[29] The middle class aspires at upper-class status, and the peasants are *moun andeyò*, people who live physically outside the urban word and who, from the point of view of the elite, exist virtually exclusively as food producers.

The Haitians have always mistrusted the state and have never expected any good to come from it. The state has been an almost physical entity in Haiti, often a person in uniform, and most contacts with it for the common Haitian have implied conscription into the army, tax collection, or some other unpleasant experience. *Vole de leta se pa vole*, says the proverb. To steal from the state is not to steal, since the state steals from the citizens. Opinion polls clearly indicate that the confidence of the citizens in politicians in general, and above all in the government, is low.[30] The latter has no legitimacy in the eyes of the people. If it ever represented anything but itself, it was the elite or the military. The army was abolished by President Aristide in 1995, but the elite are still present. According to then Prime Minister Michèle Pierre-Louis:

> All the elites – the mulatto elites, the university elites, the union elites, the peasant elites – are like a huge elephant sitting on this country and you cannot move it, because there is no political class, because there are no political parties, and everyone becomes corrupted and perverted. If you can't go into that system, the system rejects you. And so far we have not found the wrench that moves this thing.[31]

Up to now, there have not been any incentives for the elite to reform or reconstruct the country:

> The elite is a nebulous class in Haiti; its members speak French and are educated abroad, marking them apart from the 'mass population'. They probably belong to one of four powerful groups: traditional families, members of illegal traffic networks, former supporters of Aristide and the former military, now part of the Haitian National Police. These groups each have their own gangs; sometimes forging alliances; sometimes opposing each other. Different types of associations and alliances exist between these groups; they are similar to African patterns such as clans but can also be politically motivated. Elite circles are difficult to access... But... if they were all to unite, they could make the government fall at any moment. It is very difficult for the international community to understand the underground currents, links and activities of the elite, and how to work with them to foster development. They control commerce, strategic imports, hotels, telecommunications and banks. [ ] the Haitian elite could actually be classified as one of the worst elites of any fragile state.[32]

To build consensus-creating mechanisms will be an important task in post-earthquake Haiti. Hitherto, the governments have employed a top-down approach. Grass-roots initiatives have been suppressed or controlled by the governing layers of society.[33] If Haitian society is to be successfully reformed, this tradition must be broken. The support to Haiti must not end in the ministries in the capital. It must trickle down all the way to the local level.

Institution building

The reform of the state must rest on institution building. The Haitian civil service received a severe blow from the earthquake. Many lives were lost and key buildings like the presidential palace, the parliament, and several law courts and ministries were destroyed. New people have to be recruited and the destroyed premises must be rebuilt, possibly in new places. According to the action plan, priority will be given to those parts of the administration which are crucial for the reconstruction effort: the Presidency, the Prime Minister's Office, The Ministry of Economy and Finance (notably the Tax Office and Customs), the Ministry of the Interior and Territorial Communities, the Ministry of Planning and External

Cooperation, the Ministry of Public Works and Telecommunications, the Ministry of State Education and Professional Training, The Ministry of Public Health and Population, the Ministry of Justice and Public Security, and the Ministry of Agriculture and Natural Resources.[34]

Much more important than the acute needs, however, is that the fundamental Haitian institutions needed a complete overhaul already before the earthquake. This necessity remains today as well, and it has, of course, been compounded by the impact of the catastrophe.

Two of the institutions that have needed thorough reform for many years are the police and the judiciary. The security of the citizens must be guaranteed. Otherwise, nothing will work. Crime has been a serious problem for quite some time. The police force that was created in 1995 has not managed to maintain order.[35] The Haitian police has been weak, both numerically – 1500 officers during most of the 2000s, before an increase to almost 9000 in 2008[36] – and in terms of quality. It has been difficult to weed out the lemons in the recruitment process, and the present police force is perceived as not much better than the old one, a constabulary which also had military functions. Police officers on all levels have been involved in drug trade and corruption scandals.[37] The Haitians are divided. On the one hand, they are for zero tolerance against crime. On the other hand, they don't trust the police.[38]

Since 2004, a UN force, MINUSTAH (Mission de Nations Unies pour la Stabilisation en Haïti), has handled the daily police operations,[39] and also in the foreseeable future, the presence of an international police force will be necessary, probably for as long as 8–10 years.[40] In the longer run, the Haitians themselves must take charge, but then the police must be completely remodeled so the citizens can feel that it is 'their' police who are there to protect, and not harass, them. 'Ordinary' people must acquire an interest in the profession. The composition of the police corps must by and large mirror that of the population at large. Sociologically, the two worlds must overlap.

The police force must be supported by a functioning judiciary. In Haiti, there is no such thing. 'In the case of the judiciary system, reforming and capacity-building will not be sufficient. What is needed in reality is a complete overhaul of the institutions, from the foundations up', notes Amélie Gauthier.[41] The court system has not been able to handle its tasks. Between 1994 and 2004, hundreds of millions of dollars were pumped into projects which aimed at reforming the system. In spite of this, in 2004, the respect for rule of law had fallen to the lowest level since the end of military rule in 1994.[42] People suspected of crime remain in overcrowded jails during weeks, months, and years without being duly prosecuted,[43] civil cases are completely paralyzed for years on end, and the judges are both inadequately educated and corrupt. Those who are convicted often get their sentences on dubious grounds, and it is very easy to influence the judges.

Initiating a civil case in a Haitian court may easily cost more than what the object of the controversy is worth and the cases tend to be drawn out way beyond the reasonable. Such practices have a negative influence on entrepreneurship and business. If you cannot be confident that contracts will be honored, no productive activities will be promoted. The judiciary is in practice controlled by the Ministry of Justice, even though the constitution of Haiti requires it to be independent. More than half of the justices of the peace (the lowest court level) lack formal legal training. The government investigation of corruption that was published in 2007 (reported below) found a low degree of confidence in the judiciary among households, country directors, and non-governmental organizations (NGOs) alike.[44] Both the judiciary and the police were found to ask for bribes regularly.

The disaster that hit Haiti wreaked havoc in the police and the judiciary. No less than 80 percent of the Port-au-Prince justice sector was affected by it. Hence, the reestablishment of justice and public security across the entire national territory was made a priority in the action plan presented by the Haitian government during the international donor conference held in New York on March 31, 2010. Around 500 police officers are dead, injured, or missing. During the initial reconstruction phase, the aim is to replace them. Thereafter, the target is 1 officer per 800 inhabitants as of 2012, one per 600 at the end of 2015 (an increase from 9500 today to 16,000). A National School of Judges and a Police Academy will be put in place. Prisons in Port-au-Prince and Jacmel will be reconstructed and developed to reduce the density of prisoners.[45]

Fighting corruption

President René Préval has made it clear that the reconstruction and development effort must be Haitian:

> This is the opportunity for us to tell the entire world that the reconstruction of our country must be above all a national effort, an appropriate reflection of the solidarity shown right after the earthquake by all the Haitian people. It is also the opportunity for the Government to express on behalf of the nation, in a strong and united voice, its gratitude to the international community for its

> assistance in support of Haiti's strategic vision and choices for the reconstruction of our country.[46]

The action plan exhorts the international community 'to reiterate its long-term commitment to support the country in its re-establishment and to do this with respect for Haitian leadership'.[47]

Before the New York conference, the Secretary General of the United Nations, Ban Ki-moon, also underscored the importance of breaking with the past:

> As we move from emergency aid to longer-term reconstruction, let us recognize that we cannot accept business as usual. What we envision is nothing less than a wholesale national renewal.
>
> In partnership with the international community, Haiti's leaders are committing to a new social contract with their people. That means fully democratic government, grounded in sound economic and social policies that address extreme poverty and deep-rooted disparities of wealth. It also means fair and free elections, conducted with U.N. help, preferably by the end of this year. [...]
>
> During the coming days, the world's leaders will rise to stand by Haiti – a solidarity to be measured in years, long after the initial shock of the disaster has passed: I am confident that, together, we can set Haiti on the road to a very different future.[48]

The dice are cast. The long promises have been made. Delivery – the most problematic step – remains. One of the most difficult parts will be to overcome the corrupt practices of the past. On March 11, 2010, the US Department of State published its 2009 human rights report on Haiti:

> The law provides criminal penalties for official corruption; however, the government did not implement the law effectively, and officials often engaged in corrupt practices with impunity. According to the World Bank's worldwide governance indicators, government corruption was a severe problem. Corruption remained widespread in all branches and at all levels of government.[49]

Préval did not like the conclusions at all. In an interview for Reuters, he labeled the criticism 'arrogant', argued that there was 'nothing to reject or accept. It is an arbitrary judgment to which we won't respond...', and contended that the Haitian presidency should have the final say with respect to the donor-financed reconstruction projects. The interim governing board 'will analyze the projects proposed by the Haitian government and there will be an executive council for the execution of the projects once they have been approved by the governing board, and finally by the president, who has right of veto'.[50]

Unfortunately, history does not speak for Préval. Table 1 shows Haiti's position on the Corruption Perceptions Index published by Transparency International for the years 2002–09. The index runs from 0 to 10, with 0 at the bottom.

What is more, In January 2007, the final report from an investigation of corruption ordered by the Haitian government and carried out in 2005–06 was presented.[51] The results confirmed the Transparency International findings. The study was ordered by the Unité de Lutte Contre la Corruption (ULCC), created by the government in 2004, and was carried out by the Bureau de Recherche en Informatique et en Développement Économique et Social, an independent Haitian firm. It is based on interviews with households, company directors, public servants, and NGOs. The interviews were made in the capital, in Cap-Haïtien, in Ouanaminthe and in the rural community of Malpasse, on the Dominican border, opposite Jimaní.

More than 97 percent, or virtually all the interviewed households (1071 altogether), indicated that corruption in general was 'a problem' or 'a serious problem' in Haiti. No less than 93.5 percent thought it was 'serious'. Over 91 percent of all the interviewed households, almost 88 percent of the public sector employees and more than 70 percent of the firms considered corruption in the public sector to be a 'very serious' problem, and 68 percent of the households maintained that things had

Table 1 Haiti's position in the Transparency International corruption perceptions index

Year	Position from the bottom	Index	Number of countries included
2002	11	2.2	102
2003	2	1.5	133
2004	Last	1.5	146
2005	4	1.8	159
2006	Last	1.8	163
2007	3	1.6	180
2008	3	1.4	180
2009	7	1.8	180

Source: http://www.transparency.org, CPI for each respective year. Downloaded February 22, 2010.

become worse during the last 3 years. Seventy-seven percent of them stated that bribes were frequent. Even the majority of the public sector employees considered corruption to be 'widespread' or 'very widespread' in the government sector.

The customs and tax authorities and the justice sector were considered to be the most corrupt entities by households, firms and NGOs alike, and the latter two, as well as the public servants, also ranked the political parties low.[52] Around 49 percent of the NGOs considered the parliament corrupt, and so did almost 58 percent of the company directors. The worst quality in terms of public service was found in the justice, drinking water, and electricity sectors. The perception of the quality of public service by the households contrasted brightly with that of the public employees. Thus, 75 percent of the households considered the services rendered by the justice sector to be 'bad' or 'very bad', whereas 61.5 percent of the employees in the sector held it to be of high quality. Although the public employees recognized that corruption was a problem in the public sector in general, they were not prepared to admit that their own departments or agencies were affected. Close to 73 percent of the households did not believe that the government made an honest effort to combat corruption, and 70 percent stated that it encouraged it instead. Seven percent of the households and eight percent of the company directors declared that they were willing to spend money if it could contribute to the complete eradication of corruption. One of the main reasons for not denouncing corruption, however, was that the respondents perceived that no proper system that allowed them to do so existed. The households felt that denounces would not be followed up and they feared reprisals.

In a survey carried out by Oxfam in March 2010 in the areas affected by the earthquake, only 6.6 percent of all respondents thought that the leadership role in the reconstruction process should be played by the Haitian government alone, over 39 percent thought it should be played by a foreign government, and almost 25 percent favored the Haitian government in collaboration with local authorities and the civil society. Those who favored foreign leadership stressed foreign financial resources and expertise in disaster management but also the Hatian governments' lack of responsibility, poor governance, and corrupt practices.[53]

The burden of proof that the Haitian administration is not corrupt is thus on the Haitian, not American, government. It will of course be impossible to avoid the issue. The action plan puts down the requirements: 'The management framework of the different mechanisms [of the funding of the reconstruction and development effort] must comprise all the guarantees necessary for the proper and transparent management of the funds involved.'[54] The manager of the trust fund, Joe Leitmann, has stressed that the fund will apply the highest standards of financial management and procurement. '... transparency and accountability will be very much a part of what we do'.[55] The World Bank has also announced that an anti-corruption unit will be created within the interim commission.[56]

The main problem with corruption in Haiti is that it has always stemmed from the top of society, from the Haitian presidents.[57] Given this, all the other layers in the pyramid will be corrupt as well – by necessity. The signals sent from above encourage destructive income-maximizing plunder at all lower levels.[58] This kind of state is not easily reformed, If Robert Klitgaard is to be believed, however, it is not impossible.[59] Most important is to focus on corrupt *systems* instead on corrupt *individuals*. A number of 'big fish' must be 'fried' so that the citizens see that the anti-corruption struggle is honest, and it is important to show quick results, but after that, emphasis should be on prevention and reform of the systems which breed corruption. Generally speaking, corruption is worst when someone has a monopoly of goods or services, decisions are discretionary, and no accountability exists. The remedies are competition, clear rules that are made public, and transparent measurement and evaluation of operations carried out by independent entities. The issue is one of creating incentive systems which are conducive to productive, instead of destructive, behavior.

How can the struggle against corruption be anchored in the supreme command of the Haitian state? It is of course impossible to mechanically assume that a willingness exists at the top to do something about corruption. Klitgaard does not offer any panacea of how to create this willingness, but in all probability international advice and monitoring backed by legal sanctions must play a core role. Also on the highest level, clear rules and public exposure are important instruments when it comes to setting new, superior, standards. The hands of the president and the government must be tied, so that the exercise of power does not fall back into the old swamp of graft and corruption.

Economic development

It goes without saying that unless the wheels of the Haitian economy can made to turn at a considerably faster pace than in the past, it will not be possible to raise livings standards. But how is this to be achieved?[60]

As the action plan rightly points out, in the short run, 'the absolute priority... is to respond to the needs of the disaster-stricken population'. This, in the first place, includes the building of new homes, but since the living standard of those affected also received a hard blow 'it is necessary to engage in massive job creation programmes as soon as possible', all over the country.[61] Otherwise, the massive aid inflow may place a large part of the Haitian population in a state of dependence. As was made clear by the Oxfam survey, jobs are the main priority of the Haitians themselves,[62] and short-run opportunities are not lacking:

> The existing situation offers many opportunities for high-intensity labour. This relates to activities in rural areas, with the restoration of production infrastructures (irrigation systems, farm tracks) and the development of watersheds (reforestation, setting up pasture-land, correcting ravines in peri-urban areas, fruit trees). The road maintenance programmes also address this objective, using the same method as has been used for a number of years by the road maintenance fund, with an accelerated schedule. Minor community-based infrastructures (tracks, paths, footbridges, shops and community centres, small reservoirs and feed pipes, etc.) and urban infrastructures (roadway paving, squares, drainage network cleaning) follow a similar logic, as do projects relating to the cleaning and recycling of materials engendered by the collapse of buildings in the areas most affected by the earth-quake.[63]

The job creation process should give priority to families assisting disabled people and women who have suffered severely from the catastrophe. Wages are to be decent, but not high enough to lure people already employed away from their regular jobs. The projects should be economically viable sound investments and not just aim for job creation.

What will happen to the Haitian economy in the longer run is a completely open question. The targets of the action plan are an average 3.5 percent growth rate of GDP per capita between now and 2015, based on a rapid recovery of GDP in 2010–11 of no less than 10.4 percent, falling gradually to 6.2 percent in 2015. This, according to the plan, should make it possible to reduce the extent of poverty (living on less than $1 per day) from 54 to 40 percent the latter year.[64] How realistic it is remains to be seen.

The action plan emphasizes the leading role of private investment already in the first phase: '...private investment in the economy as well as in the social sector will form the backbone of the country's reconstruction.'[65] The stimulus package during the projected growth phase is, however, not spelled out in any detail. The plan simply speaks of 'a dynamic process of giving new value to the production sectors'[66] based on a very broad package of measures:

> a) structural reforms to promote competitiveness and develop comparative advantages in certain sectors, guarantee ownership rights, reduce transaction costs, and provide an effective incentive system and rational, balanced use of the territory; b) public investments in infrastructures and basic services; c) a pro-active macro-economic policy; d) the development of partnerships with the private sector based on a pragmatic approach focusing on identifying opportunities and reviving investments; e) structuring of trade associations and formalization of the informal sector; f) promoting and supervising small- and medium-sized businesses in the various sectors; g) access to loans for the various sectors of activities; h) development of regional growth hubs and exploiting local resources across the whole of the country; i) sped-up production of human capital; and j) harmonization and review of the legal and regulatory framework for businesses.[67]

A more or less balanced growth strategy is sketched: 'In this second phase, growth will be stimulated by construction, agriculture and agro-processing, tourism, manufacturing, and crafts.' Not least, half a million houses will have to be rebuilt, mainly by foreign constructors 'and a small minority of Haitian firms'.[68]

Whether the growth figures of the action plan will materialize or not is difficult to judge. Success may not be within easy reach. The damage estimate made by the Inter-American Development Bank pointed out that a full decade after such a major disaster as the one that just took place in Haiti the growth rate of GDP may be 30 percent lower than what it would otherwise have been, even in the presence of major aid inflows.[69]

Maybe one should not look too closely at the action plan scenario. Figures may not mean too much right now. It may be better to focus on some 'qualitative' facts when it comes to sketching the future course. Then, the most fundamental of all economic facts is that most Haitians are peasants, and as we have come back to several times, their income is being systematically depressed over time as a result of the interplay between population growth and soil erosion. After the earthquake, the situation has become even more severe than before, since hundreds of thousands of people have moved out of the damaged areas into the countryside.

Haiti is simply too mountainous. Less than 30 percent of the territory has a slope of less than 10 percent.[70] The kind of agriculture which is practiced in Haiti today amounts to mining the soil. If nothing is done to change this the arable area will continue to shrink. People must leave the countryside. There is no way around it. And those who remain must be brought down from the mountainsides. Unfortunately, the action plan is completely silent on this point, but the question cannot be avoided or postponed. Any argument to the contrary is simply naïve. The reduction of the rural population cannot be achieved with force, only by the provision of employment alternatives which stand out as superior both to agriculture and to moving to the already severely overcrowded capital.

Emigration

The first best solution of the employment and income problem entails moving more Haitians out of the country. Immediately after the catastrophe, the president of Senegal, Abdoulaye Wade, offered the Haitians land in his country, 'even an entire region', if necessary.[71] He will not have to deliver. Paradise is much closer. The Haitian dream is to emigrate to the United States (and Canada), and emigration during the past 30 years has been the most important social insurance mechanism.[72] James Dobbins from the RAND Corporation has consequently suggested that the United States should increase its immigration quota for Haitians temporarily.[73] His argument is an interesting one. The Haitians who live in the United States work hard, are law-abiding, and have strong ties with their families back home. Each dollar they remit in principle saves one dollar of tax-financed American aid to Haiti – an effect which is easily overlooked in the discussion of how much immigration to allow.

A similar suggestion was put forward by Nancy Birdsall from the Center for Global Development (CGD) in a testimony for the House Financial Services Subcommittee on International Monetary Policy and Trade: a Golden Door Visa for a limited number of Haitians. No great numbers are involved, and the income leverage for those admitted would be strong:

> It doesn't need to mean more immigrants, though it might; it could be made 'numbers-neutral' so that the number of all immigrants

> stayed the same but became slightly weighted toward places where people need more opportunity. It could be given in more limited numbers when the U.S. economy is weak, greater numbers when it's strong. Even small numbers would be tremendously helpful: 10,000 per year would represent a 50% increase in the number of legal Haitian immigrants, but only 1% of total U.S. immigrants. Creating some degree of flexibility in this way would help reduce the embarrassment of forcing poor people who will be trying to leave Haiti back into the disaster zone. It may also be the most successful way to help Haitians lift themselves out of poverty. According to calculations by [Michael] Clemens and CGD visiting fellow Lant Pritchett, 82 percent of Haitians who live on more than $10 per day live in the U.S. Only the top 1.4 percent of people in Haiti had that living standard even before the quake. So for most of the Haitians who left, leaving Haiti was the *cause* of leaving poverty.[74]

Unfortunately, the likelihood that the calls for increased immigration quotas will be heeded is low. This puts the burden of employment and income creation on the Haitian economy. A sector which will absorb a lot of people in the immediate future is construction, both of buildings and infrastructure: dwellings, offices, factories, public buildings, as well as roads and streets. The scope for expansion is, however, limited. Employment in construction will reach a peak and then decrease again unless the Haitian economy enters a phase of long-run, sustained growth.

Industrialization

In the longer run, the Haitian economy must be industrialized. As of 2008, manufacturing accounted for less than 8 percent of GDP.[75] Fortunately, the prospects are good. The most successful sector in the Haitian economy during the past 50-year period has been the export industry, which just before the earthquake was synonymous with the textiles and garment industry. In recent years, this has accounted for between 75 and 80 percent of total exports.[76] When it was at its peak, in 1990, it employed 46,000 people,[77] mainly women, almost exclusively in the capital.[78] However, since 2003, there are apparel factories also in Ouanaminthe, in the northeast, on the Dominican border. Clothes are produced in an export processing zone by Grupo M, the largest employer in the neighboring country. These clothes are sent across the border, to Dajabón, a mere kilometer away, and from there to the export port of Puerto Plata.[79]

The factories located in Port-au-Prince suffered considerable damage on January 12, although not to the extent that one could fear:

> Haitian industry estimates as of February 2010 indicate that earthquake damage to firms was uneven and not as severe as it might have been. Of the 28 factories operating in 2010, the earthquake completely destroyed one, killing at least 500 people, and seriously damaged four or five others. A number of factory buildings were damaged to the extent that operations will have to be moved. In general, the industry is working hard to bring production back on line, and among those factories that were not severely damaged, industry representatives suggest that production could return to full capacity by sometime in March 2010. As of the first week of February 2010, 75%–80% of [the] work force had returned. According to the ILO, as of February 25, 2010, 100% of the factories had returned to production, but not necessarily at full capacity. Many were still in need of cleaning, repair, renovation, and equipment.[80]

An estimated $25 million are needed to reconstruct damaged buildings, replace destroyed machinery and train new employees, and perhaps twice as much is required if factories with higher standards than before are to be built.[81] In the overall catastrophe context, these are modest figures, especially when you take into account that the apparel industry has the potential for creating hundreds of thousands of jobs in Haiti. It is essential to act quickly, not least with the provision of adequate finance, since if the buyers cannot rely on the Haitian producers to meet seasonal demand, they may be forced to turn elsewhere to ensure the necessary supply. As one observer puts it: 'The apparel world moves quickly...'[82] Fashions change rapidly, so fast adjustment and delivery is necessary.

It is necessary to remain competitive. In 2009, the minimum wage in the sector was increased significantly, from the equivalent of about US$1.80 per day to 3.25, that is, with more than 80 percent. This was a smaller increase than in other sectors (to $5), but the law requires parity in a few years, that is, a total increase of almost 180 percent.[83] Fully trained apparel workers already earn more than the new (2009) minimum, but possibly further increases may translate into a cost increase.[84] Paul Collier has pointed out that multi-shift operations are necessary to allow maximum use to be made of installed factory capacity. This would also increase the employment generated by a given plant, but the Haitian legislation in principle does not permit night-shift work, although recently, it has been adjusted to permit certain exceptions. Night shifts also require increased security, since workers have to travel to their work places during the dark hours, and this has turned out to be difficult both in Ouanaminthe and in the capital.[85]

Another problematic issue is the tendency for US buyers to require 'full package' production, that is, 'design, sourcing materials, organizing logistics, manufacturing the entire finished product, packaging, and delivering the final good to the retailer'.[86] As of now, skill requirements are low in the apparel sector, mainly sewing and some cutting. It is completely concentrated on mass-produced garments, but moving into higher value-added and higher wage production toward the full package end entails developing skills in such areas as printing, finishing, and washing. A long-term contract has been signed with the US Agency for International Development (USAID) to develop these skills.[87]

Industrial infrastructure

Industrial production requires infrastructure. In Haiti, the latter has been dismal for a long time, both in the capital and elsewhere. Roads, ports, airports, hospitals, electricity, water, and telecommunications left a lot to be desired already before the earthquake. This contributed to making the consequences of the quake so severe and also served as an impediment to production, especially of industrial goods. The infrastructure must be made to work as quickly and as efficiently as possible. The delivery of public goods and services has been miserable because the agencies handling them have been mismanaged. In no other field, incompetence and corruption have left so deep traces as here. The contrast between Port-au-Prince, with the worst port in the Caribbean and high electricity tariffs, and Ouanaminthe on the Dominican border, with access to an efficiently managed port and Dominican infrastructure is a memento for the future location of industry. The Ouanaminthe industrial park gets its electricity from the Dominican side and employs the vastly superior Dominican road network. This infrastructural advantage can be replicated elsewhere in the border areas.

Besides, the infrastructural requirements are not excessive:

> Production of garments is not very demanding of government: for example, Bangladesh, which has a government rated as among the

most corrupt and inefficient in the world, is able to support a garments industry for export with around 2.5 million jobs. There is thus a very high pay-off to ensuring that each of the few key requirements is met to a satisfactory standard. For each requirement it is essential to work back from a benchmark of global competitiveness and determine what standard must be met, rather than working forward from any existing plans for the activity. The main cost of garments is labour and the second is power. Since output must be exported and inputs imported the functioning of ports and customs are also critical.

There are two powerful reasons for meeting the needs of the garments industry through the creation of a few export zones around the country. One, as discussed above, is that clustering of firms reduces industry costs: zones facilitate this process of clustering and it is the standard approach in East Asia. The other reason is that it is much easier and quicker to provide the infrastructure and services that the industry needs by creating a few islands of excellence rather than by trying to improve standards across the entire country.[88]

HOPE II

Since 2008, Haiti has a cost advantage in the American market for both knit and woven products through the HOPE II (Hemispheric Opportunity through Partnership Encouragement Act) legislation. This is important, since in 2007, the United States was the recipient of almost three-fourths of Haiti's total exports, and the apparel sector accounted for over 90 percent of the Haitian exports to the United States.[89] Most important in HOPE II is that its provisions offer duty-free treatment to apparel articles 'if wholly assembled or knit-to-shape in Haiti from *materials (yarns, fabric, and components) sourced from any country* provided that a minimum proportion [55 percent, to be increased to 60 percent in 2011] of the material is produced by a country that is party to a U.S. unilateral preferential trade arrangement or a free trade arrangement'[90] for a 10-year period ending September 30, 2018. Whereas HOPE I, from 2006, required the product to be shipped from Haiti, HOPE II also allows for shipment from Dominican ports. An overall cap on imports from Haiti under HOPE II was established, at 1.25 percent of total US apparel imports, as well as specific caps for knit and woven goods for which no rules of source of inputs apply.

In order to qualify for preferential treatment, Haiti has to establish or make 'continual progress' toward a number of worker rights: '(1) the right of association; (2) the right to organize and bargain collectively; (3) a prohibition on the use of any form of forced or compulsory labor; and (4) a minimum age for the employment of children and acceptable conditions of work with respect to minimum wages, hours of work, and occupational safety and health', as 'determined and certified' by 'the President of the United States'.[91] In addition, HOPE II required the creation of an independent Labor Ombudsman's Office and the acceptance of the TAICNAR (Technical Assistance Improvement and Compliance Needs Assessment and Remediation) monitoring program which focuses on improvement of core labor standards and worker–management relationships.

HOPE II is fine as far as it goes, and Haiti is nowhere close to its limits as of now. In the future, however, further liberalization by the United States may be needed to expand exports and attract foreign direct investment in the apparel sector:

> First, the 55% value-added rule could be lowered. Reducing the 55% threshold would presumably allow more firms to take advantage of the preference. Second there is a capped (70 million square meter equivalents – SMEs) provision for both knit and woven articles that allows duty-free treatment for apparel made from third-country inputs with no value-added requirement. The rule is attractive for many apparel producers of varying size and capabilities in Haiti and the caps could be increased, exclusions reduced, or either eliminated.[92]

Also, the time period of the preferences can be extended.

A virtuous spiral?

Thus, in the end, given the good prospects for resurrecting the Port-au-Prince factories and to the extent that it is possible to build new plants closer to the Dominican border, the future looks relatively bright on the industrial employment front, thanks to the American quotas. The Dominican president Leonel Fernández suggested more than 10 years ago that a free zone ought to be established along the entire Haitian–Dominican border and cooperation between the two countries in this respect is a both palatable and realistic possibility.

If the textile industry can get going again, by virtue of the inherent characteristics of the industry, there are good reasons to expect a virtuous spiral to materialize:

> Like many other industries, global production is now organized into clusters of firms. By locating together firms reduce each others' costs. For example, they build a pool of experienced labour, and create a market sufficiently large to support specialist suppliers of necessary service inputs such as skilled maintenance of equipment. As a result, as the cluster grows the costs of production for its firms decline. This property of costs declining with expansion of the industry is unique to manufacturing; in other sectors firms typically hit some bottleneck input that becomes scarce and so beyond some point costs rise. The spectacular consequence of declining costs is that once expansion gets started it is explosive: the industry enters a virtuous circle of increasing competitiveness. In effect, there is an entry threshold of costs which must be surmounted. Until costs can be brought down to global levels firms cannot compete and so clusters cannot grow. Once over this threshold the industry can expand until it runs out of labour. This has been the experience of the garments industry globally: either countries are uncompetitive and have virtually no production, or they break into the global market and expand extraordinarily rapidly, transforming job opportunities in the societies in which they are located... The implication for Haiti is that if it can get over the threshold of international competitiveness the employment situation can be transformed.[93]

For unknown reasons, the action plan is virtually silent when it comes to the industrial sector. It states that foreign and domestic private investments 'are key to ensure the relaunching of the Haitian economy', and it speaks of a revision of the legal and financial framework so as to encourage investment in the private sector as a whole. Finally, the plan promises that an adequate incentive policy will 'be elaborated to favour the establishment of manufacturing industries, free zones, industrial areas and areas for the development of tourism'.[94]

So far, so good, but there the analysis ends. No discussion is included of the relative importance of industry, construction and agriculture for the creation of an envisaged 500,000 jobs in the private sector, and no indications are offered of how the promotion of industry is to be made, with the exception of extension of credit, mainly to small enterprises in general (not just industry), since 75 percent of the private sector losses (altogether an estimated US$2 billion) derive from medium- and small-scale businesses.[95]

The light, export-oriented industry has been the most successful sector in the Haitian economy during the past 50 years, and it is also the sector with most employment potential in the longer run. Hence, it deserves priority over agriculture and tourism, and some kind of future course must be laid down. For example, it is very important to know what a decentralized network of export processing zones will look like. Where will the zones be located and how will they connect with the Dominican Republic and with export ports within Haiti itself?

Industrial problems: Imagined and real

The export zone approach to employment creation has met with criticism in some quarters. Most common is the accusation that the factories are nothing but sweatshops which exploit poor Haitians. Admittedly, the apparel industry is a low-wage industry. Its comparative advantage is based on cheap labor, and apart from moving toward a full package delivery with a higher value-added content, there is not very much that you can do about that in the short run, especially not when alternatives are lacking. In order to advance to the dynamic, technologically advanced, high-wage sectors of the manufacturing industry, a completely different educational level than the one prevailing today is needed. No more than 54 percent of those aged 15 or more can read and write,[96] not even half of those who make it into secondary education finish it,[97] and of the latter no more than 10–15 percent go on to the university level. Vocational education is not well developed.[98] All of this must be changed if the average wage level is to increase in industry.

In a recent journal article, Yasmine Shamsie has also questioned the effects of the export processing zones and the light manufacturing industry, for slightly different reasons. The argument is a strange one. The first part of her criticism contends that this industry is part of a neoliberal globalization effort, 'the market-driven and private sector-led development process that donors favor'.[99] Haiti is extremely dependent on foreign aid (and will of course be even more so during the foreseeable future) and this, in turn, means that 'its economic development plans are also shaped by trends in development assistance',[100] 'a paradigm that privileges markets and private investment and favors public-private partnerships over state investment'.[101] That may be the case, but who would put any money into 'state investment' of the kind that Shamsie has in mind in a country with the dismal political record of Haiti?

The money that goes into the light manufacturing industry is *private* money, and that money cannot be converted into 'state investment'. It does not come from any donor funds.

The second part of the criticism states that the light manufacturing industry does not contribute to the alleviation of rural poverty. On the contrary, states Shamsie, it widens the gap between town and country and does nothing to advance country-wide poverty reduction. The assembly industries have 'exacerbated ... the long-time pattern of unequal development between urban and rural worlds'.[102] That may be the case, but the way they do it is by offering an income which is higher than in the countryside. Otherwise people would not move into the capital. By the same token they, in fact, do something about rural poverty – by moving people from lower to higher incomes. As Shamsie herself states, the rural exodus was 'fuelled by the promise of better wages in the assembly industry'.[103] It does not matter if the extent of inequality increases in the process.

The Shamsie analysis is not at all helpful when it comes to understanding how the assembly industry sector operates. It implicitly assumes that the money that goes into the latter can be used to develop the countryside or put into public investment instead, but that is of course not the case. The only other option is no investment at all, at least not in Haiti, and Shamsie fails to sketch any alternative, superior and realistic, strategy.

A much bigger problem for the industrial sector, related to the huge inflow of aid to Haiti that will take place in the near future, is that of Dutch Disease. During the first 18 months after the earthquake, over US$5 billion will flow into Haiti. Any major inflow of foreign currency, be it from natural resource based exports or from foreign financial assistance, may have two detrimental effects.[104] The first arises through the appreciation of the domestic currency when dollars are exchanged for Haitian gourdes. This serves to increase the domestic cost level in terms of dollars and hence acts as a brake on exports. The second effect operates through the increased demand that will result from the inflow of funds. With the prices of tradable goods (exports and imports) fixed by the operations of the world market, the demand increase will lead to an increase in the relative price of non-traded goods, and this will in turn serve to pull resources away from the traded goods sectors, that is, away from the export sector. Thus, exports will be held back in two ways.

The above is a not altogether trivial problem in the Haitian context, since the crucial sector in the reconstruction effort is construction, a domestic sector which produces non-traded goods, while the export sector consists mainly of the textile industry and of whatever agricultural produce that may be sold abroad in the immediate future. Even when you have preferential access to the American market, it may be more attractive to invest in the construction sector in the foreseeable future.

The difficult sector: Agriculture

In an article for *Le Monde* in February 2010, the well-known French agricultural economist Alain de Janvry pointed to the crucial role of agriculture in countries like Haiti in times of acute crisis.[105] People hit by an earthquake in a developed country would end up in the meshes of the social security net, but in poor countries like Haiti, where no such net exists, it is the agricultural sector which has to serve as a social security device. De Janvry therefore recommended subsidization of the sector in order to ease the burden imposed by the mass exodus from the capital and the other affected cities and lower the cost of food production. This is fine – but only as a short-run measure before the temporary addition of people can be removed. In the long run, subsidization is likely to have mainly negative effects, since it will lead to increased agricultural production, and hence also to increased soil erosion.

In March, President Préval stressed that he wanted most of the reconstruction aid going into Haiti channeled into the agricultural sector.[106] This is in a way understandable, since Préval is an agronomist by training, but unless the aid takes a very specific form, it makes no sense. The long-run solution must consist of a combination of alternative employment – outside agriculture – to ease the pressure on the land, and introduction of new crops and methods that make it possible to replant the mountainsides with trees capable of binding the soil.

The action plan has a section on agriculture. It leaves a lot to be desired. The plan states that the rural economy 'is largely a subsistence economy, mainly because trading opportunities are limited by the difficulty and costs of travel by road and by the lack of opportunities for storage and processing'.[107] This is a very strange statement, for two reasons. In the first place, the Haitian peasant households in fact buy most of their food. A survey taken in 1996 demonstrated that on average only 28 percent of the food consumed derived from on-farm production.[108] Secondly, rural, sub-urban, and urban markets for agricultural goods constitute one of the themes that have attracted lots of attention from economists and anthropologists for many decades. With a relative factor endowment where labor is the relatively cheap factor, the marketing chain for food crops appears as an effective one characterized by competition on all levels.[109]

A major deficiency of the action plan is that it does not stress the fundamental relationship between agriculture and erosion. It only refers to the soil destruction terms in vague terms, to some 'agricultural practices and farming choices motivated by the dynamics of market prices'[110] which reduce the forest-clad area and increase erosion. The plan also claims that the marketing structures for agricultural products contribute to the erosion problem, without mentioning which these structures may be and how they impact on the soil.

The plan suggests five different programs, based on very little analysis. The three dealing with agricultural credit, irrigation, and improvement of slaughter and preservation of meat make sense, but all need to be filled with concrete content. Road construction will of course also make it easier to transport produce and reach the peasants. Whether it will reduce the number of coffee *spekilatè* (middlemen), as suggested by the plan, is, however, a completely different matter. It could as easily have the opposite outcome – and increase the competition in coffee marketing! Facilitating the access to productivity-increasing inputs is also desirable, but it is very doubtful whether plows and (especially) tractors should be included in the package. The plow is hardly seen in Haiti. It cannot be used on steep hillsides. Few peasants have ever used a tractor. Presumably draft animals will make more sense, but it also has to be kept in mind that unless the farm is of a certain minimum threshold size, the use of a plow and a draft animal will not be profitable.[111]

The programs fail to address the fundamental agricultural problem: the damage caused by the increasing population pressure on the land. It does not contain any program for reforestation or planting of tree crops, and it does not discuss how people can be made to leave an already overcrowded sector. If these problems are not properly identified and integrated into the reconstruction effort, the economic part of it will never be successful.

The industrialization of Haiti must proceed hand in hand with the restructuring of agriculture. The mountainsides have to be replanted with trees – trees that have such a high economic value that they will not be cut down again. Mangoes are already Haiti's most important agricultural export, and the American market can absorb five or six times as much as today. They form part of the *grapyaj*, the traditional diversified mode of peasant agriculture, and the harvest season for Haiti as a whole is no less than 10 months. However, the transportation network, not least feeder roads, must be developed if mangoes are to turn into a staple export for the majority of the peasants. Credits will also be required, since it takes from 5 to 7 years before a mango tree bears fruit.[112] Possibly, the production of ecological coffee for the American gourmet market can also be developed, although it has been plagued by serious problems in the past, notably deficient administration of projects.[113]

Most fundamental is that the entire agricultural sector has to be restructured. Just putting money into the existing farms makes no sense. The present mode of operation has no future. It is low-productive, destroys the soil, and cannot meet the needs of the population. About 80 percent of Haiti's export incomes are spent on food imports.[114] An agrarian reform is long overdue. The farms are far too small, less than a hectare on average,[115] and they can hardly provide for an average peasant family. Plots are scattered at considerable distances from each other and frequently each plot contains a dozen or more different crops at the same time. Property rights are also a big problem. Few peasants have any formal titles to the land they are tilling, and land disputes are frequent.[116] To reform the agrarian structure, however, is a veritable mission impossible in Haiti. It will never meet with success unless alternative, superior, employment can be created which makes it possible to channel people out of agriculture and merge the tiny holdings of today into larger, contiguous, units.

Tourism: No short-run venture

A sector which from time to time is being held out as a possible solution to the employment problem is tourism. The somewhat amorphous service sector is the biggest contributor to GDP (51 percent), with the restaurant and hotel subsector accounting for 27 percent (of GDP).[117] Tourism as such does not play any large role in this. It has not been very successful after the mid-1950s.[118] Possibly, the earthquake can change that, but it is far from certain. So far, the main problem has been that the hotels have been located in the capital, while beaches and other attractions are found elsewhere. With Haiti's dismal road network, together with the turbulent political climate and the high crime rate, this has acted as a brake on the tourist flow.

The future is not necessarily bright either. It will not be easy for Haiti to compete with the well-developed structure on the other side of the border, in the Dominican Republic, and in the background, Cuba is waiting for a change of political regime that will make it possible once more to play the role it did before 1959 in Caribbean tourism. Developing the tourist industry in Haiti is a long-term project.

The regional dimension: Decentralization

The reconstruction and development effort has an important regional dimension. During the entire twentieth century, urban economic and political life was increasingly concentrated to Port-au-Prince while the regions decayed.[119] Between 1950 and 2010, the population of the capital grew from some 150,000–200,000,[120] to over 2 million, that is, more than tenfold. By the middle of the 1960s, François Duvalier had managed to close all the regional ports. The dominance of the capital was complete. Port-au-Prince grew until it choked. Before the earthquake, it accounted for two-thirds of all economic activity in the country and generated 85 percent of all tax revenue.[121] But the infrastructure broke down under the pressure of the population. If nothing is done, the city risks to have 6 million inhabitants in 15 years.[122]

This must not happen. More than 300,000 people left the metropolitan area after the earthquake. All of them cannot come back. Should the capital be moved then?[123] This would hardly decrease the probability of future hurricane or earthquake damage on the capital. The entire country is in the risk zone. Hurricanes and earthquakes may hit anywhere. The issue is rather how to rebuild the old capital in a way that preserves economies of scale and agglomeration and create a decent infrastructure and at the same time prevent the generation of new slum areas as much as possible.

A decentralization to cities like Cap-Haïtien, Les Cayes and Gonaïves would both contribute to the rehabilitation and development of the latter and to a decrease of future movements to the capital, and consequently also of the pressure on infrastructure and public service. Until now, however, the Haitian governments have not shown any interest whatsoever in decentralization, either administratively or economically. In the future, the regions must be provided with a good infrastructure, and – to a much larger extent than hitherto – they must be allowed to govern themselves.

For employment to be created and incomes to increase, the economy must get going, across the entire country. The action plan speaks of regional growth. This, without question, is the most important part of the entire plan. The Haitian government has decided to reverse the extreme concentration of economic and administrative activities to Port-au-Prince. To this end, the action plan envisages the creation of a number of clearly defined growth and development centers. For the Port-au-Prince area, this is Cabaret (once the notorious Duvalierville) north of the capital. Other centers are Cap-Haïtien, Les Cayes, Gonaïves,

Saint-Marc and Hinche. Elsewhere in the document, four areas are highlighted: Port-au-Prince, 'the axis between Cap Haïtien and Ouanaminthe for tourism, textile[s] and agriculture; the region around Gonaïves for agriculture and tourism; the South for agriculture, textiles and tourism'.[124]

Development of the transport network is seen as essential. The isolation of certain areas must come to an end, and the ground must be laid for clusters and sub-clusters of development across the country. The road network must connect all the Haitian towns and facilitate trade and movement of people. The smaller islands must be connected with Haiti itself. The international air traffic should no longer be concentrated to the capital but should be spread to Cap-Haïtien and Les Cayes as well. The destroyed port of the capital will be moved, probably to the Fond Mombin area north of the city, and regional ports will be either rehabilitated or constructed. The plan speaks of two more deep-water ports capable of handling large container ships.[125] In addition, a number of smaller ports will be made operational.

One of the key tasks of the renovation effort is to increase the decentralization of the administration. The plan envisages that within 5 years, 80 percent of the civil servants will be working outside the capital. At the end of this period, half the population will have local services provided by their own municipality in the areas of water, sanitation, solid waste management, and road maintenance, and by 2020 this will be the case for the entire country. Local governments will also have to provide their own resources to an increasing extent through a system of local taxation. By 2020, only 50 percent of the functional revenue of the municipalities in the development centers should be state grants, and 5 years later, this is to be the case across the entire country.[126]

The eleventh department

One of the factors that have made it possible for Haiti to survive at all during the last few decades is emigration. In 2008, there were officially 535,000 Haitians in the United States, 230,000 of whom had legal residence,[127] a figure which is probably too low, and 1 million people of Haitian origin in the Dominican Republic,[128] 150,000 in Canada, between 30,000 and 50,000 in France,[129] perhaps 50,000 Haitians or people of Haitian extraction in the Bahamas, perhaps 40,000 in Guyana and between 15,000 and 20,000 in both Guadeloupe and St. Martin.[130]

This Haitian diaspora every year remits more than a billion US dollars back home, the equivalent of almost 30 percent of GDP or more than 2.3 times the total export value (2003). Most remittances go to close family members and to the poor sections of Haitian society. Most of those sending money from the United States are young, two-thirds under 40, and they have a comparatively good education. Almost 80 percent have a college background.[131] The Haitian exiles could become a great asset during the reconstruction, above all by continuing to do what they are already doing, sending money, but also by contributing as entrepreneurs, advisers, and educators. They showed that they were willing to return after the fall of the Duvalier dictatorship in 1986. The hope for a better future had spread after almost 50 years of one-family rule. Hopefully, the negative events of the following quarter century have not deterred them from making further contributions.

It is desirable that they do whatever they can. Prime Minister Jean-Max Bellerive has asked them to.[132] Several disapora organizations lobbied for direct diaspora representation in the interim reconstruction commission, with the support of the Minister for Haitians Living Abroad, but this was denied during the negotiations of the president with the parliament – definitely not a good way of inviting much-needed support.[133]

The international community

The international community will play the leading role in the reconstruction and development effort – in several ways. Before the earthquake, Haiti had a foreign debt of $1.25 billion mainly to the Inter-American Development Bank, Venezuela, the IMF, and Taiwan.[134] Now, this debt is being written off. At the international conference in Montreal January 25, both Hillary Clinton and the IMF stressed the necessity of complete debt forgiveness,[135] and so did the Brazilian president Luiz Inácio Lula da Silva about a month later.[136] The Paris Club has exhorted all creditors to comply, The G-7 countries,[137] Venezuela,[138] the Inter-American Development Bank,[139] the World Bank,[140] and the International Fund for Agricultural Development (IFAD)[141] have written off everything.

The most important remaining creditors when the present is being written are the IMF, with US$271 million, including 114 million disbursed directly after the earthquake,[142] and Taiwan with 88 million.[143] The pressure is mounting on the IMF to do away with the rest. As of now, no payments of any kind are due for Haiti until 2012, and the country has obtained an unconditional 5½-year grace period on repayment on the interest-free loan obtained in January 2010,[144] but writing the debt off completely should not be a problem. The case of Taiwan is a bit more complicated, since the loans come from private banks.[145] However, the Taiwanese government will use public funds to help with the interest payments for 5 years, and thereafter some kind of repayment plan will be worked out with Haiti.[146]

Billions of dollars of foreign aid are now pouring into Haiti. Unfortunately, aid never worked there. In 2002, the World Bank dryly remarked that the results of its lending to Haiti since 1986 had been completely negligible. It would have been better if Haiti had never borrowed.[147] The biggest problem with aid to Haiti is to ensure that it does not end up in the wrong, corrupt, hands. Then the risk is substantial that the donors will tire and give Haiti up as a lost case which cannot be fixed even through a giant, coordinated effort. The international organizations will stand out as incompetent and inefficient, and the detractors of Haiti will be quick to point out what they already told you. The race will be finished and the common Haitians, as always, will be the ones paying the price of the failure.

The donors must point to concrete results of the aid. The reconstruction of Haiti is the largest project ever undertaken by the United Nations. Above all, failures must be avoided. The Haitian administration does not exist anymore, and a *de facto* double command has been created through the Interim Haiti Reconstruction Commission. The donors have stated that they will administer the aid in a transparent way, and indicate clearly what is permissible and what is not. This is absolutely essential. Preferably, they should work with a government of national unity while at the same time a new political leadership and new administrative cadres are trained who can handle matter alone in the longer run.

The most difficult role of all is the one played by the United States. Barack Obama took the lead immediately and without hesitation, during the first days after the catastrophe. All federal agencies were instructed to accord the highest priority to Haiti.[148] It was only the United States that could bring in help and military and police force units that could secure the catastrophe aid fast enough.

The American initiative was immediately criticized by the French minister of foreign cooperation, Alain Joyandet, who called it an occupation,[149] and by the head of the Italian civil protection service, Guido Bertolaso, who called it a 'pathetic' failure.[150] Both the French president, Nicolas Sarkozy, and the Italian foreign minister, however, hastened to express their appreciation for the American contribution. That the United States quickly seized the initiative was the best thing that could happen. That some of the operations left a few things to be desired in terms of efficiency should not surprise anyone in the chaotic situation that prevailed in Haiti immediately after the catastrophe. The United States acted quickly and the American military presence has not been prolonged beyond the reasonable. Two weeks after the catastrophe 22,000 US troops were present in the country (the peak figure). Already at the beginning of May, this figure had fallen to 1300.[151]

Sharp criticism was also voiced by some representatives of the left.[152] As always, all Haiti's problems have been created by Imperialism... No sober observer can deny that the relations between Haiti and the United States have never been simple and unequivocal. This is true above all of the American occupation 1915–34. The results were mixed.[153] The Americans never understood Haitian culture, and much of what was done was rooted in outright racism. At the same time, the first attempts were made to weed out corruption and develop the economy. The democracy issue was, however, sadly neglected. The durable results were few.

The above is not terribly interesting today. Barack Obama is not Woodrow Wilson. He is the first black president of the United States, and as such, he of course has an interest in helping the Black Republic. The Haitian colony in the United States is large, as we have already seen. Many of its members live in Florida, an important state during election years. The United States does not want any more boat people. In the short run, this can hardly be avoided but if Haiti can be reconstructed and jobs can be created, the refugee influx can be dammed. The American engagement in Haiti at the present time is, however, based mainly on simple humanitarian values. It has little to do with business. Haiti does not pose any threat to other nations, and the country is not situated in a politically turbulent region. It is time to take the American effort seriously. It's only in the Wild West that the world consists of good guys in white hats and bad guys in black hats.

* * *

Haiti has been hit by the worst catastrophe during its entire history. The rest of the world has demonstrated its willingness to provide catastrophe aid, and thanks God, the message appears to have been understood that remodeling Haiti from a heap of ruins to a country where the people do not suffer acute distress but can look to the future with confidence will not be a fast affair. It's a question of decades. As I have already stressed, the country is now balancing on a sharp knife edge. Haiti's entire history indicates that the reconstruction will founder on corrupt political structures. The earthquake, however, has struck blindly, against all groups in society. Can we hope that they will understand each other better in the future than what they did until January 12? In the best case, the catastrophe has done away with the old values and made it possible to bridge the two abysmal gaps between the elite and the masses and between the state and the citizens. Let us hope that a new generation of more cooperative Haitians can take over the helm and that the old confrontation politicians are finally put into the garbage can of history where they rightly belong.

There is a *kreyòl* word called *koumbit.* The word comes from the Spanish verb *convidar,* invite, and it is used to design the honest and egalitarian cooperation among neighbors in the Haitian countryside during the harvest and planting periods when plenty of labor is needed.[154] Can we hope for a similar cooperation both on the national level and between Haiti and the international community? It will not be easy. The past casts long and dark shadows over the present. What will happen next? Will the earthquake catastrophe become a watershed in Haitian political and social history? Does Haiti have a future? I wish I could be optimistic.

Notes

1. thoughts.com (2010).
2. USGS (2010).
3. A detailed estimate of the extent of damage is available in Government (2010b).
4. Sletten and Egset (2006), p. 44.
5. Egset and Sletten (2005), p. 12.
6. Jiménez (2010).
7. United Nations (2010a).
8. Gouvernement (2010).
9. Government (2010a).
10. Ibid., p. 5.
11. Gouvernement (2010), p. 5. The formulation is similar in the final version (Government (2010a), p. 8).
12. Ban (2010).
13. Government (2010a), p. 5.
14. Ibid., p. 50.
15. Ibid., p. 9.
16. Dominican Republic Live (2010).
17. Information about the Haiti Reconstruction Fund is available on its website: http://www.haitireconstructionfund.org/hrf.
18. Lundahl (1979), (1992), (1997).

19. Constitution (1987).
20. *LatinNews* (2010).
21. Nichols (2010), OAS (2010), Bruemmer (2010).
22. Katz (2010).
23. Nor has he been very eager to. The general impression is that Préval was far too passive during the first critical days and weeks after the quake.
24. Lundahl (1992), Chapter 14.
25. Lundahl and Silié (2005).
26. Leyburn (1941).
27. Lundahl (1992).
28. Barthélemy (1989).
29. Putnam (1993), Fukuyama (1995).
30. Lundahl and Silié (2005), p. 294.
31. Deibert (2009).
32. Gauthier and Moita (2010), p. 7.
33. Lundahl (1983), Chapter 12; Lundahl (1992), Chapters 16–17; Lundahl (2010).
34. Government (2010a), p. 41.
35. ILAC (2005).
36. Charles (2008).
37. ILAC (2005).
38. BRIDES (2007), pp. 93–95.
39. The activities of the MINUSTAH mission are described in some detail in a series of reports from the United Nations Secretary-General. The latest one is United Nations (2010b). All the reports since the beginning of the operations, in 2004, are available on the United Nations Security Council homepage http://www.un.org/Docs/sc.
40. Dobbins (2010).
41. Gauthier (2010).
42. ILAC (2005), p. 5.
43. Fuller et al. (2002).
44. BRIDES (2007), pp. 86–93.
45. Government (2010a), pp. 43–44.
46. UNDP (2010).
47. Government (2010a), p. 6.
48. Ban (2010).
49. US Department of State (2010).
50. Delva (2010a).
51. BRIDES (2007). The history of corruption in Haiti is dealt with in detail in the four monumental volumes by Leslie Péan (2000), (2005), (2006), (2007).
52. The households were not asked to evaluate the political parties.
53. Yves Pierre (2010), pp. 21–22.
54. Government (2010a), p. 48.
55. Delva (2010b).
56. BBC (2010b).
57. Lundahl (1992).
58. Baumol (1990).
59. Klitgaard (2010).

60. I will not discuss infrastructure and social sectors in the following, other than in connection with other issues. It goes without saying that schools, hospitals, drinking water systems, etc. must be reconstructed, their quality improved and their coverage extended. How to get the economy going and jobs created is a much more difficult issue.
61. Government (2010a), p. 32.
62. Yves Pierre (2010).
63. Government (2010a), p. 33.
64. Ibid., p. 46.
65. Ibid., p. 9.
66. Ibid., p. 46.
67. Ibid, pp. 46–47.
68. Ibid., p. 47.
69. Cavallo et al. (2010), p. 14.
70. Lundahl (1979), p. 59.
71. BBC (2010a).
72. Lundahl (1992), pp. 396–97.
73. Dobbins (2010).
74. Birdsall (2010), pp. 4–5.
75. Hornbeck (2010), p. 8.
76. Ibid.
77. Lundahl (2004), p. 12.
78. Other estimates contend that the high point was in the neighborhood of 100,000, in the 1980s (Hornbeck (2010), p. 11).
79. Lundahl (2004), Collier (2009).
80. Hornbeck (2010), pp. 14–15.
81. Ibid., p. 15.
82. Ibid., p. 14.
83. Ibid., p. 6.
84. Ibid., p. 14. From the social point of view the increase was necessary, since in 2008 the real minimum wage had fallen almost to half that of 2000 (ibid., pp. 6, 24).
85. Collier (2009), p. 9.
86. Hornbeck (2010), p. 14.
87. Ibid.
88. Collier (2009), p. 9.
89. Hornbeck (2010), p. 8.
90. Ibid., pp. 15, 21, cf. USAID Haiti (n.d.). Fabric for the apparel sector comes mainly from the United States, the Dominican republic and Asia, in approximately equal proportions (Hornbeck (2010), p. 13).
91. Hornbeck (2010), p. 18.
92. Ibid., p. 23.
93. Collier (2009), p. 8.
94. Government (2010a), p. 26.
95. Ibid.
96. République d'Haïti (2004), p. 104.
97. IMF (2009), Annex 3.
98. Lundahl (2004), p. 36.
99. Shamsie (2009), p. 653.

100. Ibid., p. 652.
101. Ibid., pp. 655–56.
102. Ibid., p. 658.
103. Ibid., p. 657.
104. Corden and Neary (1982).
105. De Janvry (2010).
106. Ives (2010).
107. Government (2010a), p. 22.
108. Wiens and Sobrado (1997), p. 5.
109. See Lundahl (1979), Chapter 4, for details.
110. Government (2010a), p. 22.
111. Lundahl (1979), pp. 590–94.
112. Lundahl (2004), pp. 9–11.
113. Lundahl (2006), pp. 63–64.
114. Government (2010a), p. 22.
115. République d'Haïti (2004), p. 539.
116. Lundahl (1979), deals with these problems at length.
117. Hornbeck (2010), p. 8.
118. Lundahl (2004), (2006).
119. Anglade (1982), pp. 24–33.
120. United Nations (1949), p. 31.
121. Government (2010a), p. 5.
122. Ourousoff (2010).
123. Lindsay (2010).
124. Government (2010a), p. 27.
125. Since 1996 a private project that aims at the development of a port in the Cayes area, at the Grand Bay du Mesle: the Port St. Louis, has been in progress. (See Lundahl (2004), pp. 27–30, Ashar and Woodbury (2008) for details.) Unfortunately, the project, which also aims at an international airport and several export processing zones, has got stuck in the political and administrative swamp that is Haiti. The time has come to reactivate and implement the project.
126. Government (2010a), p. 42.
127. Terrazas (2010).
128. Amnesty International (2007), p. 1.
129. *Wall Street Journal* (2010).
130. Ferguson (2003), p. 23.
131. Orozco (2006), pp. 1, 8, 12, 22, 10.
132. Dewan (2010).
133. PR Log (2010).
134. IMF (2010a).
135. Ryan (2010), IMF (2010b).
136. *El Nuevo Herald* (2010).
137. ABC News (2010).
138. Venezuelanalysis.com (2010).
139. IDB (2010).
140. World Bank (2010).
141. *Jamaica Observer* (2010).
142. IMF (2010d).

143. Shih (2010).
144. IMF (2010c).
145. GlobalSecurity.org (2010).
146. Shih (2010).
147. World Bank (2002), p. 17.
148. Obama (2010), p. 23.
149. Seward (2010).
150. Owen and Booth (2010).
151. Bajak (2010).
152. See, for example, Hallward (2010a), Hallward (2010b), Beckles (2010), and Bhatt (2010). For those interested, more is found on http://webofdemocracy.org/haiti-update-neo-colonial-p.html.
153. Schmidt (1971).
154. Lundahl (1979), pp. 110–18.

References

ABC News (2010), 'G7 to Forgive Haiti Foreign Debt', February 7. http://www.abc.net.au/new/stories/2010/02/07/2812382.htm. Downloaded February 19, 2010.

Amnesty International (2007), *Dominican Republic: A Life in Transit – The Plight of Haitian Migrants and Dominicans of Haitian Descent*. AMR 27/001/2007, March 21. http://74.125.77.132/search?q=cache:onH1pt8oSo8J:www.amnesty.org/en/news-and-updates/report/haitian-migrants-denied-basic-rights-dominican-republic-20070321. Downloaded February 19, 2010.

Anglade, Georges (1982), *Atlas critique d'Haïti*. Montréal: ERCE & CRC (Groupe d'Études et de Recherches Critiques d'Espace, Département de Géographie, Université de Québec à Montréal & Centre de Recherches Caraïbes de l'Université de Montréal).

Ashar, Asaf and Woodbury, Paul (2008), *Pre-Feasibility Assessment of a Transshipment Hub in Port St. Louis, Haiti*. May. N.p.

Bajak, Frank (2010), 'US Military Draws Down Deeply in Haiti', http://www.guardian.co.uk/world/feedarticle/9068048. Downloaded May 31, 2010.

Ban Ki-moon (2010), 'Renewal, Not Restoration, Should Be the Goal for Haiti', *Washington Post*, March 29.

Barthélemy, Gérard (1989), *Le pays en dehors: Essai sur l'univers rural haïtien*, second edition. Port-au-Prince: Éditions Henri Deschamps.

Baumol, William (1990), 'Entrepreneurship: Productive, Unproductive, and Destructive', *Journal of Political Economy*, Vol. 98, 893–921.

BBC (British Broadcasting Corporation) (2010a), 'Senegal Offers Land to Haitians', January 17. http://news.bbc.co.uk/2/hi/8463921.stm. Downloaded February 22, 2010.

BBC (British Broadcasting Corporation) (2010b), 'Haiti Fund', April 26, http://www.bbc.co.uk/caribbean/news/story/2010/04/100426_haiti.shtml. Downloaded May 26, 2010.

Beckles, Hilary (2010), 'The Hate and the Quake (Parts I and II)', January 18 and 27. www.antiguaobserver.com/?p=21616 and www.antiguaobserver.com/?p=22348. Downloaded February 9, 2010.

Bhatt, Keane (2010), 'Chomsky Post-Earthquake: Aid to Haitian Popular Organizations, Not Contractors or NGOs', Upside Down World, March 8, http://upsidedownworld.org/main/haiti-archives-51/2394—chomsky-post-earthquake-aid-to-haitian-popular-organizations-not-contractors-or-ngos. Downloaded May 28, 2010.

Birdsall, Nancy (2010), ' "Rebuilding Haiti's Competitiveness and Private Sector". Testimony for the House Financial Services Subcommittee on International Monetary Policy and Trade', March 16. Washington, DC: Center for Global Development.

BRIDES (Bureau de Recherche en Informatique et en Développement Économique et Social) (2007), *Gouvernance et corruption en Haïti. Résultats de l'enquête diagnostique sur la gouvernance. Rapport final*. January. N.p.

Bruemmer, René (2010), 'Haiti Must Hold Vote Soon: Cannon', *Montreal Gazette*, May 22.

Cavallo, Eduardo A., Powell, Andrew and Becerra, Oscar (2010), *Estimating the Direct Economic Damage of the Earthquake in Haiti*. February. IDB Working Paper Series # IDB-WP-163. Washington, DC: Inter-American Development Bank, Department of Research and Chief Economist.

Charles, Jacqueline (2008), 'Haiti Makes Strides in Modernizing Police Force', *Miami Herald*, January 16. http://www.wehaitians.com/haiti%20makes%20strides%20in%20modernizing%20police%20force.html. Downloaded February 8, 2010.

Collier, Paul (2009), *Haiti: From Natural Catastrophe to Economic Security*. A Report for the Secretary-General of the United Nations. January. Department of Economics, Oxford University.

Constitution (1987), 'Constitution de la République d'Haïti 1987', *Le Moniteur: Journal Officiel de la République d'Haïti*, Vol. 142, No. 136, April 28.

Corden, W. Max and Neary, J. Peter (1982), 'Booming Sector and Deindustrialisation in a Small Open Economy', *Economic Journal*, Vol. 92, 825–48.

Deibert, Michael (2009), ' "The Elites Are Like a Huge Elephant Sitting on Haiti". Michel Deibert Interviews Haitian Prime Minister Michèle Pierre-Louis', IPS News, July 3, http://ipsnews.net/news.asp?idnews=47515. Downloaded May 28, 2010.

De Janvry, Alain (2010), 'L'urgence haïtienne: soutenir une agriculture de subsistence', *Le Monde*, February 3.

Delva, Joseph Guyler (2010a), 'Interview – U.S. Graft Report Angers Haiti Amid Qauke Recovery', March 17. http://in.reuters.com/article/worldNews/idINIndia-46975420100316?sp=true. Downloaded March 30, 2010.

Delva, Joseph Guyler (2010b), 'Anti-Corruption Steps Key at Haiti Fund, Says World Bank', Cribbean Net News, April 26, http://www.caribbeannetnews.com/article/php?news_id=22836. Downloaded May 17, 2010.

Dewan, Sheila (2010), 'Scattered Émigrés Haiti Once Shunned Are Now a Lifeline', *New York Times*. February 3, www.nytimes.com/2010/02/04/us/04disapora.html. Downloaded February 8, 2010.

Dobbins, James (2010), Reconstructing Haiti. Testimony Presented Before the Senate Foreign Relations Committee. RAND Corporation, CT-39, January 28. http://www.rand.org/pubs/testimonies/CT339/. Downloaded February 15, 2010.

Dominican Republic Live (2010), 'Preparatory Technical Conference for Haiti. Official Statement of the Co-Presidents', March 17. http://www.dominican-republic-live.com/dominican-republic/diverse/declaration-technical-preparatory-conference-haiti.html. Downloaded May 26, 2010.

Egset, Willy and och Sletten, Pål (2005), *La pauvreté en Haïti: Profil de la pauvreté à partir des donnés de l'ECVH*. Port-au-Prince: République d Haïti, Ministère de L'Économie et des Finances, Ministère de la Planification et de la Coopération Externe, PNUD (Programme des Nations Unies pour le Développement) and FAFO Institute for Applied International Studies.

El Nuevo Herald (2010), 'Lula Proposes External Debt Pardon for Haiti', *El Nuevo Herald*, February 26.

Ferguson, James (2003), *Migration in the Caribbean: Haiti, the Dominican Republic and Beyond*. London: Minority Rights Group International.

Fukuyama, Francis (1995), *Trust: The Social Virtues and the Creation of Prosperity*. New York and London: The Free Press.

Fuller Anne; Texier Philippe; Brousseau, Michel; Lemaire, Dilia and Pierre-Louis, Patrick (2002), *Prolonged Pretrial Detention in Haiti*. July. New York: Vera Institute of Justice.

Gauthier, Amélie (2010), *Conflict Prevention and Peace-Building: Horizon Scanning and Future Needs. Haiti Case Study*, Madrid: Fundación para las Relaciones Internacionales y el Diálogo Exterior.

Gauthier, Amélie and Moita, Madalena (2010), *Vulnerability and Causes of Fragility in Haiti*, FRIDE Project Report, March. Madrid: Fundación para las Relaciones Internacionales y el Diálogo Exterior.

GlobalSecurity.org (2010), 'Taiwan Contemplating Debt Relief Decision', http://www.globalsecurity.org/military/library/news/2010/01/mil-100120-cna01.htm. Downloaded February 19, 2010.

Gouvernement de la République d'Haïti (2010), *Action Plan for the Reconstruction and National Development of Haiti*. N.p.

Government of the Republic of Haiti (2010a), *Action Plan for National Recovery and Development of Haiti: Immediate Key Initiatives for the Future*. March. N.p.

Government of the Republic of Haiti (2010b), *Haiti Earthquake PDNA: Assessment of Damage, Losses, General and Sectoral Needs. Annex to the Action Plan for National Recovery and Development of Haiti*. N.p.

Hallward, Peter (2010a), 'Our Role in Haiti's Plight', *The Guardian*, January 13.

Hallward, Peter (2010b), 'Securing Disaster in Haiti', *Monthly Review*, January 24.

Hornbeck, J.F. (2010), *The Haitian Economy and the HOPE Act*. CRS Report for Congress. March 5. Washington, DC: Congressional Research Service.

IDB (Inter-American Development Bank) (2010), 'Debt Relief', http://www.iadb.org/haiti/index.cfm?id=6470& lang=en. Downloaded May 26, 2010.

ILAC (International Legal Assistance Consortium) (2005), *ILAC Report Haiti*, January 2005. Stockholm: ILAC.

IMF (International Monetary Fund) (2009), *Haiti: Joint Staff Advisory Note of the Annual Progress Report on Implementation of the Poverty Reduction Strategy Paper*. IMF Country Report No. 09/289. August. Washington, DC: International Monetary Fund.

IMF (International Monetary Fund) (2010a), *Haiti: Debt Statistics and IMF Support*, January 27. http://www.imf.org/external/np/2010/012710.htm. Downloaded February 9, 2010.

IMF (International Monetary Fund) (2010b), 'Remarks by IMF Delegation: Donors Conference on Haiti. Statement by Ms Caroline Atkinson, Director, External Relations Department', January 25, http://imf.org/external/np/dm/2010/012510.htm. Downloaded February 18, 2010.

IMF (International Monetary Fund) (2010c), 'IMF Approves $114 Million for Quake-Hit Haiti', IMF Survey online, http://www.imf.org/external/pubs/ft/survey/so/2010/NEW012710A.htm. Downloaded May 27, 2010.

IMF (International Monetary Fund) (2010d), 'Statement by IMF managing Director Dominique Strauss-Kahn During the International Donors Conference Towards a New Future for Haiti'. Press Release No. 10/129. March 31, http://www.imf.org/external/np/sec/pr/2010/pr10129.htm. Downloaded May 27, 2010.

Ives, Kim (2010), 'Haiti Reconstruction: Factories, Not Fields', *NACLA Report on the Americas*, Vol. 43, Issue 3, 4–5.

Jamaica Observer (2010), 'You're Forgiven: Debt Write-Off for Haiti', *Jamaica Observer*, April 25, http://www.jamaicaobserver.com/news/You-re-forgiven-Debt-write-off-for-Haiti. Downloaded May 27, 2010.

Jiménez, Manuel (2010), 'Donnors Plan to Put up $3.8 Bln for Haiti Rebuilding', Reuters, March 18. http://reuters.com/article/idUSTRE62H32U20100318. Downloaded May 18, 2010.

Katz, Jonathan M. (2010), 'Haiti Prez to Extend Term if Election Not Held', http://hcvanalysis.wordpress.com/2010/05/06/pres-preval-to-extend-term-if-haiti-election-not-held-by-november-2010/. Downloaded May 28, 2010.

Klitgaard, Robert (2010), 'Addressing Corruption in Haiti', Claremont Graduate University, Claremont, CA, February. http://www.cgu/PDFFiles/Presidents%20Office/Addressing%20Systemic%20Corruption%20in%20Haiti%20_3_.pdf. Downloaded February 14, 2010.

LatinNews (2010), 'Weekly Report – March 11, 2010 (WR-10-10) Haiti: Préval Calls for Expedited Elections'. http://www.latinnews.com/lwr/LWR21973.asp?instance=1& mode=print. Downloaded March 12, 2010.

Leyburn, James G. (1941), *The Haitian People*. New Haven: Yale University Press.

Lundahl, Mats (1979), *Peasants and Poverty: A Study of Haiti*. London: Croom Helm.

Lindsay, Greg (2010), 'Can Port-au-Prince Be Saved, or Should Haiti Move the Capital?'. Fast Company. http://www.fastcompany.com/blog/greg-lindsay/aereotropolis/haiti-cities?partner=rss. Downloaded February 15, 2010.

Lundahl, Mats (1979), *Peasants and Poverty: A Study of Haiti*. London: Croom Helm.

Lundahl, Mats (1983), *The Haitian Economy: Man, Land and Markets*. London and Canberra: Croom Helm.

Lundahl, Mats (1992), *Politics or Markets? Essays on Haitian Underdevelopment*. London and New York: Routledge.

Lundahl, Mats (1997), *Towards the Abyss? The Political Economy of Emergency in Haiti*. WIDER Research for Action 40. Helsinki: World Institute for Development Economics Research.

Lundahl, Mats (2004), *Sources of Growth in the Haitian Economy*. Economic and Sector Study Series RE2-04-004, Washington DC: Inter-American Development Bank.

Lundahl, Mats (2006), 'Economic Growth in Haiti – A Mere Illusion?' *Iberoamericana*, Vol. 36, 61–87.

Lundahl, Mats (2010), 'The Failure of Community-Based Entrepreneurship in Haiti', *International Journal of Innovation and Regional Development*, Vol. 2, 112–27.

Lundahl, Mats and Silié, Rubén (2005), 'Haiti: Nothing But Crisis', in: Mats Lundahl and Michael L. Wyzan (eds), *The Political Economy of Reform Failure*, London and New York: Routledge.

Nichols, Michelle (2010), 'Haiti Able to Hold Poll by Year-End, Says Bill Clinton', Reuters, http://www.reuters.com/article/idUSN14163725._CH_.2400. Downloaded May 31, 2010.

OAS (Organization of American States) (2010), 'Assistant Secretary General Ramdin Reiterates that OAS Is Ready for Elections in Haiti', http://www.oas.org/OASpage/press_releases/press_release.asp?sCodigo=E-181/10. Downloaded May 31, 2010.

Obama, Barack (2010), 'Why Haiti Matters', *Newsweek*, January 25.

Orozco, Manuel (2006), *Understanding the Remittance Economy in Haiti*. Final draft. Inter-American Dialogue, March 15. http://isim.georgetown.edu/Publications/RCRCCPubs/Orozco/Understanding%20the%20remittance%20economy%20in%20Haiti.pdf. Downloaded February 8, 2010.

Ourousoff, Nicolai (2010), 'A Plan to Spur Growth Away from Haiti's Capital', *New York Times*, March 30.

Owen, Richard and Booth, Jenny (2010), 'US Criticised Over Haiti Aid as Reconstruction Talks Begin', *Times Online*, January 25. http://www.timesonline.co.uk/tol/news/world/us_and_americas/article7001737.ece. Downloaded February 8, 2010.

Péan, Leslie J.R. (2000), *Économie politique de la corruption (De Saint-Domingue à Haïti 1791–1870)*: Port-au-Prince: Éditions Mémoire.

Péan, Leslie J.R. (2005), *Haïti: Économie politique de la corruption: Tome II, L'état marron (1870–1915)*. Paris: Maisonneuve et Larose.

Péan, Leslie J.R. (2006), *Haïti: Économie politique de la corruption. Tome III, Le saccage (1915–1956)*. Paris: Maisonneuve et Larose.

Péan, Leslie J.R. (2007), *Haïti: Économie politique de la corruption. Tome IV, L'ensauvagement macoute et ses conséquences 1957–1990*. Paris: Maisonneuve et Larose.

PR Log (2010), 'Haiti – Post Earthquake – Haitian Disapora Challenging Haiti President to Deliver', PR Log Free Press Release, May 8. http://www.prlog.org/10633195-haiti-post-earthquake-haitian-diaspora-challenging-haiti-president-to-deliver.html. Downloaded May 26, 2010.

Putnam, Robert D. (1993), *Making Democracy Work: Civic Traditions in Modern Italy*. Princeton, NJ: Princeton University Press.

République d'Haïti, Ministère de l'Économie et des Finances, Institut Haïtien de Statistique et d'Informatique (2004), *Enquête sur les conditions de vie en Haïti (ECVH-2001), Volume I*. Port-au-Prince: Imprimerie Henri Deschamps.

Ryan, April D. (2010), 'Haitian Donor Conference Set for March in New York City', *Huffington Post*, January 26. http://www.huffingtonpost.com/april-d-ryan/Haitian-donors-conference_b_437385.html. Downloaded February 2.

Schmidt, Hans (1971), *The United States Occupation of Haiti 1915–1934*. New Brunswick, NJ: Rutgers University Press.

Seward, Deborah (2010), 'French Minister Slams US Role in Haiti', *Huffington Post*, January 19. http://www.huffingtonpost.com/huff-wires/20100119/eu-france-us-haiti. Downloaded February 19, 2010.

Shamsie, Yasmine (2009), 'Export Processing Zones: The Purported Glimmer in Haiti's Development Murk', *Review of International Political Economy*, Vol. 16, 649–72.

Shih Hsiu-chuan (2010), 'Taiwan Approves Debt Reduction Proposal for Haiti', *Taipei Times*, April 14, http://wwww.taipeitimes.com/News/front/archives/2010/04/14/2003470544. Downloaded May 27, 2010.

Sletten, Pål and och Egset, Willy (2006), 'Poverty in Haiti', *Iberoamericana* Vol. 36, 41–59.

Terrazas, Aaron (2010), 'Haitian Immigrants in the United States', *Migration Information Source*. Migration Policy Institute. http://www.migrationinformation.org/USfocus/display.cfm?id=770. Downloaded February 8, 2008.

UNDP (United Nations Development Programme) (2010), 'High-Level Haiti Donors' Conference to Be Held', http://content.undp.org/go/newsroom/2010/march/high-level-haiti-donors-confenrence-to-be-hend.en. Downloaded March 30, 2010.

United Nations (1949), *Mission to Haiti: Report of the United Nations Mission of Technical Assistance to Haiti*. Lake Success, NY: United Nations.

United Nations, General Assembly (2010a), 'International Conference Raises Almost $10 Billion As More Than 130 Donors Contribute "Towards a New Future for Haiti"', GA/10932, March 31, 2010. http://www.un.org/News/Press/docs/2010/ga10932.doc.htm. Downloaded April 1, 2010.

United Nations Security Council (2010b), *Report of the Secretary-General on the United Nations Stabilization Mission in Haiti*. S/2010/200. February 22. New York: United Nations.

USAID Haiti (n.d.), *Haitian Hemispheric Opportunity through Partnership Encouragement Act (HOPE) II Legislation*. http://www.usaid.gov/ht/docs/ege/hope_2.pdf. Downloaded February 8, 2010.

US Department of State (2010), *2009 Human Rights Report: Haiti*. http://www.state.gov/g/drl/rls/hrrpt/2009/wha/136116.htm. Downloaded March 30, 2010.

USGS (US Geological Survey) (2010), 'Magnitude 7.0 – Haiti Region', http://earthquake.usgs.gov/earthquakes/eqinthenews/2010/us2010rja6/. Downloaded January 13, 2010.

Venezuelananlysis.com (2010), 'Venezuela's Chavez Forgives Haiti's Debt', http://www.venezuelanalysis.com/news/5102. Downloaded February 19, 2010.

Wall Street Journal (2010), 'US Lets Illegal Haitians Stay, Will Turn Back Refugees', January 16.

Wiens, Thomas and Sobrado, Carlos E. (1997), 'Rural Poverty in Haiti', in: The World Bank (ed.), *Haiti Poverty Assessment, Volume II: Technical Papers*. Washington, DC: The World Bank.

World Bank (2002), *Haiti: Country Assistance Evaluation*. Report No. 23637, February 12. Washington, DC: The World Bank.

World Bank (2010), 'World Bank Pledges Half Billion US Dollars for Haiti Over 14 Months', http://web.worldbank.org/WBSITE/EXTERNAL/NEWS/0, contentMDK:22523628~pagePK:64257043~piPK:437376~theSitePK:4607,00.html. Downloaded May 27, 2010.

Yves Pierre, Raphael (2010), *Haitians Talk About Rebuilding the Country After the January 12, 2010 Earthquake.* Oxfam International, http://www.oxfam.org.uk/resources/policy/conflict_disasters/downloads/rebuilding_haiti_survey_en_130410.pdf. Downloaded June 1, 2010.

Author Index

Subject Index